ALL ABOUT FUTURES

ALL ABOUT FUTURES
The Easy Way to Get Started

RUSSELL R. WASENDORF

Second Edition

McGraw-Hill

New York   San Francisco   Washington, D.C.   Auckland   Bogotá
Caracas   Lisbon   London   Madrid   Mexico City   Milan
Montreal   New Delhi   San Juan   Singapore
Sydney   Tokyo   Toronto

Library of Congress Cataloging-in-Publication Data

Wasendorf, Russell R., 1948–
  All about futures : the easy way to get started / by Russell R. Wasendorf.—2nd ed.
    p. cm.
  ISBN 0-07-134170-6
  1. Futures. 2. Futures market. I. Title.
HG6024.A3 W37 2000
332.64'5—dc21   00-055037

McGraw-Hill

A Division of The *McGraw·Hill* Companies

1 2 3 4 5 6 7 8 9 0   BRB/BRB   0 9 8 7 6 5 4 3 2 1 0

ISBN 0-07-134170-6

The contributing editor for this book was Terry Wooten.

*The sponsoring editor for this book was Stephen Isaacs, the editing supervisor was Maureen B.
Walker, and the production supervisor was Charles Annis. It was set in Palatino by The Composing
Room of Michigan, Inc.*

Printed and bound by Sheridan Books, Inc.

McGraw-Hill books are available at special discounts to use as premiums and sales promo-
tions, or for use in corporate training programs. For more information, please write to the
Director of Special Sales, Professional Publishing, McGraw-Hill, Two Penn Plaza, New York,
NY 10121-2298. Or contact your local bookstore.

This book is printed on recycled, acid-free paper containing a minimum of
50% recycled de-inked paper.

C O N T E N T S

The Nature of the Futures Market

Philosophers throughout the centuries have said that if God didn't exist, man would have invented Him. The creation of futures markets may have been just about as inevitable a concept. Human beings have always had a love-hate relationship with the future: They can't wait for things to get better, and they fear what will happen tomorrow.

On a more mundane level, businesspeople have at least as much difficulty dealing with the unknown as the average person. How can they set firm prices for the products they sell or manufacture if they don't know what they'll have to pay for the raw materials they use? This question is at least 6,000 years old, dating back to when a futures market in rice is thought to have developed in China. By the Middle Ages there was already a sophisticated futures purchasing system for wheat and wool.

A futures market solves the basic business problem of the need to control as much of the future as possible. For example, if you are an importer or processor of crude oil, could you have dealt with the uncontrollable pricing that took place following the 1990 invasion of Kuwait by Iraq—without the futures markets? If you are a seller of capital equipment to the Japanese and are to be paid in yen 120 to 180 days from now, would you want to hedge the risk of the changing currency values of your payment? What's one of the most efficient methods for farmers to handle the price fluctuations they face each year while their crops are still in the ground?

The futures markets permit users of commodities—e.g., grains, meats, metals, financials, food, fiber, etc.—to set a price for their future requirements well in advance of when the commodities are needed. Notice that today's definition of commodities stretches well beyond the physicals and includes security market futures, currencies, interest rates, and more. Producers can likewise lock in acceptable price levels (or profit levels) before their product is ready to be sold.

However, if the futures markets were restricted to bona fide hedgers (producers or users of the commodities) only, the volume of many contracts and some entire markets would be so low that on some days they would not be able to trade. Volume is an essential key to discovering price; it is one of the most fundamental functions of all types of exchanges. The higher the volume is at any given time for a given commodity, the higher the reliability that its price reflects the current supply-demand situation. This is where speculators fit in. Speculators create liquidity in the market. They buy and sell thousands of contracts in hundreds of markets, allowing hedgers to easily transfer risk.

Confidence in understanding where the price of a commodity should be going—commonly referred to as the *trend*—inspires trading, thereby increasing volume. Additionally, high-volume markets are safer to trade. When you place an order for a trade, you have a better chance for it to be filled when trading volume is high. Therefore, the market function of the speculator is to create volume, so that anyone who wants to trade has a market. The speculator's personal objective, naturally, is to make money from the ever-changing ebb and flow of prices.

Who should be a speculator is a much more important question. The term *speculate* means to engage in risky business transactions on the chance of generating great profits. There are three key terms: risky business, chance, and great profits.

Risky business distinguishes futures speculation from gambling. Gambling generally involves sport and pure chance. Futures speculation is more intellectual, involves research, strategies, and planning.

Detractors of futures trading have always tied their arguments to the second key term, *chance*. There is always the element of chance when you attempt to forecast what is expected to happen at some time in the future. This is true for commercial real estate investors, insurance companies, bank officers who set interest rates, and even individuals who buy homes. The speed at which the futures markets fluctuates is what makes its detractors wrongly classify it as a game of chance.

The last key term, *great profits,* is what attracts aggressive investors to this form of investing. A goodly percentage of individual speculators wish to make a lot of money fast. They are greedy. This may be the single most important reason that most small traders lose. Success in the futures markets requires the patience to wait for high-quality trades, to manage money judiciously, to study the markets and do the research required, to control emotional responses to fast-moving opportunities when they are moving for or against your positions, and to have a clear head when everyone around you is losing theirs.

There are rules to follow in the market that are designed to protect you against catastrophic losses, but you can't teach someone to trade successfully. "Natural traders" are as rare as "natural shooters."

The purpose of this book is to teach you enough about the futures markets and its rules so you can protect yourself. However, this knowledge is not a guarantee that you won't get wiped out. The market has a will of its own. Never forget that! If it moves violently against your position, you'll get burned.

The futures market is a zero-based market. At the end of each day, the books are balanced. For every buyer, there is seller. For every seller, a buyer. That means one side wins and one side loses—every day. And every day, the losers must pay the winners in the form of margin money or reduced equity in their trading account.

Some days you'll win. More often you'll lose. Your objective is to be a net winner in terms of dollars invested. The risk may be heavy, but the possibility of reaping very large profits over very short periods of time attracts the aggressive investor.

Futures trading is not for everyone, but careful study will give you an excellent overview of futures and options on futures. This will help you decide if futures trading will assist you to reach your financial goals; and if so, how you go about entering the markets, what alternative approaches are available to you, and how you can develop strategies to reduce or control risk.

CHAPTER 1

Is Futures Trading for You?

Key Concepts
- Financial and Psychological Suitability for Trading
- Five Personal Attributes of the Effective Trader
- Four Major Obstacles to Success

The title of this chapter implies that you have some general insights into how the futures markets work. You likely know that futures prices and price trends reflect the composite response to the current supply-demand equation of everyone who is in the market. If the overall attitude is bullish, the market moves higher. If traders are bearish, it plunges. If nobody is sure or opinions are conflicting, it slides sideways.

Next, you must determine if you are suitable to trade futures. This is a question your broker must also determine, as mandated by the federal regulators that govern the industry. Your broker is charged by the National Futures Association (NFA) and the Commodity Futures Trading Commission (CFTC) to find out if you are indeed suitable. That's why you are asked a series of personal questions. What is your net worth? Profession? Age? Investment experience?

With this information, your overall suitability is reviewed on several levels. Your broker makes the first screening. Your account forms or account papers are then passed to the supervisor, who is usually at the introducing broker (IB) level. From here, it goes up the ladder to the futures commission merchant (FCM). The FCM is the entity that actually does the trading in the pits. It is the clearing (as in clearing trades through the system) member of the exchanges. An IB is the link between you (the general public) and the FCM. It introduces you to the market.

WHO'S SUITABLE AND FOR WHAT?

There are a variety of ways of determining suitability for futures and options trading. One of the measures is the person's net worth, annual income, and liquid assets.

Before getting into specific evaluation methods, you should understand the difference between futures and options trading. That difference is simply the amount of risk. With futures, the risk is unlimited. The options trader can lose 100 percent of the amount invested, but the amount is known in advance.

If you are in a futures position and the market makes a limit move against your positions, you must immediately meet the margin call if your account does not include excess equity. Also, there could be more than 1 day in a row of limit moves. For example, once the live hogs contract limited down 6 days in a row. The limit move was $600 per day, or $3,600 for those 6 days. If you had 10 positions, it would have been over $36,000 when you include commissions and fees. And this doesn't account for days when the limit might have been extended. Margin calls can be in the millions of dollars.

Buying exchange-traded futures options involves a more defined risk. It equals the amount of the premium for the option and the transaction costs. These latter costs are defined as the broker's commission and fees. (There are NFA, exchange, and FCM fees to be paid on both futures and options trades.) Here, buying options refers to calls or puts. If you write options, you'll have the same risk as a futures trader if the options are exercised. Basically, you are contracting to deliver a futures position.

This analysis of the risk facing both types of traders explains why the net worth and liquid asset requirements differ for each type of account. The FCM, which is the entity that holds the investor's capital and executes (or arranges to execute) the trades, sets the standards.

When approving an account for trading, the FCM compares the prospective customer resources with their anticipated trading activity. Are they financially suitable? For example, many FCMs will not approve an account that plans to trade more than 10 percent of the customer's liquid assets. When and if a margin call is made on the account, the customer has 24 hours or less to meet it. Therefore, only liquid assets can be considered in the evaluation.

If customers have a high annual income (in excess of $100,000 per year), they may be approved even if their net worth is unremarkable. If they are not very wealthy, they may be approved to trade (buy) options since the risk is defined and the entire investment is usually made in advance.

A customer's financial position, however, is not the only consideration. Brokers are required by federal regulations to "know their customers." They have to know the customer's true name, address, approximate age, principal occupation or business, and an indication of the customer's previous investment and futures trading experience.

Also, the FCM and the federal regulators (the NFA and the CFTC) want to get an insight into the experience and sophistication of the investor. For example, very young or very elderly people may require additional investigation by the FCM before they are accepted. Investors who have traded futures in the past or traded stocks on margin would be considered reasonably experienced.

RISK TOLERANCE

Besides learning about an investor's financial background and previous investing experience, good futures brokers delve into the risk tolerance of their customers. This is a critical consideration when developing a trading plan designed to reach specific objectives. The plan must be one the customer is comfortable trading.

When doing this, a good broker attempts to classify the customer's attitudes toward risk. Each customer is an individual, and each one reacts differently to risk. If a broker doesn't deal with this, a lasting bond of trust will not be created.

When classifying attitudes to risk, economists use the term *utility*, which is a measure of personal satisfaction. If something provides a feeling of greater satisfaction than whatever it is compared with, it is said to have greater utility.

As experienced brokers discuss trading strategies and risk-to-reward ratios of specific trades with their clients, they learn to classify customers as averse, neutral, or aggressive risk takers. For example, a risk-averse person may not be interested in a trade that would be projected to return a dollar for every dollar at risk. These traders want to take little or no risk and are satisfied with low, but dependable, returns. If you fit the risk-averse description, you probably should not be trading futures.

The risk-neutral traders may consider trading options and / or what appears to be the most conservative of futures trades. The aggressive risk takers are the ones most commonly thought of as futures traders. These people are willing to take the risks required to get high utility (satisfaction) from making successful trades.

When you consider your suitability to trading futures, look closely at all three of these areas—financial situation, investing experience, and risk tolerance—before you fill out the account papers and send in your check.

PERSONAL ATTRIBUTES OF SUCCESS

Just because you are suitable doesn't mean you'll be successful. Studies of futures traders indicate most lose money. So who will be successful in the futures market? What is the most important element of a successful trading system?

When active traders get together at a conference or seminar, there is often a heated discussion about trading systems. Which one works best? Can the fundamental trader know and evaluate all the possible facts that influence the supply-demand equation? How reliable are technical signals and how should they be interpreted? When you are using technical and fundamental analysis and you selectively override your system, which are you relying on—skill or luck?

The answer lies in certain common characteristics found in successful people of every profession, namely the personal attributes of self-knowledge, persistence, discipline, patience, and independence.

Self-knowledge in successful people is an innate understanding of themselves and their mission in life. They seem to have a little secret that guides their lives. They have clearly defined goals.

Persistence in working hard each day to achieve these goals is essential. Objectives are usually reached in stages, with each step of the journey clearly defined. How does this apply to the futures traders? Why do, as conventional wisdom tells us, 95 percent of futures traders end up net losers?

Discipline must be exercised in setting realistic goals. Some people get in the market on a whim. Someone gives them a tip that corn is going to $4 or silver to $10 in the next 3 weeks. They call a broker and put on a futures position or buy an option. Conversely, a broker might have called them with the "trade of the century." Their odds of winning are the same as someone who purchases a lottery ticket. Very few win; many lose.

Patience must be used by the serious futures trader. The trader is no different from the serious athlete. The professional football player starts playing in grade school, going on to 8 or 9 successful years at the high school and college levels. And yet, after 10 to 12 years of hard work, the player is still a rookie! More years of sweat and bruises and the player may be taken seriously in the NFL, and make it eventually to the Pro-Bowl or Super Bowl. Most commodity traders do not spend 10 years preparing for their first serious season in the markets, but in the long run they must learn the regimen.

Independence in knowing yourself and staying focused is important. It really doesn't matter what type of trading system is employed. Systems of all sorts have proven successful. It is important that you choose a system that fits your personality and unique character so that you will be consistent with the elements of the systems that are profitable, but will maintain the individuality to change the system when necessary.

Here are a few oversimplified examples. If you look at a head-and-shoulders topping chart formation that projects a 22-point move lower and feel "in your heart" it is all hocus-pocus, you should not be a technical trader. Or if you feel totally overwhelmed by all the information processed by a fundamental trader, that's probably not your calling either. Any system must suit the individual or it will fail. Traders who develop sophisticated systems requiring 1 or 2 hours of daily updating may be frustrated to learn they don't have the time or inclination to service such a system.

Your system must suit you, your psychological makeup, and the time you have available to administer it. Additionally, you need to believe in your system, and trust it, work with it, and refine it until it makes money for you. Without the patience, persistence, and discipline mentioned earlier, you'll never succeed as a futures trader.

OBSTACLES TO SUCCESS

This brings us full circle to the secret of success. It's not the "magic system" that reaps success in the markets. You need achievable objectives, a plan to reach those objectives, and a system in which you have faith—a system that matches your personality and helps you withstand the setbacks you'll experience on the way. Last of all, you must learn to conquer four major obstacles everyone faces— *fear, pride, hope,* and *greed.*

The ancient Greeks would easily relate to how an intelligent, aggressive trader with a strong market position ends up taking a massive loss on that position. The Greeks coined a word for what often happens to otherwise skillful people: *hubris.* Its common definition is simply "overbearing pride." Be wary of the trader who says, "I *know* where the market is going!"

You'll often find the four witches of greed, pride, hope, and fear accompanying hubris. This foursome has brought more people who could have been successful in the market to their financial knees than just about anything else.

Why are these emotions so prevalent among traders, and why must they be minimized or reduced for the trader to be successful? The first part of the question is easy to answer. These emotions are simply human nature, and it is hard to separate human nature from any task.

The trader on a roller coaster of emotion is not a pretty sight. Take the trader who establishes a long position in crude oil futures. There really isn't a specific trading plan, other than just a feeling or hunch the market is going to rally.

Indeed, the first week in the market, crude oil rises by 50 cents a barrel. The trader has realized a profit of $500 (not including broker commissions and other trading fees). The trader says, "I made $500 in one week. That's pretty good, but I want to make a $1,000 profit on this trade."

At the beginning of the second week, crude oil is continuing to rally strongly and prices rally by another 50 cents. As prices rise, sentiment becomes more bullish. (Remember that sentiment is most bullish at market tops.) The trader knows there is already a $1,000 profit, but can't resist the bullish news and the hope of gaining even more profits. Greed is setting in.

Toward the end of the week, some negative fundamental news surfaces that sends crude oil prices plummeting by 75 cents a barrel. In one day the trader has lost $750 in profits. "It's just a correction; this market is still headed to new highs," the trader thinks to himself. "Besides, media reports are still being heard on all the bullish factors in the crude oil market. I had $1,000 in profits and I need to get back to that level, and then I'll get out."

The next day the market drops another 75 cents a barrel— putting the trader at a loss of $500 on the trade. Now the fundamentals in crude oil are not quite as bullish as they were, according to the media reports. The trader says, "I'm not going to lose on this trade. I had $1,000 in profits just last week and lost it. Now, I just want to get back to even money. When I get to even money, I'll exit my position and try another market." This trader is hoping to get back to even so as not to be a loser on this trade. Nobody likes to lose.

The last day of the week the crude oil market falls sharply by $1 per barrel as bearish news hits the market. The downdraft in price is so sudden and so late in the trading day that the trader is not able to exit his position by the time the market closes.

Now fear has set in. But hope is still at play—the unlikely hope that prices will rocket higher just as fast Monday as they fell on Friday. A more realistic hope is that prices will stabilize enough to just get out of the trade without any further damage.

Having a specific plan of action when initiating a trade will greatly reduce, and—the hope is—eliminate, the emotions that can be so damaging to the trader. Know your entry and exit points. Know how much profit you think you'll realize—or how much loss you will tolerate. Then, when you've got your trading plan all laid out and you've entered the trade, don't let emotions change your strategy. Don't listen to what the "herd" is saying. The herd is usually wrong. Calm, cool, and collected traders stand a much better chance at success than do traders who ride all their emotions during a trade. This is where that personal attribute of independence comes in to play.

The answer may also be hidden in the past. Just as the ancients offered an ox or a goat to the gods, you must make a sacrifice. We often refer to it as "swallowing one's pride." One way of doing this is being brutally honest with yourself in your trading journal. Let's say your system flashes a sell signal while you are holding a long position. You override it, only to watch your profits evaporate as prices head lower. In your journal, if it is to be of any real value to you, you must state how you violated your system. Your journal must force discipline upon your trading. If it does only this, it will be well worth all the time and trouble it takes to maintain.

One way to prove to the market that you have conquered or at least can manage greed is to take windfall profits. Let's say you're short silver. Your analysis indicates it should go down a quarter over the next 30 to 90 days. Shortly after you get your order filled, silver drops a half dollar, 25 cents more than you expected. Do you take your unexpected profit, wait for it to go down further, or place a close stop to protect profits?

If you selected take the profit, you profit $2,500 minus transaction costs. If you wait for it to go down, you are blinded by greed, and this could lead to a devastating loss. If you place a close stop, you are still fighting greed, but you have shown some management. You're still in the market. You still have a profit, at least on paper. If all goes well, you'll eventually be stopped out with a profit.

If you trade multiple positions, you can demonstrate your mastery of greed by closing out part of your position when it becomes profitable by disciplining yourself to trade in three lots. You're long corn. It moves up to within a range from one-half to two-thirds of your objective. You close out one position at this point. Then you close your second when your objective is hit, and you speculate with the third using a stop.

Eternal hope can put you in the poorhouse. You may survive on hope in your personal life, but it can be extremely damaging in the markets. The usual scenario revolves around a position that is moving against all your best judgments. Just about everything indicates you are wrong, but you keep hoping the market will turn in your favor. Hope is addictive, numbing your discipline. Open your journal and write down why you are staying in this market. If you're frank with yourself and write "because I hope it will go my way tomorrow," you are in trouble. Cut your losses short. If you still think the market will turn, place a stop reversal order in the market. However, do it only after reevaluating the situation and entering it as a complete new trade that meets all your criteria for a new trade.

Where greed and hope abound, fear is close by. It is faced daily in the markets. Fear of losing money, fear of making a stupid error, fear of looking foolish in the eyes of peers. Probably the most effective way of controlling fear is by sacrificing a portion of profit. The old adage—bears win, bulls win, hogs lose—comes into play. You can limit some market fear by not trying to pick tops or bottoms. If you are riding a bull market to seventh heaven, get off at the sixth cloud. Take your profits and bank them. Or you can hedge your position. If you are into a large position on the long side, consider buying some puts that are near in-the-money as protection. This is not a sign of weakness. It is a sound business decision. Another suggestion is to continually take excess profits out of your account. Then, when you do have a drawdown, it is not as crushing. You still have profits to show. You don't feel as threatened, and fear doesn't overwhelm you.

Futures trading is a very personal challenge. To check your preparedness, complete the Financial-Psychological Worksheet in Figure 1.1.

FIGURE   1.1

Financial Psychological Worksheet

1.   Never invest more than you can afford to lose in highly speculative investments such as futures and options trading. Don't invest more than 10 percent of net liquid assets (those that are cash or can be converted to cash within 24 hours) in the futures market. And don't put more than 10 percent of this 10 percent amount in any one position.

Net liquid assets (NLA)
Cash-savings/checking accounts $_____
CDs and money market funds $_____

(continued)

F I G U R E **1.1** (Continued)

Bonds——Treasury, etc. $_____
Publicly traded stocks $_____
Other $_____
Total $_____
Risk capital*—10% of NLA $_____
*If this is less than $5,000, consider trading options rather than futures.

2.   Before opening a futures or options trading account, have the following:

_____   Adequate life insurance
_____   A sufficient net worth to sustain your lifestyle in the event all or
            part of the NLA is lost

3.   Examine your attitude toward risk.

_____   Risk averse (avoid futures trading programs)
_____   Risk neutral (consider options or managed programs)
_____   Aggressive risk taker (consider futures and managed programs)

4.   Determine the annual percentage rate of return you desire from the funds
committed. The higher the expected return, the higher the risk will normally
be.

_____25%   _____100%
_____50%   _____150%
_____75%   _____200% or higher

5.   Qualify your past investment experience.

_____ Minimal   _____Adequate   _____Experienced

6.   Access your personal knowledge of the futures market.

_____Very good   _____Medium   _____None

7.   Measure your reaction to pressure.

_____ Checks for $10,000 or more for an investment increase heart
         rate.
_____ Losing money causes sleepless nights.
_____ Taking the good and bad in stride is no problem.
_____ Gambling and taking chances are enjoyable.
_____ Seriously describe behavior when under financial pressure:

_____

_____

8. Rate your ability to accept the follwing negative facts of trading:

_____ Numerically, there are more losing trades than winning ones.
_____ Trading accounts will regularly experience drawdowns of equity.
_____ Occasional margin calls are inevitable.

9. Check off what trading successfully means to you:

_____ Cutting losing trades short and letting winners run
_____ Controlling pride, greed, hope, and fear
_____ Writing a plan that includes goals
_____ Keeping a trading journal
_____ Developing a trading system
_____ Selecting a broker that complements my character and limitations
_____ Funding my account adequately

There are no right or wrong responses to these items. After answering them honestly, review your answers with someone you trust. Then carefully and thoughtfully make your decision about whether you are ready to become a futures trader.

Understanding the Basics for Futures Trading

Key Concepts

- The Development of the Futures Market
- Forward Contracts versus Futures Contracts
- Standardization of Contracts
- Manage Up (Bull), Down (Bear), and Sideways Moving Markets
- Discovery of Price Trends

When you buy a futures contract, you agree to be contingently liable for accepting delivery of a specific amount of a specific commodity at a specific time in the future at a specific price. Every futures contract is carefully defined as to size, quality, quantity, delivery location, and delivery date. (See Figure 2.1 and the Appendix.) When you buy a contract, you are considered to be "long" the commodity. It "be-*longs*" to you. You own it at a given price.

On a cash commodity basis, when you are long, you have physical possession of the commodity. For example, a farmer with 5,000 bushels of No. 2 corn in a bin on the farm or at a grain elevator is long cash corn.

When you sell a futures contract, you contingently agree to deliver a specific amount of a specific commodity at a specific time in the future at a specific price and location. If you are a seller of a futures contract, you are short. You are currently "short" of the com-

F I G U R E   2.1

Basic Futures Trading Strategy

Offset positions at a better price than you originally paid for them.

Long the Market

Objective:	Buy low, sell high.
Example:	You decide to go long the deutsche mark because you believe it is going higher.
Initial position:	Buy 1 June d-mark at 55 cents on the IMM Exchange
Offsetting position:	Sold 1 June d-mark at 60 cents on the IMM Exchange
Results:	A 5-cent profit was realized. Since 1 cent equals $1,250, a total profit of $6,250 was earned. From this, a brokerage commission and NFA, FCM, and exchange fees would be deducted, or approximately $100.

Short the Market

Objective:	Sell high, buy low.
Example:	You decide to short gold because you believe it's going to decline in value.
Initial position:	Sell 1 August gold contract a $500 per ounce on COMEX.
Offsetting position:	Buy 1 August gold contract at $450 per ounce on COMEX.
Result:	A $50 per ounce profit was realized. Since each COMEX contract contains 100 troy ounces of gold, a total profit of $5000 was earned. From this would be deducted the transaction costs (brokerage commission; NFA, FCM, and exchange fees), which could be $100 more or less.

Note: See the appendix, "Contract Specifications." An offsetting futures position must be for the same commodity, delivery month, quantity, and exchange, but on the opposite side of the market, as the initial position.

modity. On a cash basis, a farmer would be short corn if it is currently not in the inventory. It has been agreed to accept delivery of a specific number of bushels of corn of a specific grade (quality) at a specific location (grain elevator) at a specific time and price.

A little historical perspective may help in explaining this basic concept. The modern futures markets began to develop in the early 1800s. Chicago, because it was a strong financial center in the heart of the corn, cattle, and hog country, was one of the early centers. It is still a leading center today.

SURPLUS TO SHORTAGE PROBLEMS

At harvest each year, farmers hauled to town the grain they could not use as livestock feed. Chicago became a natural basin for this excess grain because of transportation routes. Harvest was a time of surpluses. Grain users (feed companies, stockyards, processors, etc.) pressed for low prices, often forcing farmers to accept ridiculously low offers.

Grain merchants stockpiled as much grain as they could afford at the low harvest prices, but storage facilities were limited. As the year progressed, the supply of stored grain shrank and users were forced to bid aggressively for the remaining supply still stored on farms. Thus began the annual cycle of surpluses to shortages. Violent price swings from harvest lows to late-season highs drove the grain industry to search out an alternative marketing method. Forward contracts were born.

FORWARD CONTRACTS—A USEFUL MARKETING TOOL

It's impossible to appreciate the development of the modern futures contract without taking a close look at the forward contract—a still popular vehicle that allows users to manage risk. A forward contract is an agreement between two parties. The first party agrees to deliver a certain product to the second party at a specified time for a price agreed upon in advance. The term *forward* refers to a date forward in time.

Forward contracts have been around for ages, but they gained particular popularity in the Midwest in the early and middle nineteenth century as farmers began to cultivate the vast prairie. Finding themselves far from the market centers in the East, producers often had little choice but to transport their excess grain long distances.

Meanwhile, Chicago, located on the shore of Lake Michigan, was establishing itself as a center of trade in grain, livestock, and other physical commodities. As the city grew and roads, canals, and, eventually, railroads connected to it, Chicago cemented its position as the supplier of grain to the more populous East, as well as to much of the rest of the world.

While Chicago became a ready market for Midwestern grain, farmers had little to insulate themselves from cyclical price swings. Without much in the way of storage, producers usually had to take their crops to market soon after harvest. What's more, the farmers had no choice but to take the price offered. Often, prices plummeted as the harvest progressed and the grain markets were flooded with supply.

Eventually, a small group of farmers sought a more efficient way to price their crops, striking agreements with buyers to deliver grain at a set price in the future. If nothing else, the arrangement guaranteed the farmer a set price for the grain. While facing the risk of missing out on added profit if the price fell before the grain was delivered, the farmer was seemingly guaranteed not to suffer should the price plunge.

Farmers benefited because price risk was being transferred in part to the buyer. Millers benefited as well. While they would miss out on a bargain if prices fell before the grain was delivered, they didn't have to worry that prices would rise sharply.

It was a great idea in theory. The shortcomings of these early forward contracts, however, included the fact that they were difficult to enforce. Since the contracts were agreements jointly between the buyer and seller, farmers were often tempted to wriggle out if prices rose before they made delivery. Millers were also known to renege on their obligations if prices had fallen in the interim.

INADEQUACIES OF FORWARD CONTRACTS

Forward contracts suffer from an inherent problem. They lack flexibility. To understand the limitations of forward contracts, consider the following situation. On July 15, a farmer has 100 acres of land planted to corn. The crop seems healthy, and the farmer expects 100 bushels of corn per acre, or 10,000 bushels. On the same date, a corn oil refiner checks the inventory and decides 10,000 bushels are needed at harvest time to meet the production schedule.

The farmer feels confident that 10,000 bushels of corn will be delivered at harvest, and a buyer needs to be found willing to set the price. The corn oil refiner is sure that 10,000 bushels of corn at harvest time will be needed and wants to lock in a price.

As the corn buyer and the seller bargain, they hammer out the specifics of a forward contract. They agree upon:

A price—$2.50
Quality—No. 2 yellow corn
Quantity—10,000 bushels
Delivery place—the refiner's site
Time of delivery—October 10

The seller of the grain signs the contract, obligating himself to deliver.

If the price of corn declines during the contract period, the seller would be protected, but the buyer would have a loss of opportunity—the opportunity to buy at a cheaper price. If the price rose, the buyer would enjoy the lower price, but the seller would lose the opportunity to sell at a higher price.

Suppose that after signing the forward contract, the corn farmer experiences a major crop failure that cuts production in half. The forward contract obligates the farmer to deliver 10,000 bushels, so the farmer would have to purchase corn in the cash (open) market, thus compounding the loss.

A similar problem could arise for the refiner if a decline in the value of corn oil were to dictate a reduction in oil output. The refiner is contractually bound to accept delivery of and pay for 10,000 bushels of corn. A portion of this corn would likely have to be sold in the open market at a lower price if it is not used for oil production.

The forward contract was an improvement over producing and holding grain in the hopes of higher prices; however, it still proved to be an inefficient and inflexible way to market crops when supply or demand changed unexpectedly. Grain buyers and sellers needed more flexibility.

DEVELOPMENT OF CONTRACT STANDARDS

As forward contracts became more common, speculators appeared on the scene. They hoped to make a profit by assuming temporary buy or sell positions in forward contracts. For example, a seller wants to create a forward contract to price for future delivery of grain but lacks a commercial buyer. A speculator might step in and sign the buyer's side of the contract with the objective of finding a commercial buyer at a later date. The speculator hopes to profit by reselling the forward contract at a higher price.

Assume that a speculator takes the buy side of a wheat producer's forward contract. Shortly afterward, prices of forward contracts begin to rise. The speculator realizes that the forward contract can now be sold at a profit—say, 10 cents per bushel higher. The contract can be sold to a commercial grain buyer for a profit. In that case, the grain buyer must be willing to accept the specific details of the original contract. The speculator's profit is the 10-cent difference between the original contract price and the resale price. On a 10,000-bushel contract, $1,000 has just been made.

As you can see, trading or speculating in grain by forward contracts can be cumbersome, inefficient, and restrictive. The Chicago Board of Trade, established in 1848 with 82 members, was formed in large part to encourage a smoother transfer of forward contracts. The existence of a centralized marketplace highlighted the need for streamlined trading procedures. Over time, these forward contracts acquired specific standards for quantity, quality, commodity, delivery place, and date. They, thus, became similar to modern futures contracts—one of the most flexible, innovative pricing mechanisms in the history of commerce.

Although the Chicago Board of Trade was charged initially with promoting commerce in general, one of its first accomplishments was to set standards for wheat, as well as to implement an inspection system. By 1865, following years of volatile global and local price action due to the Crimean War and, later, the U.S. Civil War, the exchange had adopted rules that defined the first real futures contracts. While modifications and additions were to come, the modern futures contract had been born.

Essentially, futures contracts differ from forward contracts in several key ways. First, futures contracts are traded on exchanges, while forward contracts are two-party agreements between a buyer and a seller. Second, futures contracts rely on standards that determine the product being delivered will be of uniform quality. Also, a futures contract sets a specific quantity to be traded, while the size of a forward contract is set by the buyer and the seller.

Forward contracts require counterparty vigilance. Since futures are traded on an exchange, buyers and sellers needn't worry whether or not the person they trade with will make good on the contract. That's because the exchange clearinghouse guarantees that the other side of the trade will be fulfilled if either the buyer or seller defaults. There's no clearinghouse to stand between a buyer and seller in a forward contract. That means both parties in a forward must keep close track of their trading partner's creditworthiness.

Forward contracts don't allow users to easily change marketing plans. Futures provide more flexibility. For example, a farmer who sold, or went short, a November soybean futures contract in March, expecting the price to go down, could see a summer drought push the price of soybeans substantially higher. At that point, the farmer could buy back the November contract, eliminating the short position—leaving the farmer long the cash soybean market based on the crop that is in the fields. With a forward contract, the producer is locked into delivering the soybeans to the local elevator at the price established in March.

A forward contract's value isn't "marked to market" until it comes due. Exchanges require that each futures account be marked to market at the end of each trading day. That means that each position in the market is assigned a value based on the day's closing price. A trader holding a losing position may be required to post additional margin or else close out the position. This keeps big losing positions from accumulating and lowers the risk of default. Since forward markets aren't marked to market, the risk that a trading partner could default in a volatile market is higher.

Forward transactions are often more complex than futures transactions. Complex financial transactions can often be executed more easily in the futures market than in the forward market. A bank whose client wants to borrow money in September, and repay in December, would be exposed to interest rate risk if it quoted a fixed rate. To offset the risk in the forward market, the institution would have to make two trades, lending to September and borrowing from December. Futures would allow the bank to execute a single trade, selling 3-month Eurodollar futures for settlement in September.

If the bank wanted to unwind the position before September, it would simply offset the futures position by buying back a September contract, eliminating the short position.

FUTURES CONTRACTS

Futures contracts have only one buyer and one seller at any moment in time. The creation of a contract simply depends on one buyer and one seller agreeing on a price. This is accomplished by "open outcry" in the pits on the floors of the exchanges. All other specifications, except for the number of contracts to be bought or sold, are standardized.

You, as a trader, transmit your trading order (to buy or to sell a futures contract) to your broker. Your broker in turn communicates with the order desk on the floor of the exchange that trades the specific futures contract you want to trade. The floor order desk gives your trade to the floor trader in the pits. Once your order is filled, the process is reversed and your broker calls you with your fill (the price at which you bought or sold the contract).

To offset your position in the futures market, you need only to find a substitute seller or buyer. You do this by giving your broker an equal but opposite order to your current futures position. Only about 3 percent of futures contracts are actually delivered. Therefore, initiating and offsetting futures positions are carried out in the same way.

Because futures contracts are standardized, ownership, transfer, and substitutions are accomplished without endangering the original purpose of the forward markets—which is to set price, facilitate delivery, and transfer risk. Futures contracts can change hands many times before their delivery date (expiration). Historically, the increased use of futures by speculators makes the market more efficient and actually reduces price fluctuations.

Without active involvement of speculators, buyers' and sellers' price differences (the bid and offer price spread) would widen and prices would fluctuate more dramatically. Furthermore, without this speculative activity, the consumer would have to pay higher food prices to compensate grain dealers for the risk of violent price swings resulting from temporary gluts and shortages.

THE IMPORTANCE OF STANDARDIZATION

As stated previously, the Chicago Board of Trade's adoption of standardized contracts for delivery of grain in 1865 marked the birth of the modern futures contract. While forward contracts can be written for any quantity of any commodity for delivery at any time the two parties desire, futures contracts are rigidly defined.

Futures exchanges establish all the key parameters of a contract. They define its size, the specific grade and class (U.S. No. 2 yellow corn, 30-year U.S. T-bonds) of the underlying commodity or product, the month that delivery will take place, and the time period within that month when delivery can occur. The exchanges also determine where delivery can take place.

For example, a Chicago Board of Trade corn futures contract sets terms for delivery of 5,000 bushels of U.S. No. 2 yellow corn to be delivered to an exchange-approved clearinghouse. Available delivery months are March, May, July, September, and December.

STANDARDIZATION SIMPLIFIES AND EXPEDITES PRICE DISCOVERY

By defining all the key characteristics of the commodity or product to be delivered, buyers and sellers need only worry about how many contracts they want to trade and at what price. When a customer phones the broker and places an order to buy two contracts of corn for December delivery, the broker needn't worry what type of corn is wanted or where it will be delivered. All orders flowing into the corn pit are for the same commodity. There's nothing left for the traders to shout about other than the price.

STANDARDIZATION PROMOTES LIQUIDITY

Standardized delivery grades mean virtually anyone with sufficient capital can enter the market easily to hedge or speculate. Because the contracts are standardized, there's no confusion about what's on the block. A speculator who spots what is believed to be a trading opportunity can move into the market quickly, without first haggling to determine exactly what to buy or sell or when it will be delivered.

Similarly, hedgers know whether or not the product being traded can be used to offset their own risk in the spot market. Both speculators and hedgers can move in or out of the market with ease.

Increased participation by speculators and hedgers increases liquidity, and increased liquidity means lower transaction costs. Of course, for a contract to be a success, it's crucial that the specifications meet the requirements of end users or liquidity will suffer. A contract that doesn't provide delivery of grain when mills most require it offers few advantages. Similarly, delivery of a class of commodity or product that doesn't fit the commercial user's hedging needs will also have difficulty attracting liquidity.

Speculators must also be accommodated. While the terms of a grain contract should readily accommodate both farmers and millers, it must also be of a size that's attractive to speculators. A contract that is too big may force potential speculators to pony up a margin beyond their means. Similarly, a contract too small may attract investors unsuited for the volatility of a particular contract.

STANDARDIZATION PRODUCES MORE RELIABLE PRICE INFORMATION

Futures markets offer buyers and sellers more reliable price information than cash and forward markets. Forward markets often offer a number of delivery dates and locations. For most users, particularly nonprofessionals, it is often difficult to determine the market price. That's not the case with futures, which offer numerous products and designate a single delivery date for settlement.

What's more, futures quotations offer a combination of the price for a spot commodity plus the "carrying cost" (interest, insurance, etc.) of holding the commodity until delivery—a feature usually not found in spot market quotations.

ROLE OF INVENTORY MANAGER

To really get into the swing of what moves the markets, put yourself behind the desk of someone responsible for managing an inventory of a specific commodity, soybeans for example. Begin at harvest time when the bean supply is plentiful.

One of the first insights an inventory manager needs is how this commodity reacts to changes in supply and demand. The principle of elasticity can be defined as a characteristic of commodities which describes the interaction of the supply of, demand for, and price of a commodity. A commodity is said to be elastic in demand when a price change creates an increase or decrease in consumption. It is said to be elastic in supply when a change in price creates a change in the production of the commodity. Inelasticity of supply or demand exists when either supply or demand is relatively unresponsive to changes in price.

Most food and feed commodities respond to changes in price. If soybean prices shoot up, users look for a substitute or ration their usage of soybeans. Livestock feeders use other sources of protein. Vegetable oil producers and users have a wide variety of substitutes available such as sunflower seeds, corn, palm, and coconuts.

The professional inventory manager knows soybean prices are elastic. The price stretches and contracts (rises and falls) in relationship to supply and demand. It is known that supplies are usually plentiful and prices are relatively low at harvest because many farmers do not have or cannot afford storage.

Studying the season price information indicates cash soybeans can be expected to bottom approximately three out of four times during the October–November period each year. Therefore, the inventory manager looks at harvest as a buying opportunity. Then the question becomes how much to buy or whether to wait and buy as the beans can be used. The next step is to make an evaluation of the overall supply and demand (also known as *fundamental*) of the market. In late fall, the South American crop is planted. How many hectares? What yields are expected? How aggressively are the governments of Brazil and Argentina promoting production and exportation?

Most American farmers are on a cash basis accounting system and often carry soybeans for sale into the next tax year as a way of balancing their income. Traditionally, farm real estate debt comes due on March 1. This generates another buying opportunity for the inventory manager. Within the same time frame, the South American crop is being harvested and supplies are again plentiful if the crop is good.

In other words, the inventory manager must decide in November how much to buy between then and spring. Technical analysis can be a big help. What do the charts indicate? Are prices near long- or short-term support areas? How much volatility is in the markets? This gives insight into how wide or narrow the trading range is expected to be. Keep in mind that beans are elastic. They will respond to changes—often widely.

When you put yourself in the inventory manager's seat, all known and unknown variables come into sharper focus. This is true for virtually any commodity traded. Suppose you wish to trade the financials. You can evaluate interest rates from the standpoint of a bank officer inventorying money. What about the S&P 500? Put yourself in the shoes of a mutual fund manager. If you have a $20 million stock portfolio to manage, what do you do?

The object of this exercise is to gain an overview of the market you are interested in trading. Is the trend likely to be up, down, or sideways? If your analysis indicates it is up, you would go long on the futures or buy call options. If it is down, go short or buy puts. If it is sideways, stand aside or learn to trade within the price range.

Before trading, you must also gauge the strength of your conviction. Hold back when you get conflicting signals from the seasonals, fundamentals, and other technicals. Your confidence should increase when everything is synchronized.

Timing can make all the difference—even when your analysis is absolutely correct. You can be dead right and still lose in the futures market, especially in the short term. In the long term, you must have the money and the patience to wait for the right time or to get in and out of the market with small, controlled losses until the timing is right for a big win.

Also, you can never assume your analysis is infallible. There are always unknown factors—dock strikes, floods, droughts, governmental intervention, etc.—that can stampede the market against your position. That's why you need to use special techniques such as protective stop orders to cover your positions.

The beauty and value of the futures market is that every contract eventually reverts to the cash market. When a contract expires, it is either deliverable in the commodity or settled on a cash basis. The cash and the futures markets become one!

If you chart the cash price of a specific commodity at a given location and its futures price, particularly in the nearby delivery month, you'll find these two prices usually move together. One does not mirror the other, but the patterns are usually similar. Keep in mind that the cash price quote comes from a delivery point such as a grain terminal. This geographical point has specific local influences that explain minor discrepancies that distinguish the cash and futures markets.

Also, the futures price is just that—a price for the commodity at some chronological point in the future. News, crop reports, cycles, seasonals, and all the other influencers of price usually affect the futures price first and with more impact than in the cash market. Then the price influencers trickle down into the cash market. It is common to see a 2- or 3-week differential in the trend changes between the futures and the cash markets. Eventually, they become one price at the expiration of the futures contract. This keeps the market honest and true to the supply-demand situation.

This is the reason users and producers closely follow the futures market even if they don't trade it. They know that what happens in the pits will eventually be felt in the fields, or the mines, or the bank vaults.

Additionally, the inventory manager can be a hedger, shifting the risk of futures' usage to a speculator. This would be another reason to closely follow the futures markets.

Once you accept this close relationship, you gain insight into how to anticipate price activity by viewing the markets through the eyes of the inventory manager. Now, look at some specific price-trend moves and decide what action an inventory manager would take.

MANAGING AN UPTREND

The inventory manager of a large soybean crusher is responsible for maintaining a 30-day inventory of beans. The inventory manager's annual bonus is based on the profitability of the operation. For the sake of profitability, the inventory manager must time bean buying carefully.

Harvest is now over. The seasonal trend is up, and the South American crop is in trouble. Each time the manager goes into the market, the price is higher. Faced with this prospect, most inventory managers begin to build inventory. Each purchase becomes a little larger.

What does this do to the uptrend? It causes the trend to move sharply higher. As prices begin to skyrocket, everyone panics. Herd psychology takes over. The buyers buy at any price. The sellers hold the product off the market because they think it will be more valuable tomorrow. The poor inventory manager fears being completely shut out of the market and out of inventory.

At some point prices become ridiculous—$13 per bushel. The manager of the soybean processing plant instructs the inventory manager to quit buying. Prices are too high to process the beans and generate a profit. It makes more sense to shut down the plant.

About the same time, the sellers realize they have a windfall and begin to send raw materials into the cash market. Shorts in the futures markets take delivery, thus squeezing the cash market even more. Then sellers begin to fear they are going to totally miss the boat. This causes them to sell as fast as they can, which drives prices down—just when the buyers have backed off. This behavior helps explain why markets tend to top with sharp peaks and fall twice as fast as they rise.

MANAGING THE DOWNTREND

If the soybean market was trending downward, the inventory manager would not build inventory. The inventory manager would buy from hand to mouth because each subsequent purchase would be made at a lower price. Patience may pay off, but at some point abundant supply fosters increases in usage and increases demand. A base is eventually built and prices level off.

MANAGING CONGESTION

What does the inventory manager do when prices are in a sideways or consolidating pattern? As prices move in a channel, the buyer perceives the top of the price channel as being too high or prohibitive. The buyer backs off. Prices move lower and become a "bargain." The buyer steps in and his buying generates support at the bottom of the channel.

Eventually something upsets this pattern. It could be some fundamental news, such as a drought or news of record yields. The supply-demand scale tips one way or the other and a new trend begins.

Your emotional or instinctual reaction to price changes is a valid input. After all, the market is the sum total of all the players' reactions to what has happened, what is happening, and what everyone expects to happen. In short, it can be said that a commodities futures price is the composite opinion of all market participants and influencers.

GET THE RIGHT HAT ON!

When you put yourself in the position of an inventory manager, you must first give some thought to the specific situation you'll be facing. An inventory manager can just as easily represent a country as a company. Therefore, you want to match the commodity and the situation with the inventory manager's motives. If you are looking at the long-term outlook for grains, you may want to look at the situation from a variety of viewpoints. Then you will be able to anticipate what each player will do and the cumulative impact on the price of grains.

The motivation of the inventory manager from a South American country, which is a net exporter, differs substantially from that of an inventory manager of an Eastern European country, which is a net importer. You must also sort out the political motivations of countries like the United States, which has a history of using food as foreign policy. In our current situation, the grains appear to be making a technical bottom. What is going through the minds of inventory managers around the world?

The United States Department of Agriculture (USDA) has the administration pressuring it to reduce its budget. Therefore, the USDA wants to force the price of grain higher to reduce subsidy payments to farmers. At the same time, the State Department and the White House refuse to issue credits to the foreign country because of its human rights violation. Your analysis indicates that political pressure will be strong enough that the USDA will win. Credit will be given. This will have a positive effect on price.

The people in South America, who control the flow of grain, are also under a lot of political and financial pressure. They need the sales badly. Therefore, they will be aggressive sellers, but they are not in a financial position to offer credits. This means they will probably discount prices.

As an inventory manager, you must analyze the net impact of this tug-of-war. You conclude that the need or the demand is so strong, it will push prices higher. However, it also looks as if prices will move up slowly and in an orderly manner because there are many willing sellers but the aggressive buyers are cash poor.

Historically, big net importers of grain, like the Commonwealth of Independent States (the former Soviet Union), have been very active buyers of U.S. grains around harvesttime. This is the cyclical low for the grain market. Inventory managers for these countries would naturally be buyers at this time of year. You have just seen what a bottoming market looks like. What positions do inventory managers take when a market is topping?

First, you must distinguish whether you are thinking like an inventory manager for a seller or a buyer of the commodity. As a market tops, inventory managers for buyers try to hold back as much as they can—buying from hand to mouth. They are hoping the market will break before it breaks them.

Inventory managers for sellers might also hold back, expecting to sell their commodity at an even higher price tomorrow. This drives prices into a blow-off top, sometimes followed by a short-term rebound.

OPEN INTEREST IS A KEY TO THE ACTIONS OF INVENTORY MANAGERS

Another key to understanding both topping and bottoming situations is open interest. It can be defined as the sum of all long or short futures contracts in one delivery month or one market that have been entered but not yet liquidated by an offsetting transaction or fulfilled by delivery. This information is reported by the futures exchanges and published daily in the major financial newspapers. Inventory managers, by virtue of their size, have a noticeable impact on open interest when they act.

If open interest increases when a market is near record lows and prices start to stabilize or move higher, inventory managers for users are aggressively accumulating inventory. If, on the other hand, prices are topping and open interest is declining, the inventory managers for producers are selling. Generally speaking, as the inventory managers go, so go the markets they trade.

The strongest hands that ever hold a commodity are those belonging to a bona fide hedger. The bona fide hedger is a producer or someone with a business need for the commodity. Plans are made to sell it or use it. Business can't be conducted without it. The bona fide hedger is not easily swayed by transient political or economic pressures, but is neither crazy nor foolish. If prices get too far out of line, hold will be relinquished on the commodity in question.

ANATOMY OF A BULL MARKET

Understanding the concept of bull (uptrend) and bear (downtrend) markets is critical to success in the futures market.

There are usually seven distinct stages in every major bull market. You must learn to recognize each stage before it is in full swing. By developing this skill, you'll be able to trade with the trend, which is often the difference between winning and losing in the markets.

1. *The birth of the bull.* Surprisingly, the origins of a bull market are found in surplus situations. Surplus commodities widen the arteries, fill the pipelines, and foster new sources of demand. An industry whose raw materials are in surplus is likely to expand usage. Low-priced, surplus supplies build confidence in users—the confidence to expand, to develop new uses (corn sweetener, oils, gasohol, etc.), to solicit new customers, and to contract long-term commitments. All these factors result in an increased appetite and a wider demand base.

From a technical analysis perspective, a surplus market is observable as a rounded bottom, the early signs of which are progressively shallowing downtrends and narrower trading ranges. The absolute bottom of a rounded bottom often occurs when the fundamental information is the most bearish while the commodity price meanders sideways in a narrow range. You can be comfortable, for instance, with a major market bottom when all the news reports say that corn is going to the "price of gravel" while the corn price wanders aimlessly in a 2-cent range. Passive market activity in response to bearish news is your first bull sign.

2. *Shallow uptrend.* The next benchmark is modestly increasing prices at the right side of the rounded bottom. It is a very shallow uptrend, usually accompanied by wider price ranges. Fundamentally, there is little change in the supply of the commodity, but commercial interest in the commodity does change slightly. A "what-if" stage develops among the fundamentalists. What if there is a short wheat crop in Canada? What if Brazilian coffee has a freeze? What if housing starts increase by 10 percent? What if war breaks out? Due to the intangible nature of the what-if stage and the fruitless nature of most what-if scenarios, stage 2 offers very little price improvement other than the gradual increase in price due to carrying charges. Yet this is the place to begin to build your position as the momentum picks up.

3. *The breakout.* The third stage of development is a very interesting one that often occurs with very little public supply and demand information. It is frequently described in business publications as a "technical breakout." This is a way of saying, "The market has made a dramatic move, but we don't know why."

Technically, the market is breaking out of the rounded bottom, and it usually shows a modest rally for a few days, sometimes weeks. This rally often subsides without fundamental follow-through and develops a platform or plateau. This is sideways market activity at the area of the rounded bottom breakout and a time of confusing information. Fundamental and technical data are often conflicting and often contradictory.

4. *The rally.* Stage 4 of the bull market develops as market information becomes more detailed. Often, seemingly minor fundamental (supply and demand) information comes into play, such as erratic weather patterns across the Midwest affecting the grain market. More what-if scenarios also begin to develop. This nervous rally tends to be choppy, with labored price increases and sharp, quick dips. The rallies and subsequent dips are usually able to hold a 45-degree trend line. Traders feel confident in buying when prices dip back to the trend line.

5. *The explosive newsmaker.* On a technical basis, gaps are often left on the charts during this phase, while the bullish fundamental scenario gains wider acceptance. Users scramble to purchase raw material, while sellers become reluctant to release supplies. Interestingly, advisory newsletters during this stage usually become nervous and indicate a bias that the market may be topping.

6. *The steep rally.* The sixth stage of the bull market is typically a steep rally with few market retracements and wide trading ranges fueled by bullish fundamental information. Often, public attention turns toward the market rally, and people who have never traded commodities suddenly think about trading the long side. During this period the news media report on users who are going bankrupt because they have left themselves exposed to price increases in raw materials.

7. *The shearing.* Stage 7 occurs when investors decide to sell their blue-chip stock at a loss and go long in the commodity market just when bullish information is being offered to the public, inspiring them to become involved. When you read about it in the *Wall Street Journal,* check to make sure you have your protective stop orders properly placed. Technically, the market will gap higher with limit up moves, even for 2 or more days; then, the sheep are shorn. It is after stage 7 that the futures industry is plagued with outcries for greater regulation.

BEAR MARKETS

Bear markets usually move down faster than bull markets move up. One of the reasons is lower volume. The less volume, the more erratic and violent market moves become since there is less activity to absorb and cushion the fall. Low-volume markets are very dangerous to trade for this reason. Staying informed is essential. The volume of each market is reported by exchanges and published daily in the major financial papers.

Like bull markets, there are several stages to these markets.

1. The first stage occurs when bullish news enters the market but the market doesn't move higher. It appears that either nobody believes the news or everyone believes the market has already taken the information into consideration.

2. Next, the market makes a severe retracement—usually 33, 50, or 66 percent of the previous bull move. A lot of traders on the long side, often small individual traders, lose money and are forced out of the market. Since no new longs enter the market when this retracement starts, the market is said to "fall by its own weight."

3. Once the market finds some support, completing the retracement stage, there may be a period where the market moves sideways or even up. This is a bear market rally. Traders are often very confused during this time period.

4. Sooner or later, the bullish news becomes scarce or nonexistent. At this point, the market makes its final descent to the point where inventory managers can't resist building inventories. This actually brings the bear market to an end.

THE PRICE DISCOVERY PROCESS

Obtaining a firm grasp of how the market discovers price is a key to successful trading. What may appear to the novice trader as totally random price movement eventually conforms to recognizable and tradable patterns.

Think about the futures market as a public poll. The futures brokers are the pollsters. They go out and survey the general trading public. "Where do you think the price of gold is headed?" "In your opinion, is the price of crude oil too high or too low?" The answers to all the questions are communicated to the trading pits, where they are processed. The results are published daily in various financial papers, are transmitted on the financial wire services, and can be found on several websites.

The people who answer these surveys are very sincere about their answers. They have backed their opinions with margin money. Collectively, they represent all the thoughts, research, and emotions surrounding the entire financial community. The people polled may have been influenced by the media, their personal financial situation, and what has happened or is happening in the world.

Can studying and evaluating all these surveys be meaningful? Yes, they help in the discovery of long-term trends. If you look at the trends—as someone like John Naisbitt, author of *Megatrends,* would do—you begin to think about them as being the collective response to stimuli. By reading, studying, and collecting a wide array of seemingly unrelated data, experts can deduce, with a good deal of accuracy, various interesting trends that planners and businesspeople can use.

This work is very similar to fundamental analysis of the futures markets. However, even if you can deduce the overall, long-term trend, it doesn't necessarily tell you which specific opportunity or trade to take. Nor is it much help when it comes to timing. Most traders revert to technical or chart analysis at this point.

LEFT- AND RIGHT-BRAIN TRADING

As learned from scientific research, the brain has a left and a right hemisphere. The left side deals primarily with the logical side of our nature, the right with the creative or artistic.

In selecting trades you use your left side to do fundamental and technical research. Once all your homework is done, either by yourself or in consultation with your broker, you digest the facts. At this point, the hard data moves to the right side of the brain for interpretation. The artist in the trader uncovers the patterns in the charts. Intuition takes over in many successful traders. They may trade what appear to be hunches, but are, in reality, a synergistic blend of the left- and right-brain functions. A behavioral pattern is often seen in successful traders and brokers, where they study the facts, sleep on the information, and trade successfully the next day.

Good commodity trading advisers (CTAs) substantiate their analysis at different times with different analytical tools. One time a CTA may seem to be a fundamentalist; the next, a strict technician.

The experienced analyst selects the correct analytic technique based on the current market conditions. Some techniques work well when the markets are trending up or down, but are useless or dangerous in choppy, trendless markets. Some chart formations are more reliable than others. Sometimes, the fundamentals are clear and meaningful. At other times, they are conflicting.

Nowadays there is so much access by traders and advisers to both technical and fundamental information, the well-known signals become self-fulfilling prophecies. Everyone sees corn break a trend line or drop through a support level. This causes a rush to the short side of the market. The lower prices foretold by the broken trend line are realized.

Wouldn't a totally automated system be best? True enough, a freestanding computerized trading system would eliminate the need for subjective judgment on the part of the analyst. However, you wouldn't want this any more than you would want to ride in a plane that didn't have human pilots who have the capacity to override the autopilot when conditions warrant it. Futures trading is a blend of cold, calculating statistics and a warm, human touch. Traders who rely too heavily on either—to the neglect of the other—are not usually successful.

You must accept the law of probability to be able to handle the stress of futures trading. Futures trading can be a hit-and-miss investment. Some trades work; others don't. You must keep trying one trade after the other until you pick the profitable trades. "Cut losing trades short and let winners run" is the rule to go by.

You diversify your portfolio by trading several different markets in order to increase the probability of being in the right trade at the right time. This requires discipline and money management. Both are essential for you to survive the markets and utilize the law of probability to your best advantage.

CHAPTER 3

Setting Goals and Creating a Portfolio

Key Concepts
- Set Realistic Goals
- Have a Written Trading Plan
- Keep a Written Trading Journal
- Select Trading Portfolios

The futures industry, more than just about any other, is filled with stories of office clerks becoming millionaires virtually overnight. Some of these stories are even true, but the reality of the situation is that most small individual traders lose money. For this reason, it is very important that you develop realistic goals. These are milestones you can use to measure your success. Learn to do this often, so you know when you are ahead and when you're falling behind.

SETTING REALISTIC GOALS

Success in achieving goals often depends upon putting them in writing. This makes them more real. More importantly, you have a better chance of reaching written objectives because they don't go away.

At the same time you dictate your goals, also prepare a list of your limitations. What will limit your success in reaching your futures trading goals? It could be lack of, perhaps, equity, or knowledge of the markets, or a tested trading system, or time to devote to the market. Or it could be something you have too much of, like optimism, greed, or self-confidence. Or it could be an equipment limitation. You can't day-trade without tick-by-tick price quotation equipment. You might need a computer to run the trading system you wish to use. Does your current work keep you out of touch with the markets during the day or for other periods of time? No matter what your limitations are, you must take them into consideration as you develop your goals.

The primary goal of just about every trader is, or should be, to take money out of the market. The question is usually how much and how fast. Do you want to double your equity every quarter? Or make 200 or 400 percent or more return on your trading equity?

The more aggressive your goal, the greater the risk you have to take. Keep in mind that one of the keys to reaching financial goals is being in the right market at the right time. You may have to diversify to do this and trade several markets at the same time.

In the futures market, an account can trade only a few markets at a time. Even if the analysis is absolutely right, your timing may be a week or two off. Once the trader loses some money (drawdown of equity), it may not be possible to get back into the market when the time is right. For this reason, goals must be tempered with whatever limitations you impose or are imposed on you from without.

DEVELOP A WRITTEN TRADING PLAN

A written trading plan doesn't have to be formal or extensive, but it should answer the following questions:

Trading Plan Checklist
1. Am I psychologically and financially suited to trade in the futures markets?
2. What are my goals?
3. What are my limitations?
4. How will I keep a trading journal?
5. Will I trade futures, options on futures, or both?
6. What commodities and contracts will I trade?

7. How will I do my analysis?
8. What trading system will I use?
9. Do I have hard-and-fast money management rules?
10. What trading strategies will I use?
11. What type of orders do I plan to use?
12. What do I need from my broker?

Once you have answers to these questions, you're ready to begin the broker selection process.

KEEP A WRITTEN JOURNAL OF OUTCOMES

Another important record you should maintain is a daily trading journal. A good written record of your trading activity could separate you from the majority of traders who fail. The function of the journal is twofold. First, it reminds you why a trade was selected or rejected. Second, it provides an audit trail.

Why bother is a common attitude among futures traders. They just don't see the value of chronicling their trading activity. They have the attitude, "I get a monthly statement—isn't that enough?"

The most important piece of information missing from your monthly statement is the reason you got into the trade in the first place. What did you expect to happen? What was the risk-to-reward ratio? What alternative trades did you turn down in favor of the ones you took? What fundamental or technical signals triggered your trading decision? What attracted you to the trade initially?

Remember the quotation (Santayana), "Those who cannot remember the past are condemned to repeat it." Trading is an extremely personal and emotional endeavor. Our minds interpret the inkblots on the price charts and rationalize trading decisions. Some great traders talk about their instincts. According to them, they can smell a trade when it is still 10 ticks away!

The essence of what these traders are saying is basically believable, but writing stimulates thought and clarifies thinking. Researchers who have studied the papers of some of the world-class traders indicated that their trading wasn't by the "seat of their pants." The great traders documented what they did before, during, and after the markets were open. Learn from mistakes. Why repeat them? Learn from success. Why not repeat it? This historical record overcomes the tendency to mold the past by the perception of it in the present. Without the facts it is difficult to be brutally honest.

For these two reasons, you should put your thoughts and emotional reasons for each trade on paper before you call your broker. This is needed even if all you have to go by is a "gut feeling that corn is going higher." Record when you first noticed that feeling as well as what might have triggered it. Was it a news story, a chart formation, or what? Later on, you may be able to piece the puzzle together and make concrete sense of it.

Reliable instincts are as meaningful in commodity trading as they are in any other human activity. The price trends and patterns of the futures market reflect the instincts and emotional state of every trader that is getting in or out of the market at a given time. You may be able to instinctively sense where a market is going at times, just like a hunter can sense where game can be found.

Your trading journal helps you hone your instincts and/or rid yourself of them if they are not valid. You really learn to sort out unfounded hunches from brilliant insights, but what should be included in a trading journal? When do entries need to be made, and where do you keep your journal? The journal reflects your trading system. Start by asking, "How do I select trades? What are my key indicators? What are my goals?" For example, the first thing many traders do is determine if the trend is up or down for the markets they are tracking. This may be your first entry. You would then do the same for the other signals that you regularly check. Be consistent in your logging of this information.

How often do you need to make an entry or update your journal? There are a couple of ways to look at this. First, do you normally trade for the long or short term? Second, do you trade slow-moving markets like oats or speedier ones like the S&P 500? You should make an entry each time you "check" your markets. Checking means evaluating your current position and giving serious consideration to entering or exiting a trade.

What format is best for a trading journal? It might be hieroglyphic notes scratched on a Daytimer by a day trader or an elaborate record maintained on a computerized word processing program. The what, when, where, and how of keeping a journal is a lot like the question of how long should a person's legs be? Long enough to reach the ground. Your journal should satisfy your needs.

It is created only to help you trade more successfully. The worst thing it can become is a chore. If you find yourself dreading the thought of updating it, something is wrong.

Simplicity often makes diaries more meaningful. Say you receive a weekly charting service that you update once or twice throughout the week. You could make your journal entries right on the charts as you are filling in the daily trading ranges. Then cut out the charts you use and put them in a three-ring binder. Once a trade is closed, record the results. Then page back through the chart pages and evaluate your performance. On the last page, write a two- or three-sentence summary. It can be as simple as that.

SELECTING A TRADING PORTFOLIO

Your portfolio choice could help you compensate for a shortage of margin money or trading equity, two common trading limitations. For example, the amount of margin money required to trade one futures contract varies by commodity. The various exchanges (Chicago Board of Trade, Chicago Mercantile Exchange, New York Futures Exchange, New York Board of Trade, etc.) set the margin requirements for each commodity traded on their exchange. The margin is set based on the size of the contract and the amount of price volatility of that specific market. It can range from a few hundred dollars to several thousand and can change dramatically depending on market conditions. It is always recommended to keep at least twice the margin money required in the trading account to cover unexpected price swings.

The purpose of margin money is simply to ensure that traders stand behind their trades. This is critical since the books on every trade are balanced every day. The oats futures contract has a low margin requirement, usually less than $500 per contract. The Chicago Board of Trade contract specifies 5,000 bushels. The price per bushel has ranged from less than $1.00 to just over $4.00 over the past 25 years. Most of the time, however, the price range was between $1.00 and $2.50. This calculates to a total contract value of $5,000 to $20,000.

The price swings in this contract are usually small on a day-to-day, and even week-to-week, basis. It is a market with low price volatility. Therefore, a trader who wishes to trade futures with a small amount of equity would do well to start with oats. One or two contracts could be traded at a time. As an oats trader, what kind of return could you expect? What should your income goal be? Is it worth your while?

During a 5-year period the author's in-house trading system, the Wasendorf Trading System (WTS), generated a simulated profit of $11,425 trading one contract of oats. This doesn't include a deduction for brokerage commissions and fees, which could vary widely. If you divided this gross simulated profit by 5, you have $2,285 per year. To produce this profit, approximately 7 trades were conducted each year. If you paid $125 for commissions and fees, you would still have netted over $1,400, or about 3 times the margin money required, and your $2,500 equity would have increased by about 50 percent. There were periods of time during that 5-year period when the simulated performance record lost money. That's why funds over and above the margin required by the FCM could be needed. Always remember that whenever someone discusses past performance of a system, it is not necessarily indicative of future performance.

A complaint often heard is that it is dull to trade oats contracts. If you only make 5 to 10 trades a year, that's less than 1 per month. Additionally, 3 or 4 of these are routine rollovers. That's when you transfer your position from one contract that is expiring to one that is still trading. For example, you could roll over from the June oat contract to the September oat contract. You do this to stay in the most liquid or most heavily traded option. This is done so you can quickly fill an order if you need to when the trend changes against your position. You can then reverse your position and go from long to short or short to long. Of course, you could always choose to get out of the market by "standing aside."

CHOOSING A FULL PORTFOLIO

One of the keys to selecting a full portfolio is diversifying your risk over as wide a spectrum as possible. The theory is both offensive and defensive. It's offensive in that it is designed to put you in the right place at the right time. By taking a position in several markets, you have a greater possibility of catching a major market move. No one can anticipate exactly when a given market will make its next big move up or down. Therefore, the more markets you are covering, the greater the chance you will be successful.

From a defensive stance, by spreading your investment capital over a wide variety of markets, you won't always be caught in the wrong market at the wrong time or even the right market at the wrong time.

Experience teaches that the different commodity groups are normally negatively correlated. That means they do not move up and down in unison. When one group is bullish, another is bearish and a third may be moving sideways. For example, if the price of grains is high and going higher, it puts pressure on livestock producers because it cuts their profit margin. More livestock are subsequently sent to market sooner, and livestock prices become bearish, moving lower as the cash market is flooded with animals. Negative correlation can help you from getting caught with all your eggs in one basket.

Therefore, a diversified portfolio would look like this:

Grains:	Corn, oats, soybean oil
Meats:	Feeder cattle, live hogs
Food/fiber:	Coffee, cotton, sugar
Metals:	Gold
Petroleum:	Crude oil, heating oil
Financials:	Japanese yen, Dollar Index, Muni-Bond Index, S&P 500 Index

A 15-market portfolio, like the one outlined above, requires $40,000 to $50,000 in margin money under normal conditions. In times of extreme stress, such as the U.S.-Iraqi war (January 1991), some of the margins in these markets were out of reach. During that conflict, crude oil and gold margins exceeded $20,000 each on a per-contract basis. The exchanges and the FCMs raise margins during these periods of stress in an attempt to control volatility. The individual trader is often forced to stand aside certain markets because of the inflated margin requirements.

STOCK INDEX PORTFOLIOS

How do you select which markets you should trade? If you have a decent-size stock portfolio or a lot of experience trading stocks, you may decide to get involved in the futures market by trading the stock indexes.

To begin with, you have several choices when you decide to trade the stock indexes. Additionally, some of them, such as the S&P 500, have an option liquid enough for the average trader to utilize. Prior to the bull rally in stocks, traders only had three other indexes besides the S&P 500 to track—the Major Market Index (MMI), the New York Stock Exchange (NYSE) Composite, and the Value Line. As the bull market has flourished and developed a strong technology sector, there has been a proliferation of indexes. It is very important to understand the composition of these indexes in order to attempt to predict how they will react to changing market conditions. Several indexes have a broad base of stocks, while one, the MMI, contains only 20 (see Figure 3.1).

The Value Line is the broadest-based index. It includes both blue-chip and smaller-capitalized stocks. About 80 percent are on the NYSE, 14 percent are over the counter (OTC), and 6 percent are from the Amex. The Russell 2000 Index, which has become a leading measure of small-capitalization stocks, has also become popular during the past few years.

On the opposite side of the spectrum is the MMI. It includes only blue-chip stocks, 85 percent of which are also part of the Dow Jones Index. Therefore, it would be the futures stock index contract that most closely tracks the Dow.

Do the blue chippers perform differently from the smaller-company stocks? Yes, blue-chip stocks usually lead the rest of the market in a bull move. Once a bull stampede starts, individual investors rush to buy "undervalued" secondary issues that are still affordable. This segment of the market then catches up with the blue-chip segment, as institutional buyers seek out bargains among the lesser issues.

As a major bull move exhausts itself, the prices of the blue chips are traditionally the first to level off. Unfortunately, the prices of the less capitalized stocks often continue to surge. This is where small investors are just getting into the market and are often the ones hurt, as it is so late in the move. They end up holding inflated stock while the market moves sideways or down.

The activity of institutional buyers is usually an indicator of what to expect. Just as the institutional buyers' rush for the blue-

F I G U R E   3.1

Index Composition

S&P 500:	500 stocks, mostly NYSE issues
S&P Midcap 400:	301 NYSE, 7 Amex, and 92 Nasdaq
NYSE Comp:	All NYSE common stocks
Value Line:	Approximately 1,650 NYSE, Amex, and OTC stocks
MMI:	20 blue-chip stocks, all NYSE, of which 19 are on DJIA
Russell 2000:	Small-cap stocks, 858 NYSE, 84 Amex, 1,022 Nasdaq
Nasdaq 100:	All 100 listed on Nasdaq Stock Market
Indice de Precios y Cotizaciones (IPC):	Main index of the Bolsa Mexican de Valores (BMV); 35 stocks, all traded on the BMV
Nikkei 225:	All listed on the Tokyo Stock Exchange

chip stocks often foretells a bull move, their movement from stocks to cash instruments may warn of a bear market ahead. This lack of confidence in the overall stock market causes a flight to quality; thus, the blue-chip stocks tend to hold their price level longer in bear rallies.

BULL, BEAR, SIDEWAYS MARKET

This strategy puts you in the position of deciding whether the next move of the Dow will be to 12,000 or 7,500. You must also accurately predict what stage of the current move you are in and what to use as an indicator.

Since the MMI most resembles the Dow, it would make sense to go long the MMI at the early stages of a bull, or short it just before a bear move. Once the move is well under way, you might want to trade one or more of the other more broadly based indexes.

Since the S&P 500 has a liquid option, you could buy a call at the same time you go long the MMI. Once the small stocks catch up with the blue chips, you would exercise that option or take profits on it.

A SPREADING STRATEGY

Another alternative would be to spread the MMI against one of the other indexes. A spread is when you simultaneously buy and sell in the same or related markets. This strategy allows you to take advantage of expected changes without having to predict accurately the overall market direction. You are basing your decision on the strength of one contract compared with another or the strength of the blue-chip stocks relative to that of the broader-based issues.

This approach may give you more protection in very volatile markets than taking an outright long or short position. You sell the weaker contract and buy the stronger. Regardless of the overall trend, you can win.

RISK CONSIDERATION

There are no risk-free futures trading strategies, including spreads. If your analysis of which contract is stronger is incorrect, the spread moves against you. You can close out the unprofitable leg and hold the profitable one. The move must be large enough for you to recover what you lose on the unprofitable side and pay your transaction costs. If the markets move only slightly or sideways and there's no change in the spread between the two contracts, you still must pay transaction costs.

Also, keep in mind that the NYSE Composite and the S&P 500 settle in cash at the opening value on the last trading day, while the MMI and Value Line settle in cash at the closing value. If you are holding an MMI-NYSE Composite spread until expiration, at the opening of the last trading day you would be holding an outright position in the MMI until closing. This might be risky considering expiration-day volatility.

THE EVOLUTION OF PROGRAM TRADING

Program trading on the stock market can have a significant impact on the volatility of the stock indexes, although the exchanges have moved to lessen the effect since the sharp fall in the markets in 1987. The New York Stock Exchange and the other exchanges that trade stock index futures have established circuit breakers, trading-collar levels, and price limits in an attempt to cool down volatility that might result from program trading.

Program trading at present encompasses a wide range of portfolio-trading strategies, which involve the purchase or sale of a basket of at least 15 stocks with a total value of $1 million or more.

By 1960, block trading of stocks had become common. These are characterized as trades of 10,000 or more shares at one time. In the beginning, only one security at a time was block-traded. It wasn't until the mid-1970s that block trading occurred in a variety of stocks at one time.

In 1974, the ERISA law was enacted requiring pension fund managers to use "skill, prudence and diligence" to minimize risk. This is sometimes referred to as the "prudent investor" or "prudent expert" legislation. Like most regulations, it requires managers to "prove" they are being prudent, as well as actually being prudent. How do you prove prudence? You don't put all your eggs in the same basket! This led to the first highly diversified index funds that attempt to mimic the performance of the S&P 500 or the NYSE Composite Index.

Enormous amounts of money were flowing into mutual funds at this time. Portfolio managers had to devise a method of moving quickly and efficiently from cash to equities and back, depending on the daily influx of cash and redemptions.

"MAY DAY"

May 1, 1975, brought the end to fixed brokerage fee schedules. Portfolio managers were now free to negotiate commissions. This led to the trading of packages of stocks because the portfolio's performance was now less affected by transaction costs. Brokers were more than willing to provide volume discount packages.

You could hardly move a block of 5,000 shares in 1965. Trades of 10,000 shares later became commonplace. This had an impact on volatility. The major brokerage firms developed five basic portfolio-level trading packages. These are usually referred to as the agency, open-hand, blind-bid, blind-blind-bid, and incentive trade packages. The cost per share traded ranges from a few cents to a few dollars. The wide range reflects the amount of risk the broker assumes in the trade.

The highest commissions are paid when a brokerage firm is required to guarantee the price in advance. This is done even when the individual stocks and timing of delivery are not identified to the broker. The broker is given a general description of the types of stocks to be traded.

How does a brokerage firm handle the risk of a blind-bid package? This is where the futures and options on futures come into play. In 1982, index futures became available and a year later index options. This allows the brokerage firm to hedge the transaction. If the package or program trade resembles the S&P 500 and the client is selling, the brokerage firm goes long the S&P 500. Between them, they are neutral or flat the market. When the trade actually takes place, both legs of the hedge are offset. The brokerage fee naturally includes the cost of the hedge.

On the opposite end of the spectrum are portfolio-level trades where the brokerage firm assumes no risk. It simply agrees to handle the transaction whenever the client decides to do it, offering no price guarantee. This is the agency package. The three packages in between include various methods of sharing the risk and rewards between broker and client.

THE IMPACT

How does program trading affect you as a futures trader? The most obvious answer is the volatility of the stock market and its related impact on the futures index markets.

A study conducted by the NYSE several years ago indicated that the impact of a typical program trading market order at that time was 0.2 percent. This equates to a 6-point move when the Dow Jones is at 3,000. (At 10,000, the effect would be a 20-point move.) But these program trades usually hit the market in waves of two, three, four, or even ten at a time. If the average trade was nearly 200 stocks worth $10 million, what's the impact of four of these in a 10- or 15-minute time period? And the typical trade can double in size if it is the result of some negative news.

From a longer-range perspective, there was a pattern of increased volatility on the NYSE in the mid-1980s as program trading grew. Between 1983 and 1985, prior to the widespread use of index arbitrage, or spreading, volatility exceeded 2 percent on 13 days. In the 1986–1988 period, 2 percent volatility days were up to 87. During the same periods, 3 percent volatility days increased from 1 to 26 and 4 percent volatility days went from 0 to 14.

MANAGE THE VOLATILITY

Stock trading curbs were first put into effect after the near-catastrophic 500-point DJIA plunge in 1987. As the bull stock market rampaged into higher and higher ground, stock and futures exchange officials established measures to control volatility. The NYSE system of circuit breakers and trading-collar levels is aimed at controlling program trading when the market is in a free fall or wild surge upward. The futures exchanges put into effect their own price-limit rules.

The circuit breakers and collars are reviewed each quarter and changed if necessary. Circuit breaker points represent the thresholds at which trading is halted marketwide for single-day declines in the DJIA. There are decline levels of 10, 20, and 30 percent. For example, the circuit-breaker points adopted for the fourth quarter of 1999 would have worked in the following manner:

- A 1,050-point drop in the DJIA before 2 p.m. (Eastern Time) would halt trading for 1 hour; it would halt trading for 30 minutes if it occurred between 2 p.m. and 2:30 p.m.; and it would have no effect if it occurred at 2:30 p.m. or later.
- A 2,150-point drop in the DJIA would halt trading for 2 hours if it occurred before 1 p.m., for 1 hour if it occurred between 1 p.m. and 2 p.m., and for the remainder of the day if it happened at 2 p.m. or later.
- A 3,200-point drop would halt trading for the remainder of the day, regardless of when the decline occurred.

Trading collars would be implemented as follows:

- When the DJIA declined 210 points or more. Such a drop would require all index arbitrage sell orders of the S&P 500 stocks to be stabilizing, or "sell plus."
- When an advance in the DJIA of 210 points occurred. All index arbitrage buy orders of the S&P 500 stocks are then required to be stabilizing, or "buy minus."

The "buy plus" and "buy minus" order formulas are designed to reduce the possibility that index arbitrage orders would further depress or inflate a market that is already falling or rising sharply. Exchange officials hope the delays will take some of the fervor out of the markets.

If you plan to trade the stock index futures markets, you should be familiar with the trading-curb rules of the stock exchanges and the futures exchanges. Be aware that they may change each quarter.

Even with the curbs, you must learn to protect yourself from the risk of increased volatility in the stock market and the index futures markets. The use of trading stops or options as stops can help. Holding an uncovered position, on the other hand, can entail major risk.

Placing Trades and Working with a Broker

Key Concepts

- ◆ Selecting a Broker
- ◆ Opening an Account and Types of Accounts
- ◆ Understanding and Completing Account Papers
- ◆ Knowing the Kinds of Orders
- ◆ Recognizing the Role of the Clearinghouse

To implement your trading plan, you need to be able to communicate closely and clearly with your broker. To do this, you must have a broker you can rely on and relate to. You must also educate yourself with the terminology of the markets in order to avoid misunderstandings.

SELECTING A BROKER

It pays to find a knowledgeable broker backed by a strong order desk. This way you can explain in plain English exactly what you wish to do and let the broker convert it to the trade jargon. For example, you can place what amounts to good-till-canceled (GTC) orders, or out-of-range orders, with your broker. The broker and the order desk track them for you and place them in the market each day until you get a fill or they are within range. Your broker should also constantly review your positions with you to be sure none get entered without your knowledge. This way you won't lose track of a GTC order or get an unexpected and unwanted fill.

To begin with, there are professional commodity brokers and there are futures order takers. You must decide which you need. This also determines whether you trade through a discount or full-service brokerage company. In the past few years, the technological revolution has made it possible to trade directly online from your own computer. Both full-service firms and discounters now offer online trading.

The per-trade cost at a discounter ranges between $25 and $35, depending on how much you trade and how long you have been with the firm. In most cases, the trader places a toll-free telephone call to the order desk at the discounter headquarters. An order clerk takes the order and relays it to the order desk at the appropriate exchange. You may also place the order online to some brokers, with the cost likely to be about the same, $15 to $30.

To utilize either a discount service or an online broker, you need a lot of experience. The order clerk is not in a position to assist you in choosing or evaluating a trade. The clerk's function is strictly to execute orders. In most cases the clerk will not even provide current price quotes or other information you may want at the time you are placing your order, such as highs, lows, trading ranges, trends, or market news. As a general rule, the discount cost matches the service. Discounters serve full-time traders who have the time and money to generate all the information they need to trade.

Full-service firms are set up to work in tandem with both experienced and inexperienced traders who need assistance in gathering and interpreting information about the supply and demand situation of the commodities being traded. Commissions with full-service firms may run from $100 to $110 per trade, but this will likely include analytical advice and other services usually not available from discount brokers.

HOW DO YOU SPOT A GOOD BROKER?

First off, the key word is *good*. It means good for you, your trading style, your personality, and your needs. If you require no assistance in selecting trades, tracking them, money management, technical and fundamental information, order placement, exchange floor reports, and the like, you should seriously consider using a discounter or trading online.

One of the best places to develop a list of what you want from a broker is to review your list of limitations. Your broker should become your partner; you make money together. The broker's commission must be earned.

There are at least four common limitations most individual traders must overcome. The first is to follow the markets and to sort out the important information from the false rumors that clutter the pits. The second is the flow and cost of information available about the markets. As fast moving as the futures markets are, you often need tick-by-tick price quotation equipment. Additionally, you need immediate access to the wire services and other forms of news. Therefore, you require some expensive and sophisticated equipment, which most individuals cannot justify as part-time traders.

Third is the experience that only comes from trading the markets day after day, year after year, facing bull markets and bear rallies, spotting the major moves early, and avoiding getting whipsawed by false breakouts. Last of all, there is just an enormous amount of background information you need at your fingertips to trade and avoid making expensive errors. You need to know all the specifications of the contracts you're trading, the hours the markets are open, the days they are closed, and if they are closing early for some reason. You also need to know how to place orders, when important government reports that will impact markets are to be released, and what rumors are sweeping the exchanges. The list goes on and on.

To look at it from another perspective, here are some serious errors that could happen if you get into the futures markets without enough knowledge or assistance.

A farmer has hedged on corn. There were 100,000 bushels in the bins, and 100,000 were sold on the Chicago Board of Trade. When going to offset the short futures position, the broker was told to buy 20 at the market. Since each corn contract is 5,000 bushels, it was thought 100,000 bushels were being offset—the quantity the farmer was short. But grains are traded differently than all other contracts are, as mentioned earlier. The number refers to each 1,000-bushel unit. The farmer's broker did as instructed and bought 20 at the market, or 4 contracts. Since 100,000 actual bushels of corn were sold on the cash market, the farmer was still short 80,000 bushels. The farmer was at extreme risk. For every cent the corn market goes up, $800 is lost.

Something as seemingly simple as placing an order to be filled within the closing range can prove expensive and risky. For example, there is the case of the trader waiting to place a market order in the last 15 minutes of trading to fulfill a trading strategy. Because of a clock running late, the order was received on the floor too late. The customer had to take the risk of holding the position overnight and exiting in the morning. The broker could have used a market on close (MOC) order, if the situation had been fully understood by both parties.

Therefore, develop your list of what you are going to look for in a broker before you begin to interview (usually by telephone) broker candidates. Use all the skills you learned over the years in hiring employees or vendors, selecting schools for yourself or your children, and making other critical buying decisions. Make a "T" list of positives and negatives on all candidates after you talk with them (see Figure 4.1). If you do this for each broker you interview, the selection process becomes much easier. Review the Trading Plan Checklist as you develop your T list.

Some characteristics common to "good" brokers include:

Availability. Good brokers are available to their customers whenever they are needed. This often equates to long hours from covering the early grain markets to the evening Treasury bond sessions. When they aren't personally available, they see to it that an assistant or associate is. You're never out of touch. Ask prospective brokers about how "reachable" they are. Then, when you open an account, test them (call them at 8:00 a.m. and again at 8:00 p.m.) before a market emergency occurs.

Responsiveness. You need a broker who'll help you overcome your limitations and satisfy your needs. Therefore, this person must be responsive. In the interview process, request some obscure piece of information, such as when the Federal Reserve is releasing the next beige book. Find out in advance how the broker performs. Ask how fast you'll get fills. Try to discern how hard the broker will push to respond to your needs.

F I G U R E   4.1

Broker Selection "T" List

Broker's Name: _____

Firm: _____

Phone Number: _____

My Needs and/or Limitations	Pros	Cons
1. Live time quotes	X	
2. Market experience	10 years	
3. Reliable trading system		?
4. Track record		Unclear
5. Personality	Excellent	
6. Reliability	Good	
7. Commission		$72/rt
8. Reference	Check out	
9. Firm		Unknown
10. Trade presentation		Unorganized
11. Type of trader	Technical	
12. New services		Limited

My overall impression is:

_____

_____

Note: It's important to customize the T list to suit your needs and/or limitations. This list is for illustrative purposes only.

Honesty. Naturally, you must trust and have confidence in your broker. You can often learn a lot about sincerity when you ask about the risk of futures trading or a specific trade. If the broker evades or glosses over the high risk involved, beware. You should receive a serious, no-holds-barred discussion from prospective brokers about the unlimited nature of the losses that can be sustained in futures trading. Regarding the buying of options, the risk is limited to the cost of the option (premium) and the transaction costs (brokerage commission and fee), but you can lose 100 percent of this amount. Most options expire worthless. Few traders make money in options. If you're told this is a serious investment with high risks, it's a big plus.

Dealing with losses. Under the stress of losing other people's money and the pressures of trading, many brokers come apart. The first sign is often a lack of communication with the losing client. This is almost impossible to detect in the early interview stage of the selection process. However, when you start to trade, you should become sensitive to it. If possible, ask for references from past customers. Ask them how the broker performed when the account was in a drawdown. The best brokers don't let it bother them, because losing money is a large part of futures trading.

Trading. Find out how they trade. What system do they use? Are they fundamentalists, technicians, or a combination? Have them "sell you a trade." Just ask them what their trade recommendation for today is. You want to learn how well they present an opportunity to you. Is it well thought out? Convincing? Have they done their homework?

Discipline. Good traders and brokers are very disciplined. They spend hours studying the market and refining their system. Bad brokers will try to emotionally sell you the "hot trade of the day." Probe to get a feel for the daily routine of prospective brokers. Do they keep a trading journal? What do they do each day that assures that your positions will be reviewed?

Experience, knowledge, track record. If you know more or have traded more than a prospective broker, who's going to help whom? Find out what they have done, what they know, and how that's going to make you more successful.

The question of a trading track record is tricky. Most brokers do not have one. If they do not take total discretion in an account (power of attorney that permits them to actually trade the account as if it were their own), the customer approves each trade. Therefore, the broker is merely a consultant and the customer is the trader. The broker cannot use these accounts to create a track record, as per CFTC regulations.

Next, there are some very stringent regulations imposed by the CFTC regarding track records. These regulations make it difficult and expensive for a broker to prepare a track record. This is another reason most brokers do not have one. Personally, if a broker shows or offers a track record that is not part of a full-blown disclosure document that has been reviewed by the CFTC, you should be very suspicious.

These are just a few of the areas to which you must be sensitive as you select and work with a broker. Always remember that it is your money that is being invested in the market. You are the one who is financially responsible.

OPENING AN ACCOUNT

Let's quickly review the different types of commodity futures trading accounts you can open and the basic forms you'll be asked to sign or acknowledge understanding of. Some of this will vary slightly from one FCM to another, but there should not be too much variation.

The types of accounts include:

Individual account. An individual account represents the account of one customer as an individual.

Sole proprietorship. A sole proprietorship is the same as an individual account except that the account is in the name of a sole proprietor.

Joint account. A joint account represents an account established in the names of two or more people. Joint accounts require information on all parties to the account.

General partnership account. Basically, a general partnership is a business arrangement between two or more individuals or business entities, each of whom is a general partner conducting a business in the name of a partnership. Each general partner can make decisions on behalf of the whole partnership. The business of the partnership is usually conducted pursuant to an organization's agreement in accordance with state law. A general partnership can be established to conduct a full-time business, such as commodity merchandising, or for a specific investment or trading activity, such as futures trading. An important aspect of a general partnership is that each general partner is liable for commitments and debts incurred in the partnership.

Limited partnership. A limited partnership is primarily established for investment, rather than for general business activities. It is usually established and operated pursuant to an organization agreement in accordance with federal and state law. An important aspect of a limited partnership is that the limited partners are not involved in the management of the partnership, and each limited partner's liability is generally limited to the amount of the individual's investment in the partnership.

Corporate account. A corporate account is an account established by a corporation. The information for individuals is not required, but corporate information must be submitted. Additionally, a corporate resolution allowing the corporation to trade futures and options on futures must be completed, and it must be signed by at least two officers of the corporation. The account papers must indicate who is allowed to trade on behalf of the corporation. In addition to this document, the corporation must submit either a personal guarantee or a copy of the firm's most recent audited financial report.

Trust account. A trust property is controlled by one person for the benefit of another. For example, a father may create a trust (and be the trustee) for property held for the benefit of his minor children. Or a pension fund could hold funds for the future benefit of members of that fund. In order for a trust to trade futures, the trust agreement must specifically authorize it. A copy of the trust agreement is usually requested with the account papers.

The package of forms you'll receive to sign is generally called the *account papers.* Each FCM prepares its own account papers, but all papers must meet the requirements of the regulatory agencies (the CFTC and the NFA). (See Fig. 4.2.) For this reason, there is a strong similarity among all the forms you'll see.

One of the first things your broker is charged to do, by the National Futures Association in its Compliance Rule 2–30, is obtain information about you. The broker must be able to prove to the NFA that you are known and you are who you say you are. Specifically, your broker needs (1) your true name and address, (2) your princi-

F I G U R E   4.2

Futures Industry Structure

U.S Congress
    Commodity Futures Trading Commission (CFTC)
       National Futures Association (NFA)
          Exchanges
             Futures commission merchants (FCM)
               Introducing brokers (IBs)
                 IB branch offices

pal occupation, (3) your age, and (4) your previous investing experience.

The purpose of this information is to assess your suitability to trade futures. You will be asked to answer a series of questions and / or fill out some sort of financial statement. In addition, you'll need to supply information about your previous investing experience.

The next part of the account papers includes a variety of risk disclosures. The purpose is to make you fully aware of the serious risk involved in investing in these types of investments.

The *Non-Cash Margin Disclosure Statement* is a statement provided so that you understand and acknowledge that in the unlikely event that the FCM becomes bankrupt, funds not held in segregation (i.e., held as T-bills) will be returned to you based upon your pro-rate share of all property available for distribution.

The *Commodity Account Letter and Customer Agreement* should be read carefully. It highlights the following areas: order entry, margining, commissions and fees, commodity options, delivery and short sales, security interest, liquidation, foreign exchange rates, customer representations and warranties, market recommendations and information, communications, credit, recordings, terms of the agreement, and miscellaneous provisions. The customer must sign this acknowledgment indicating that it has been read and understood. All parties to the account must sign and date this agreement.

The *Lending Agreement* comes into play when a customer

makes or takes delivery, which is unusual. If the balance in the customer's account is not adequate to pay for the delivery, and the delivery creates a deficit in the customer's account, a signed Lending Agreement allows for the FCM to use the commodities or evidence of ownership of the commodities as collateral for a loan. The proceeds of that loan are used to pay for the delivery until redelivery of the commodity and/or payment in full by the customer can be completed.

The *Permission to Cross Agreement* allows the FCM to unintentionally take the opposing side of any trade that may have been placed on behalf of a customer. The CFTC requires the FCM to get your permission to take the opposite side of trades. Since the FCM handles so many trades each day, it asks for your blanket approval because it doesn't have any practical way of keeping track of all the possible conflicts of interest.

The *Options Disclosure Statement* informs you of the risks associated with trading options, as well as describes the different types of options traded.

The *Transfer Form* should be completed if you are transferring your account from one FCM to another.

The *Pre-dispute Arbitration Agreement* allows for the filing of an arbitration conducted by a self-regulatory or other private organization rather than pursuing the matter through civil court litigation. The arbitration agreement does allow you to request a Section 14 reparations proceeding before the CFTC. You have 45 days from the date of such notice to decide. NFA rules prohibit the signing of this agreement to be a condition of opening an account.

The *Risk Disclosure Statement* discloses to you the various risks associated with futures trading. CFTC Regulation 1.55 requires that each customer receive and sign a copy of this statement before an account can be approved to trade. If an account executive ever plays down the importance of this document, you should be concerned. It's important that you read and understand what you are getting into.

Once you complete the account papers, you send them to your broker. They are reviewed by the supervisor. This is usually done at the introducing broker level. From here, the papers are sent to the new account department at the FCM for its approval.

When your account is approved, it must be funded before trading can begin. This is usually carried out by bank wire or by check. Therefore, if you're anxious to trade, send funds with your account papers.

THE KINDS OF ORDERS

Understanding the types of orders and when to place them is one of the investor's greatest safeguards. Study the following carefully:

Market Orders

Market orders are orders to buy or sell at the current price as quickly as possible. In the trading pits, they are the first orders to be executed because they can be filled at any price. You use them when you want to get into or out of the market quickly. You're trying to catch a move, and you don't want anything to slow you down. There are no contingencies placed on the orders.

When you get the fill back, it may or may not be close to the market price when you placed the order. If the market is on fire, there may be a substantial difference. With orderly markets, it may be right on the money.

When you place a market order, you pass the responsibility to the floor brokers to fill the order as best they can. These brokers are governed by CFTC and exchange rules to give you the best possible service. And they do. But you don't have any control over the market. You never do. When markets are choppy with a lot of volatility and low volume, you may not want to use a market order because you don't know when or at what price it will be filled.

Stop Orders

In special situations, you may want to use stop orders. You place buy stops above the market if you are bullish on prices or sell stops below the market if you are bearish.

Stop orders become market orders when the price trades, or is bid, at or better than the stop price. What you're trying to do is catch a move just as prices break out of a trading range or an area of congestion. Once your stop orders become market orders, you take on all the risk of a regular market order. Namely, you may or may not get a fill with which you are satisfied. Prices could spike up or down to hit your stop and then move against you. By the time your order gets filled, it's way above or below the price you were hoping for. That's the risk of market orders.

Stop orders are often used to close out or protect profitable positions. They are called *trailing stops.* As your long futures or call options-on-futures positions gain value, you place sell stops just below them. You continuously move the stop up as your trade becomes more profitable. If the market moves against you, your sell stops are hit. They become market orders and you offset your positions. This is referred to as being *stopped out of the market.*

If you are short futures or holding puts, you can do just the opposite with buy stops. Just place your stop orders above your positions. You wait for the market to "pick off your stops" and close your positions, at, it is hoped, a profit.

Placing a stop takes some skill and experience. If you place it too close to your position, a slight move in the wrong direction removes you prematurely from the market. If you put it too far from your position, you can give up too much of your profit before your stop is hit.

To select the right position for your stop, you need to get a handle on volume and volatility. What have the daily trading ranges been recently? Is the volume high enough to smooth out the markets?

MIT Orders

The opposite of stop orders are the market-if-touched (MIT) orders. These are sometimes referred to as *board orders* and possess two of the characteristics of stop orders: (1) They are activated when their price is hit. (2) Once hit, they become market orders.

The difference is that buy MIT orders are placed below the current market price. (Remember that buy stops are placed above the current price.) Sell MIT orders go above the current price. (Sell stops go below the current price.) MIT orders can be used to establish new positions or close out existing ones.

MIT orders are not officially recognized on the Chicago Board of Trade, but a broker can accept them at the risk of the customer. They can be used on the Chicago Mercantile Exchange and on some of the other exchanges. You need to check the individual exchange rules before you make your decision to use them.

Limit Orders

If you don't like being left to the mercy of the market when your stop or MIT order becomes a market order, you can use a limit order (sometimes called a *price order*). Limit orders are used to buy or sell at specific price levels. Buy limit orders are placed below the going market price. They can only be filled at or below the limit price. Sell limit orders are placed above the current market price and can only be filled on, at, or above the limit price.

Keep in mind that orders other than a straight market order have a lower priority. This means that market orders get filled first. In fast-moving markets, you may not get filled at all. Or the market may not move to a point where your stop, MIT, or limit contingency allows your order to be filled. This may keep you out of the market, which may or may not be a good thing.

Stop Limit Orders

A variation on limit orders is stop limit orders. Buy-stop limit orders are activated when the futures contract trades or is bid at or above the stop level. These orders cannot be filled unless the price level subsequently stays at, or moves below, the limit level. Sell-stop limit orders are activated when the commodity is offered at, or trades at or below, the stop level. These orders are not filled unless the price subsequently remains at or moves above the limit level.

Now, the stop price and the limit price need not be at the same price level. For example, an order might state: "Buy 90:16 stop 90:20 limit." This order would be activated when the price hit 90:16, but would only be fired if the price remained below 90:20.

Stop orders are sometimes used for protection in fast-moving markets. They let you place orders within price ranges.

Time Limit Orders

Besides putting conditions on the price of your orders, you can also put time restrictions on when your orders can be executed. These contingencies tell the floor brokers when your orders are to be activated.

Kill or fill (KOF) is an example. These orders must be filled immediately or they are canceled. Traders use them when they spot a trading opportunity. But since kill-or-fill orders are not market orders, they do not have top priority. On the other hand, floor traders try to accommodate these orders.

Another common type of time limit order deals with placing your orders in the opening or closing trading range. *Market-on-open* orders must be filled within the opening trading range, just as *market-on-close* orders must be filled within the closing trading range.

You may want to place standing orders. These are good-till-canceled orders. Theoretically, these orders will stay in the market until filled. You risk the danger of losing track of these orders—only to have one filled just when the market turns against you. GTC orders are not recommended under normal conditions.

Another type of time limit order lets one order replace another. These kinds of orders are called *one-cancels-other* (OCO) *orders*, where a new order replaces one already in the market.

PRIORITY OF ORDERS

Floor brokers in the trading pits fill the order they have in their books in the following order of priority: (1) market orders, (2) stop orders, (3) limit orders, and (4) limit-price, stop, time. Also, keep in mind that all orders are assumed to be day orders unless otherwise specified. Therefore, if your order is not filled during a trading session, you would have to reenter it when the next trading session begins. Some markets, bonds for example, have two trading sessions each day. Orders entered in the day session may not automatically be carried over to that evening's session, depending on your FCM's trading rules. You may have to reenter your orders in the evening session or, if you choose, reenter your orders in the next day's trading session.

Good-till-canceled, or open, orders do not always do what the name implies. Many exchanges will not accept them. If an order is not filled during a session, it becomes *unabled.* An unabled order is simply one that cannot be filled during a specific trading session or within the given price-time limit.

Your orders may also be characterized as *out of range.* This means that the orders are out of the normal trading range for that commodity. The trading range reflects the daily trading limit. For example, the daily trading limit for corn is 10 cents per bushel. If your order is more than 10 cents above or below the opening price, it would be out of range. Most exchanges will not accept out-of-range orders. With options on futures, there are no daily price limits.

Take note also that grain orders use a different nomenclature than other futures contracts. Grain orders must be stated in thousands of bushels, rather than numbers of contracts. For example, if you'd like to buy 10 corn contracts, you'd tell your broker to "go long 50 corn." Since corn trades in 5,000-bushel contracts on the major exchanges, you would be long 10 corn contracts. If you decide to offset this position and place an order to go short 10 corn, you only offset 2 of your 10 contracts. You still would be long 8 contracts. This could be a very expensive error.

The Mid America Exchange in Chicago trades *mini* contracts in several commodities. The mini corn contract is for 1,000 bushels of corn, rather than 5,000. This is another important alternative the novice trader should consider.

THE CLEARINGHOUSE

After you get into trading, it's good to know just how the process works after your broker places the order and it is taken up by another trader. That's where the clearinghouse comes in.

A market won't function without integrity. Buyers and sellers will abandon or at least be loath to use markets where losers don't pay up and winners can't collect. Indeed, such problems with forward contracts led to the evolution of the modern futures contract in the first place.

How can exchanges guarantee that a buyer will take delivery of a commodity or product or that a seller will make delivery as promised? Moreover, with contracts changing hands thousands of times before delivery, how can a trader keep track of who is on the other side of the transaction?

Fortunately, the trader doesn't have to worry about that, thanks to the role of the exchange clearinghouse. Essentially, a clearinghouse takes the other side of each trade on the exchange.

Clearinghouses are made up of brokerage firms that are also members of the exchange—though not all exchange member firms are clearing members. Clearing members must buy stock in the clearinghouse relative to the volume of business that they clear. They are also required to pony up a substantial sum that goes into a clearinghouse fund that guarantees all trades will be fulfilled in case of default.

Exchange member firms that aren't clearing members must clear. That is, they must have all trades verified and guaranteed through a clearing member.

How does the clearinghouse guarantee trades? By the end of the trading day, all trades conducted on the exchange are recorded by the clearinghouse. At that point, the clearinghouse takes the opposite end of each trade.

Suppose trader A sold a December Japanese yen contract to trader B. At the end of the day, the clearinghouse would stand between the two traders. Essentially, the clearing firm that represents trader A would be short a yen contract against the clearinghouse, while the firm representing trader B would be long a yen contract against the clearinghouse. If trader B sold the contract to trader C, then the firm representing trader C would be long against the clearinghouse, and trader B's obligation would be canceled. Meanwhile, trader A doesn't need to worry about keeping track of trader C. And trader C can sell the yen contract, transferring the obligation to yet another participant, without seeking trader A's approval.

This differs substantially from the forward market in which a trader must always be fully aware of the changing identity of the trading partners, as well as their credit worthiness. A futures trader must also worry about creditworthiness, but concerns need only center on two entities: the brokerage firm and the clearinghouse.

Overview of Some
of the Active Markets

Key Concepts

- ◆ Overview of Grains and Oilseeds (Soybeans, Corn, Wheat, Oats)
- ◆ Overview of Meats (Live Hogs and Pork Bellies, Live and Feeder Cattle)
- ◆ Overview of Food and Fiber (Sugar, Coffee, Cocoa, Orange Juice, Cotton)
- ◆ Overview of Metals (Silver, Gold, Copper)
- ◆ Overview of Energy (Petroleum and Petroleum Products)
- ◆ Overview of Stock Indexes
- ◆ Overview of Debt Management (Interest Rates)
- ◆ Overview of Foreign Currency

The following is neither an exhaustive list nor an exhaustive summary of the markets available to futures investors. These are merely markets that now have and will have enough trading volume to make them acceptable for traders new to the futures markets.

Nonliquid markets—those that are lightly traded—cause serious problems for experienced and inexperienced traders alike. These should be avoided because their thinness causes minor trading activity to result in a disproportionate amount of price movement or volatility. Additionally, the low volume can, at times, make it difficult to open or close positions. You can be unwittingly trapped in these markets or have them unexpectedly move violently against your position.

The professional trader learns the markets inside out to avoid being blindsided by an unexpected market event. Use the following information as a starting point for basic information you may need to know to trade successfully.

GRAINS AND OILSEEDS

OVERVIEW OF THE SOYBEAN MARKET

Soybeans have been commercially cultivated for at least the last 5,000 years, primarily in the Orient and specifically in China. Cultivation of the "wonder bean" is relatively new to the United States (circa 1930), even though the United States is now the world's largest producer, with about 2.8 billion bushels in 1998. Beans are grown in this country from the Southern delta to the Canadian border. Iowa and Illinois are the largest producing states.

From a fundamental analyst's point of view, you must determine what will influence supply and demand. Think of it as a balance scale. When supplies are heavier than demand, the price declines. When demand outweighs supplies, prices increase.

Supply Side

One of the keys to the soybean price equation is production. How many acres will be planted? What will the yield be?

The key to production is weather, but it is a very difficult factor to predict, especially over the growing seasons throughout the entire world. Is there enough moisture to germinate the crop? Will there be rains through the growing season? Will harvesttime be dry and free of snow?

In the Northern Hemisphere, August is a particularly sensitive month in which the crop can be made or lost. Pod filling occurs primarily during the first 2 weeks of August. You should be particularly attuned to rainfall markets during this month. The slightest shower, particularly in Chicago, can send prices plummeting. Any prolonged dryness and prices will take off like the space shuttle.

Several South American countries, particularly Brazil and Argentina, have complicated the production side of the supply-demand equation over the last 25 years. Brazil's production grew from 364 million bushels in 1974 to 1.139 billion bushels in 1998. Argentina produced only 18 million bushels in 1974, compared with 680 million bushels in 1998.

The crop year for these countries is essentially the opposite of that of the United States. They plant in November and harvest in March and April.

Soybeans also have a lot of competitors. When the bean is crushed, it produces oil and meal. Oil competitors include sunflower, palm, and coconut oil. The main meal (or protein) competitor for replacement feed is wheat.

Demand Side

The meal is used as feed for livestock. Therefore, you also need to keep an eye on hog and cattle prices and numbers. Also, such factors as the acreage, yield, and weather for the other oil producing crops mentioned earlier must be tracked closely.

Demand or usage depends on the beans being in the right place at the right time at the right price. Therefore, you need to be aware of any export problems (e.g., embargoes, dock workers strikes, etc.) or transportation problems (e.g., frozen rivers in inland waterway systems, barge rate, etc.).

Since about 50 percent of the United States crop is exported, the strength of the dollar is critical. The lower the dollar, the greater quantity foreign countries can purchase. One of the largest importers is Japan. Being aware of another country's needs for food and feed and its economic condition can make the difference between picking a winning trade or not.

Technical Factors

As you can see, following the fundamental side of the market is a staggering task. That's why so many professionals rely on technical analysis.

One of the most reliable tools is a seasonal analysis. At harvest, you can expect a lot of beans on the market. Therefore, prices are likely to be lower. Prior to harvest, processors use up last year's production and prices tend to increase.

This analysis has been finely tuned. Studies indicate that 70 percent of all seasonal tops occur between April and July. By the end of July 80 percent of all seasonal highs are made. Price bottoms—up to 80 percent—occur between August and November.

The theory of cycle analysis states that price action will repeat itself in a predictable fashion. For soybeans, two dominant long-term cycles, a 24- and a 39-month cycle, have been identified by the Foundation for the Study of Cycles. Weekly and even daily cycles have also been isolated.

Chart analysis of soybean price activity has been known to be quite reliable. It is often a trending market that can be interpreted fairly accurately. But certain chart formations, like triangles, are very unreliable. Other chart formations, like head-and-shoulder formations, are very reliable but are seldom formed.

OVERVIEW OF THE CORN MARKET

Corn is a member of the feed grains family, which includes corn, sorghum, oats, and barley. Corn is the single largest member of the group, accounting for more than 80 percent of the total U.S. production of feed grains.

The crop year for corn begins October 1 and ends September 30 of the following year. Since corn is a commodity that can be stored for a reasonably long period of time and can be moved long distances, keeping track of the amount available worldwide is important. For this reason, the U.S. Department of Agriculture releases regular projections of production and disappearances (usage).

Corn is grown on every continent except Antarctica. The United States is the largest producer of corn, providing more than 40 percent of world production. China is the second largest producer, with just over 20 percent. Brazil, the European Union, and Mexico are the other producers of note, although they lag far behind the leaders. Corn is grown in more countries than any other crop, but most consume all their production and do not export.

The United States exports a significant amount of its production, ranging from 18 to 30 percent, depending on the size of the crop and the economic conditions around the world. The Pacific Rim region (in Asia) has emerged as the world's fastest-growing market for U.S. corn. There, most of the corn is fed to livestock to produce food for humans. The majority of the world's population is located in the Pacific Rim region.

Fundamental Factors

Pipeline supply is the key issue. How much corn is in farm and how much is in commercial storage (that is, left over from the previous crop years)? How much is expected from the current crop that's still in the ground? These numbers are then compared with what is expected to be used. The supply-demand equation looks like this:

Beginning stocks + production + imports = total supplies
Feed, seed, residual + food + export = total usage or demand
Total supplies − total usage = ending stocks or carryover

In the United States, the import figure is not significant because of high production. However, the export figure can make or break a market. If there is an abundance of inventory, prices are depressed. If supplies are scarce, prices soar.

Supply Side

Water is the key to the production of corn, which requires about 5,000 gallons of water per bushel. During the growing season 18 to 24 inches of rain are required to produce 100- to 175-bushel yields. For every pound of dry matter (leaves, stalks, ears, etc.) produced, 372 pounds of water are needed. Normal rainfall during the growing season provides only half of the needed moisture. Therefore, subsoil moisture is critical.

Water can be a problem at planting time and at harvest. In Iowa and other Midwestern states, wet fields in the spring can delay planting. If planting is substantially delayed, farmers may switch to soybeans. Heavy rain at harvest can knock down stalks, slow harvest, and reduce yields. There's usually no such thing as a "normal" year. Either you get too much or too little rain.

One of the most critical periods occurs when the plant pollinates—usually for about 10 days around mid- to late July in the Corn Belt. During this period, corn needs moisture—either rainfall or subsoil. Additionally, the temperature cannot be excessively high.

A week of 100-degree-plus temperatures during pollination sub-stantially reduces yields.

Demand Side

About 80 percent of the U.S. corn crop is used domestically, con-sumed as feed for livestock, for human food, for alcohol, and for seed. Livestock feed is by far the most important. Alcohol usage has been boosted in recent years as ethanol has become popular as a fuel blend to enhance octane and as an oxygenate to reduce air pol-lution.

Domestic and overseas livestock industries consume about 80 percent of all corn grown in the United States, feeding it as ground grain, silage, high-oil, and high-moisture corn, according to the Na-tional Corn Growers Association.

From just over 10 million gallons of production in 1979, the U.S. fuel ethanol industry has grown to more than 1.8 billion gallons of annual production capacity. The USDA estimates that ethanol pro-duction uses about 500 million bushels of corn a year, and projects a 1.7 percent average growth rate during the next 5 years.

Demand depends quite a bit on the financial conditions of live-stock producers and the cattle cycle. Are animal numbers increas-ing or decreasing? Are herds expanding or contracting? Demand for feed can be estimated when you can get a good fix on these numbers.

The price of wheat must also be taken into consideration. Farmers will use wheat as a substitute feed when its price drops enough to make it economical.

Exports are another major demand element. Although the United States only exports about 20 to 30 percent of its crop, this rep-resents about 75 percent of the world's feed grain trade. Most coun-tries produce their own feed, primarily in the form of silage. Only a handful of countries grow enough corn to be a real force in the ex-port business. Of these countries, none is considered a steady and reliable supplier. They export only when they have a particularly abundant crop.

Price Forecasting

It's almost impossible to analyze corn prices using fundamental analysis! Keeping track of the the impact of the worldwide weather patterns on yields alone is a Herculean task. Further, you must accurately forecast cattle and hog numbers as well as usage for alcohol, seed, and food. There have been several attempts to develop econometric models to manage all the variables, but none has proved exceedingly successful. Technical analysis has been more dependable. For example, seasonal patterns are reliable. Price highs are usually made in late July or early August; lows come in November or April. Several reasonably reliable long- and short-term cycles have been isolated.

Chart analysis also works pretty well. Head-and-shoulder formations can be traded with an acceptable amount of confidence. The price activity of corn also responds to other predictive formations, such as flags and triangles. Once a solid trend is established, you can work the trend line for all it is worth. Corn is a very popular market and almost always has plenty of liquidity.

OVERVIEW OF THE WHEAT MARKET

Like sugar, wheat is a universal crop, grown all over the world and harvested year-round. Carvings found in Egypt indicate wheat has been cultivated since at least 1000 B.C.

Wheat belongs to the grass family. Its kernels grow in compact heads on the end of hollow stalks, making it easy to harvest. China, India, the United States, Russia, the European Union, Canada, Argentina, and Australia are among the top wheat-producing nations. China and Russia, although major producers, usually consume what they produce and are often net importers.

About 50 percent of the U.S. production is exported. Canada is also a major exporter. From time to time, depending on crop conditions, other countries can make a major impact on world pricing. Subsidized exports by the 15-nation European Union, particularly from wheat producer France, cut into the amount of wheat the U.S. can sell in such areas as North Africa.

Since most countries consume the wheat they grow, the production of the exporters must be watched closely. Also, the wheat price analyst needs to be aware of the amount of supply available worldwide. Since wheat is primarily a food, prices are elastic. The price is very responsive to changes in the supply-demand equation.

Wheat is unique, as far as the price analyst is concerned, in that the type of wheat available is an important consideration. Wheat produced in the United States, consistently the world's largest exporter, can be classified as common and durum wheat. Common is further classified by color (red or white) and by hardness (hard or soft). It can also be classified by the time of planting (spring versus winter). The U.S. crop is about evenly divided between spring and winter wheat.

Supply Side

Winter wheat is planted in the fall, lies dormant during the winter (ideally with a snow cover that prevents the erosion of soil and seed and that will provide moisture for germination in the spring), and is harvested between late May and June. Spring wheat is planted as early as possible and harvested in late summer.

Hard red wheat, the majority of the U.S. production, is valued worldwide because of its high protein content. The hard reds also contain a large quantity of strong, elastic gluten, which is ideal for breadmaking. These wheats are produced in the dry climates of Kansas, Nebraska, Oklahoma, and northern Texas.

Soft red wheat is produced in areas with high rainfall, such as the Great Lakes, Atlantic Coast, and eastern Texas. Its primary use is for making pastry, crackers, biscuits, cakes, and similar products. It has a lower protein content than hard red.

The last major type of wheat produced in the United States is durum. Grown in North Dakota, South Dakota, and Minnesota, durum wheat is used for making semolina, which is particularly suited for pasta.

Demand Side

Worldwide demand for wheat is caused by the need to feed billions of people every day. Most countries consume all they produce. In the United States, demand also comes in the form of export, which can be through either commercial firms or government programs.

Food is a very politically sensitive subject. A well-fed country is usually a politically stable country. The opposite is also true. For years, the U.S. government exported large amounts of wheat in hopes of stabilizing client countries. Therefore, politics can play an important role in demand.

Wheat can be used as a feed substitute for corn in livestock enterprises. However, the quantity of wheat used for this purpose is very insignificant. The impact, if any, is on the price of corn and is usually short term.

Price Determinants

Worldwide weather is the dominant factor affecting wheat prices. Refer to the supply-demand equation given in the section on corn. Particular attention must be paid to China and other large, importing countries.

Government policy is the second most dominant determinant of wheat prices. If a shortage occurs in a controlled society, to what extent will the government go out on the open market to replace the shortfall? Or will the government tell its people to tighten their belts? How will the foreign policy of a major exporter, like the United States, have an impact on pricing?

Other important determinants are exchange rates (a strong dollar hurts U.S. exports), level of carryover stock (the higher the level, the lower prices will be), availability of storage and transportation (these have a short-term impact on prices), changes in production and consumption patterns (these produce gradual changes), and seasonality.

Prices tend to decline in harvest months as supplies become plentiful and increase toward the end of the year.

Technical Analysis

Wheat is a very popular futures contract. It usually has plenty of liquidity and responds well to basic technical analysis.

OVERVIEW OF THE OAT MARKET

Oats are cereal grasses that grow well in cool, temperate climates and are produced all over the world. Farmers have always found them useful because they actually do best in poorer soils. Even in areas with an abundance of high-quality ground, you'll find oats grown on the lesser fields.

Supply Side

The Commonwealth of Independent States, made up of countries of the former Soviet Union, is the world's largest producer, followed by the United States, Germany, Canada, and Poland. Oats have been displaced during the last decade or so by higher-value crops. But the USDA, in a recent outlook, projects that the long-term downward trend in U.S. oat acreage will bottom out in the early 2000s. U.S. production was estimated at 167 million bushels for 1998. The United States has been importing food-quality oats for many years, and is expected to continue to do so. The USDA projects production will range from 155 to 165 million bushels during the next 8 to 10 years, with total use remaining at about 270 million bushels. This will mean around 100 million bushels will be imported.

Oats are a lot like wheat in that the producing countries consume just about all they produce. Less than 5 percent of the world's production finds its way into export channels.

In the United States, the major producing states are South Dakota, North Dakota, and Minnesota. The United States primarily grows white oats, although some red and gray are produced. Oats are planted in early April or late May and are harvested between mid-July and late August.

Demand Side

The single largest use of oats (nearly 95 percent) is as livestock feed. Worldwide, livestock consume most oats on the farms on which they are grown. They are a particularly excellent feed for horses, breeding animals, young stock, and poultry because oats have the highest amount of protein among the cereal grains. They are also high in carbohydrates, which provide energy.

The decline in oat acres and production in recent years has been the result of a decline in the number of horses and mules employed as work animals.

A small amount (less than 5 percent) of oats is processed into food for humans. These are made into oatmeal and other food products. Recently, results of clinical tests indicate oat bran can be used in human diets to reduce the amount of cholesterol in the blood. This may increase food consumption. It, however, won't be significant to the overall world production. Also, a small portion of each year's crop is held back for seed for the following year.

Seasonality

Like the prices of most crops, oat prices tend to weaken as we move into harvest when supplies are plentiful. This puts the lows in the July–August time frame. After harvest, prices usually increase, with the high being hit most often in January.

Price Determinants

Oats, as previously stated, are primarily used as feed for livestock. Therefore, the number and mix of livestock and poultry on feed is the primary price determinant. Analysts must pay close attention to all the USDA's livestock and crop reports because oats compete with other grains—corn, sorghum, and even wheat—as feed.

A partial list of reports you'll want to monitor if you trade oats include Planting Intentions, Prospective Planting Report, Monthly Crop Production Reports, Monthly Eggs, Chickens & Turkeys Report, Quarterly Hog & Pigs Report, Livestock and Meat Situation, Cattle on Feed, Weekly Roundup of World Production & Trade, U.S. Export Sales, Stocks in All Positions, Grain Market News, Feed Market News, Wheat Situation Report, and others. Additionally, you'll want to review various state agricultural reports, particularly those of North and South Dakota.

Another important fact to keep in mind when you do your analysis and begin to compare oats with other feeds is that oats are lighter than other feeds. A bushel of oats weighs only slightly more than half of what a bushel of corn weighs. This equates to its feed value, which is slightly more than half that of corn. Therefore, a cattle feeder would have to buy more oats than corn to feed the same number of cattle or poultry. It's not a one-to-one comparison. In general, if you compare oats with corn by weight, oats sell for about 85 to 90 percent of the price of corn.

As with any crop, weather is an important price determinant. However, oats are a hearty crop. They are less vulnerable to bad weather than most. This is documented by the fact that so much of it is grown in North and South Dakota, states that are not known for their pleasant climates.

Carryover of stocks from one year to the next is another critical factor when forecasting price levels. Refer to the supply-demand equation in the corn overview. The higher the amount of carryover, the lower prices will usually be. Also, keep in mind that you must compare the oat carryover figures with those of other feed crops, particularly corn. If one is high and the other low, feed users will switch to the more plentiful, usually less expensive, feed.

Uncle Sam has a heavy hand in the process of determining future price levels. You must know if there is a government program affecting oats, how it works, and what is its expected impact.

Trader Notes

The speculative use of the oats futures contracts is very similar to that of corn, but there are some important differences. Because of the enormous size of the corn crop and the tremendous amount of hedging that goes on, moves are usually slow and ponderous. It often takes "forever" to get a major trend change in corn under way. This market can absorb large jolts, such as foreign countries unexpectedly entering the market to buy several million metric tons.

Oat futures contracts are much thinner than those of wheat and corn, and therefore much more responsive to trading activity. Many traders use this characteristic to advantage by using oats as a leading indicator of the grain complex's direction.

If oats make a major change in trend, the traders then position themselves to take advantage of this in the corn and wheat markets. If you trade oats, just remember that a thin market is often very volatile and dangerous. On the other hand, the margin money required to buy a futures contract in oats is usually the lowest of all the commodities.

MEATS

OVERVIEW OF THE LIVE HOG
AND PORK BELLY MARKETS

On a worldwide base, the United States ranks third in pork production, behind China and Russia. However, there is a negligible import-export business and so your knowledge should primarily cover the U.S. markets.

Iowa has the largest production in the United States. Nine other states (Georgia, Illinois, Indiana, Kansas, Minnesota, Missouri, Nebraska, North Carolina, and Ohio) are major producers. Together these 10 states account for approximately 75 percent of total U.S. production.

Pork producers have a special vocabulary of their own that you will need to understand. *Farrowing* is the act of giving birth. *Gilts* are female swine that have not given birth to a litter. *Boars* are male hogs used for breeding. *Stags* are boars castrated after sexual maturity. *Barrows* are male hogs castrated before maturity.

The reason for castration is simple. It increases the rate of weight gain and reduces aggressive behavior (fighting). The production cycle for hogs is relatively short. The gestation period is approximately 4 months. Sows are bred twice a year. Litters range from 5 to 15, with an average of approximately 9, of which 7 reach maturity. Gilts reach sexual maturity and slaughter weight at 6 months. At this point, they can be held back for breeding or sent to the packinghouse. Barrows reach slaughter weight (220 pounds) at 6 months. It takes about 1½ years from the time a pig is born to the time a pork chop from its offspring reaches the dining room table.

Supply Side

Hog farmers often integrate their production. It is common for producers to grow much of their own feed (corn or soybeans), farrow their own feeder pigs, and finish them out to slaughter weight. It is not unusual for a pig to spend its entire existence until slaughter in the same building or adjacent buildings—moving only from the nursery to the feeding floor. These pig farms are known as "farrow-to-finish" operations.

In the past when hogs farrowed in pastures and were fed in open lots, all females were bred in the spring and fall. This gave a seasonality to production. Now, with more sophisticated facilities, production has leveled off somewhat.

A 220-pound market hog yields an average 153 pounds of pork, trimmings, and lard. Fresh hams account for about 18.5 percent; pork bellies (bacon) 17.5 percent; loins 15 percent; trimmings 18 percent; picnics 8.5 percent; and others 22.5 percent. The six commercial cuts are hams, loins, picnics, Boston butts, bellies, and spareribs. These represent 40 percent of the live weight and 90 percent of the value of a hog.

Demand Side

Pork has always been an important part of the American diet. During the last 20 years, pork has faced some stiff competition from beef, chicken, and fish. It has been fighting back for a market share in the media, in recent years as producers have bred a leaner product and promoted it as "the other white meat."

Unlike beef, of which most is consumed fresh, pork is mostly processed or stored—smoked, canned, or frozen. Pork bellies, for example, can be stored (frozen) up to 1 year before processing. The ease of storage of pork products means that the forecasters of futures prices must take supplies, as well as production, into consideration.

What Are Pork Bellies?

The pork belly is the layer of meat and fat from the underside of the hog. Each hog has two bellies, one on each side, which extend from the front to the rear legs. They weigh between 10 and 20 pounds. Most bellies weigh 14 to 16 pounds. Almost all bellies are cured, smoked, and sliced into bacon. A well-developed cash market exists in bellies, which impacts the futures markets.

Fundamental Analysis

Fundamental analysts usually take the pipeline approach. What is the farrowings number? How many feeder pigs are available? How many gilts will be held back for breeding? How many market hogs are in the system and at what weights? What are storage levels? You must consult USDA quarterly reports (Hogs and Pigs Report) released in March, June, September, and December for numbers. They cover the top 10 producing states.

Hog Cycles

The hog cycle is considered to be a 4-year cycle. It may range from as low as 3 years to as high as 6. During the last 50 years, there have been 12 cycles averaging 4.1 years. The expansion phases lasted 2.4 years on average, and the contraction phase 1.7 years.

Seasonality

As mentioned earlier, the seasonality of the production cycle has become somewhat less meaningful over the years as production techniques have changed. Still, hog prices tend to have a definite seasonal pattern. Hog prices tend to bottom in late spring and the fourth quarter. Most highs are made in August. With pork bellies, the inventory level on hand tends to impact any seasonal pattern. There is also the BLT factor—demand in late summer for bacon, lettuce, and tomato sandwiches.

Price Determinants

Naturally, the supply-demand equation is the most important price determinant. You must be on top of the size of the pig crop, hog slaughter, slaughter weights, direction of two-way gilts, etc. Other determinants are:

1. *Hog-corn ratio.* This is the price of corn (major feed component) compared with the price of hogs. If the ratio is low, feeding is profitable. If high, it isn't. With the increased investment in buildings and the cost of feed supplements, this ratio has become less reliable in recent years
2. *Weather.* Unusually hot or cold weather can impact weight gain. This is somewhat mitigated by the confined feeding systems currently being used, but not entirely.
3. As mentioned in past sections of this series, such things as fashion, health considerations, and promotions can impact prices by influencing demand.

Trading and Technical Analysis

Pork belly contracts are a favorite of day traders and aggressive position traders because of the wide price ranges in which the contracts trade. But the volatility factor should be taken as a warning to neophyte traders.

Both the bellies and the hogs lend themselves well to spread trading strategies. Nearby contracts usually gain enough on the distant in bull markets—and lose enough in bear markets—to make the spreads attractive, especially when you take the lower margins and somewhat more manageable risk (compared with a straight futures position) into consideration.

Always trade these markets with stops. They respond violently to unexpected news, weather, or reports.

OVERVIEW OF LIVE AND FEEDER CATTLE MARKETS

The production of beef requires the breeding, raising, and fattening of cattle. As with pork, this industry has a unique vocabulary that you need to understand.

Cow. A mature female that has had a calf

Heifer. A female under 3 years old that has not yet produced a calf

Bull calf. A male calf, not yet castrated

Steer. A castrated male

Bull. An uncastrated male, capable of reproduction

Yearling. A calf that has been fed on pasture for approximately 1 year

Another unique aspect of beef production is its cycle. There are 14 to 18 months between when a heifer calf is born and when that calf is bred. The gestation period of a calf is 9 months.

There are 17 to 19 months between when a bull calf is born and when it can be slaughtered as a fed steer. It takes over 2-1/2 years from the time a cow is bred until a steak from its offspring is in the butcher's case. A lot can happen from the beginning of the production cycle to the end. The cattle go through several stages and hands.

There are three distinct sectors of the cattle industry:

The first is the ranch, called the *cow-calf operation.* Calves and feeder cattle are produced here.

The second sector is the feedlot. The feeder cattle are fed out in preparation for slaughter. When ready for market, the feeder cattle are called *fat cattle.*

The packer is the third segment of the industry. It converts the live cattle to beef and by-products.

Supply Side

The cow-calf operation produces calves. It is the driving force that moves the cattle business. A typical breeding herd in the United States consists of 75 cows, with 1 bull per 20 cows. Depending on the climate and rainfall of the ranch, it may take from 5 to 200 acres to support 1 cow-calf unit.

The herd is usually bred in the summer, with the calves born in the spring (as noted earlier, a 9-month gestation period). The calves are weaned after 6 to 8 months, when they weigh about 300 to 500 pounds.

The weaned calves are two-way cattle. Either they can go directly to the feedlot for fattening, or they can be put on grass for another 6 to 10 months, until they weigh 650 to 800 pounds. The decision is based on cattle prices, production costs, and economic conditions. Additionally, the cow-calf operation must hold back up to 20 percent of its heifers as replacements for cows that become barren.

The feedlot sector takes the calves from the cow-calf operator and fattens them for slaughter. Usually steers are fed until they weigh 1,000 to 1,200 pounds and heifers until they weigh 850 to 1,000 pounds.

There are basically two types of feedlots: commercial and farmer. The most common distinction between them is that the commercials have a larger capacity. They can feed 1,000 or more heads at a time. Anything less is classified as a farmer feedlot. The commercial feedlots tend to be more efficient with better rates of gain per head, higher gains per day, and shorter feeding time.

The last sector is composed of the packers. They purchase the fed cattle, slaughter them, and sell the beef and just about everything else (hide, trimmed fat, bones, blood, and glands). The carcass, which is approximately 62 percent of the live weight, will yield about 50 percent steaks and roasts. The rest will be hamburger, except for about 5 percent that becomes stewing beef, on an average.

Demand Side

After the packer, the beef enters the retail food chain. Beef is almost exclusively produced for human consumption, with a small amount used in dog food. Beef has a lot of serious competition, such as pork, chicken, fish, and other types of meat and poultry. Several vegetable products, soybean fillets, and meat substitutes attempt to compete directly or indirectly.

Fundamental Analysis

Because of the lengthy production cycle and the limited ability to store beef, one popular approach to analyzing price is the *pipeline method*. Users of this analytical tool estimate the supplies at hand in each of the various sectors of the industry. They attempt to anticipate the decisions of the managers of each sector. Will cow-calf operators hold back more than 20 percent of their heifers this year to increase the size of their herd? Which way will two-way cattle go?

The basic source of information on the status of the pipeline comes from quarterly reports issued by the USDA. They are called the Cattle on Feed Reports and cover the top 13 cattle-feeding states, or about 85 to 90 percent of all cattle on feed. Since the typical length of feeding is approximately two quarters, you can anticipate slaughter numbers. The USDA also publishes data on fed cattle, slaughter, and beef production which can be compared with earlier forecasts.

The Cattle Cycle

The size of the cattle herd has a distinct, long-term cycle. There have been 8 cattle cycles identified since 1896, averaging 12 years in length. They have ranged from 9 to 16 years in length. On an average, the national herd expands for 7 years and contracts for 5. The primary reasons for the cycle is the length of the production cycle and heavy investment (land, equipment, and cattle) required to enter and stay in the business.

Seasonality

There are no set planting or harvesting time periods for cattle, as with other agricultural products, but there is still is a seasonal cycle. Most calves are born within 45 days of April 1 and weaned within 45 days of October 1. The 350- to 500-pound calves are usually kept on grass until they gain 250 to 350 pounds. Then they are sent to the feedlot to gain 2 pounds a day for the next 210 days. At that point, the steer is 26 months old, weighs 1,150 pounds, and is ready for slaughter.

Price Determinants

Several factors impact the price of beef besides the supply-demand equation already discussed. Feed costs account for approximately 30 percent of total production costs. Low corn prices stimulate production and enable more weight to be put on fat cattle. This increases beef supplies and lowers prices.

Since cattle production is capital-intensive, interest rates can stimulate or stifle production. Weather can also impact production. Particularly hot or cold weather reduces weight gain. Taste, fashion, and sales promotion can influence consumers. Is eating beef the "healthy thing" to do? Will TV spots increase usage or switch consumers to the "other white meat"?

Trading and Technical Analysis

The length of time required to make major changes in the cattle cycles causes the market to develop long-term trends that are ideally suited for technical analysis. This can also result in the market trading for long periods of time within narrow ranges, making it difficult to trade it profitably, except on a very short-term basis.

FOOD AND FIBER

OVERVIEW OF THE SUGAR MARKET

Two types of sugar exist: cane and beet. Historically, cane accounts for about 60 percent of the world's production. Cane sugar is a perennial crop with an 18-month growing season. After harvesting, the stubble left in the fields produces another crop. With each successive crop, the yield diminishes. Eventually, it has to be replanted.

Cane sugar is grown in many countries around the world and is one of the few crops harvested year-round. The major producers are Brazil, the European Union (EU), India, the United States, and

China. They account for almost half of the world's production in a given year. Brazil has increased production by 90 percent since 1993–1994 and now accounts for about 15 percent of the world's sugar output. It has about 25 percent of world exports.

Beet sugar accounts for the other 40 percent of total production. The EU produces more than 75 percent of beet sugar. Sugar beets are an annual crop, so plantings can be estimated in the spring and followed throughout the year. Because the European crop accounts for so much of the world's production and the cane crop is harvested all year long, the beet crop critically influences the supply-demand equation.

Supply

The statistical sugar season begins September 1 and ends August 31. Like all food commodities, year-end stocks play a big role in price analysis. So does estimated production. The first official indication of the size of the new crop each year is made by F. O. Licht's estimates of European sugar beet plantings. The first estimate of the total world crop is not released until October of each year.

The supply side of the supply-demand equation is further distorted by the impact of competitive products. High-fructose corn syrup (HFCS) is a popular sweetener as a result of depressed corn prices. Also competing with sugar are such nonnutritive sweeteners as aspartame (NutraSweet), saccharin, acesulfame K, and sucralose.

Demand

Sugar consumption has grown steadily over the years, usually averaging about 2 to 3 percent a year. Since sugar has a well-defined usage pattern, it is relatively easy to project consumption from year to year. Total world consumption during the last 7 years of the 1990s grew from 112 million to 129 million tons. Although consumption was flat in marketing year (MY) 1994–1995 compared with MY 1993–1994, there was a jump of about 6 million tons in MY 1995–1996 and an increase of about 3 million tons each year through MY1999–2000.

Reasons for the steady pattern are:

1. Governments exercise strict controls on sugar prices in many countries by limiting imports. Only about 27 percent of the world's annual usage requirements are traded on the free market. Domestic usage by producing countries is high.
2. There is no substitute for its use in many products.
3. Even when HFCS can be substituted, this is done reluctantly because of the fickle nature of consumer tastes. This has been particularly evident in the soft drink industry, where changing formulas is a high-risk decision.
4. In nonindustrial usage, demand tends to be inelastic because the cost of sugar is not a significant amount of the user's budget.

Therefore, projecting consumption can be relatively simple. If there has not been an extremely active bull market in recent seasons that would substantially increase plantings (especially of perennial cane sugar), the previous usage gains for the last two to four crop years can be used. If there has been a bull market recently, then you can anticipate a modest consumption decline.

Price Forecasting

Sugar pricing has an unusual pricing history. Many analysts liken it to the "tulipomania" that occurred in seventeenth-century Holland. It was a period of speculative frenzy that drove tulip bulb prices to incredible heights—only to crash with equal momentum.

The 1974 bull sugar market is a good example. At the market height in November 1974, sugar prices had increased eightfold over 1973 levels. In the final months of this wild bull rally, futures prices shot up 36 cents per pound in 2 months. Thirty-six cents is three times higher than the prior post-World War II high!

It started with some very bullish fundamentals. The year-end (1973–1974) stock-consumption ratio was a low 20 percent. The sugar beet crop in Europe was faced with some adverse growing conditions. Fundamentals might account for 20- or 30-cent sugar, but it more than doubled that price to over 65 cents. There was talk of dollar-per-pound sugar. Then it came down faster than it went up, leveling in the 15- to 20-cent range. A similar market "panic" occurred in 1980. It was not as severe, but sugar rallied to 45 cents a pound that time.

The price differential between world raw sugar and U.S. No. 14 raw sugar can be great at times. During the first quarter of 1999, the gap between the two was the largest since 1987—an average 22.48 cents per pound for the U.S. product compared with about 6.75 cents per pound for world raw (f.o.b. Caribbean Contract No. 1). The differential occurs because the United States controls the imports of sugar, whereas the world price can be affected by surplus sugar being dumped onto the market, particularly from the European Union which has sugar price supports about 40 percent above U.S. levels.

The point is that sugar has a propensity to move way beyond what could be expected based on fundamentals. It can be a very emotionally driven market. Remember that if you're thinking of trading sugar.

Technical Analysis

Because of its emotional nature and unusual pricing history, sugar can be traded using technical chart formations. They will catch the big moves.

The seasonal pattern projects the annual low around September and the high in January or February. The cycles for sugar have been described as "bizarre." They are characterized by extremely sharp but relatively short-lived upside bursts, followed by extended periods of dormancy at depressed levels. This may be the result of some fundamental factors, such as the year-long harvesting of the crop.

OVERVIEW OF THE COFFEE MARKET

The first common usage of coffee has been obscured in antiquity. Most scholars of the subject believe it was probably first used in ancient times in Ethiopia. From there, its popularity spread throughout the Arab world and then Turkey. Around 1600, its use moved through Italy to the rest of Europe, including England, where coffeehouses became important centers of commerce in London. Tea later became the favorite drink in the United Kingdom and its colonies, including the United States, until the American Revolution changed tastes here. Today the United States is the world's largest coffee consumer.

Arabica Versus Robusta

There are basically two types of coffee. The most popular and most in demand is arabica. It is a mild coffee grown mainly in Brazil, Colombia, and other parts of Latin America. Arabicas make the richest blends. Best-quality arabicas ("milds") grow from 2,000 to 6,500 feet, with quality rising the higher above sea level one goes. Brazil's arabicas (the less esteemed "natural" type) are grown from 650 to 2,500 feet.

Robusta coffee comes mainly from Africa and Asia, but also increasingly from Brazil (the conilon type). It is grown from sea level up to 2,500 feet and is more resistant to pests and heat, but not to frosts, than arabica. Robustas, which have a more powerful taste and are less aromatic than arabicas, are used mostly in blends and for instant coffees.

Young coffee trees begin bearing at about 4 years of age and continue for about 25 years. Each tree produces enough beans (on an average) to make one pound of marketable coffee each year. The trees begin the process by producing a white flower, followed by a berry, usually called a "cherry" because that is what it looks like. The cherries are originally green and turn red as they ripen. At harvest, the berries are handpicked and consist of sweet pulpy fruit usually covering two flat beans.

Once picked, the fruit can be processed into coffee beans by one of two ways—both today are equally as common. The wet method, whereby the beans are washed in fermentation tanks after the outer pulp has been mechanically removed, is used almost exclusively for mild arabicas, and the dry method is used for robustas and natural arabicas. Here berries are mostly dried in the sun to remove the pulp, so dependable weather is very important.

When the initial process is complete, the beans are sized and graded. Then they are packed into heavy bags (132 pounds each) for storage or shipment. Most beans are moved to New York, New Orleans, San Francisco, Le Havre, or Antwerp for roasting, blending, and packaging for the customer.

Supply Versus Demand

Even though the United States is the world's major consumer of coffee, coffee is not consumed to quench thirsts, nor does it have any nutritive value. Its popularity depends on its use as a stimulant (caffeine). It tends to be emotionally addictive. Millions and millions of people "need" a cup of coffee to get going in the morning.

This makes a very inelastic demand situation. Prices have to increase drastically to make an impact on demand. Therefore, the short-term demand can be calculated fairly accurately. The long term is not as clearly defined. Soft drinks, many of them with caffeine as part of their formula, have made an impact on usage. Many young adults prefer a soda in the morning, rather than a cup of coffee. This has already slowed the demand growth rate, particularly in the United States and some European countries. This, along with saturation in some mature markets, is a potentially negative long-term factor. Moves have begun in the United States, however, to encourage the young to rediscover the "coffee habit."

The supply side of the equation is the one that often impacts pricing. The coffee tree is not a dependable producer. Its yield can vary sharply, partly because of the tree's biennial cycle, but weather and husbandry practices are also key determinants.

In Brazil's coffee zone, where there is a perennial danger of frosts in June and July, subzero temperatures, or just the threat of them, will send prices soaring. Toward the equator, areas above 6,000-feet sea level are also vulnerable to freezes. Another threat to production, especially in Brazil in September and October, is drought, which can hamper the trees' flowering and thus fruit production. Although coffee needs plenty of rain (at least 40 inches a year), very heavy downpours can damage the flowers. Other problems include high winds, pests, and diseases.

Seasonality

Coffee is unique in that there is no clear-cut seasonality to its pricing, partly because the commodity is harvested throughout the year.

As long as there are no supply shocks, beans are usually readily available, while demand can often be met from stocks, as green (unprocessed) coffee can be easily stored for long periods without loss of quality.

Price Determinants

As discussed earlier, weather is the major determinant of price in the short term. However, there are other factors you must track. Transportation is one. Coffee must move from its origin to where it will be processed and consumed. Anything that interferes with this movement (dock strikes, war, etc.) will impact price.

Inventories can help limit the market's upside potential at times of crop problems. Roasters (processors) have, during the 1990s, become accustomed to living with much lower stock cover than would once have been thought safe, as they increasingly follow a just-in-time buying strategy. This is potentially very risky, as the 1997 price boom proved.

Government restrictions can also figure in. The producing countries are considered to be somewhat unstable in some circles. Brazil at one time went as far as to burn much of its crop in an attempt to manipulate prices.

The International Coffee Agreement, administered by the London-based International Coffee Organization (ICO), was a key factor in pricing from 1963 until mid-1989. Its system of export quotas aimed at keeping the market within a price band acceptable to its importing and exporting member countries collapsed. Following the failed attempt in 1992/1993 to renegotiate the returns of ICO quotas, the Association of Coffee Producing Countries (ACPC) was formed. This producer cartel aims to ensure market stability through the imposition, if necessary, of limits on exports. However, it has had little impact because all sales limits are voluntary and are often ignored. The fact that 30 percent of world production is outside the ACPC's orbit is another drawback. However, the agency's activities need to be watched, as the agency has the potential to become a force in the market. The ICO today is a clearinghouse for statistics on coffee and a talking shop for its producer and consumer members (which no longer include the United States). No moves are envisaged to restore its old market-regulatory powers.

Understanding the impact of the supply-demand equation requires attention to a lot of data available from the USDA, the NCA, and the ICO.

Trader's Notes

Trading weather markets is a tricky business at best. Trading coffee is that much more complicated because it is a very thin futures market. This means that even a small amount of trading activity can result in very wide price swings. In other words, it can be very dangerous.

Since arabica contracts are traded on the New York Coffee, Sugar and Cocoa Exchange and robusta is on the London Exchange, some traders spread these two types of coffee depending on the price relationship. Intracontract spreads are less interesting because there is basically no crop year.

OVERVIEW OF THE COCOA MARKET

Cocoa is an ancient crop and drink of Central America. At times, it was important enough to be used as a medium of exchange. Cocoa appeared in Europe in the sixteenth century, but it wasn't until 1828 that a Dutch processor discovered that the fat of the cocoa bean, called cocoa butter, could be extracted. Combining sugar with the cocoa butter produced chocolate. Later, nineteenth-century Swiss candy makers pioneered the use of adding milk to the cocoa butter and sugar and gave the world its first milk chocolate.

Supply Side

Cocoa beans grow on trees in tropical climates. They grow in an area that is between 20 degrees north and 20 degrees south of the equator and require at least 50 inches of rain per year. It takes 5 years for the trees to produce a bean crop. After that, the trees yield for another 40 to 50 years, with peak production coming around the fifteenth year.

Output was once fairly price-inelastic. However, it has become much more sensitive to market movements, starting in the 1990s, because of deregulation, which has put an end to state-guaranteed prices to farmers nearly everywhere (including the Ivory Coast in

1999). The main reasons for the decade's underlying upward production trend, however, were productivity gains from the extensive replanting with high-yielding clones in Africa and the steady rise in Indonesia's planted area.

In the major producing countries (Ivory Coast, Ghana, Indonesia, Nigeria, Brazil, Cameroon, and Malaysia), the main crop comes in from October through March. This accounts for three-quarters of the world's production. A "mid-crop" is harvested from May to August. The reason for these long harvesting periods is that the cocoa bean matures slowly and unevenly. With the production in the tropics and the majority of consumers in the temperate zones, the bulk of the crop must be shipped to the confection manufacturers. This makes transportation an important part of the price equation. The bean cannot be stored in the tropics without being processed. Historically, all the processing (and therefore, inventory held) was done in the developed, user countries, especially the United States and Europe. Producing countries, however, are now doing more processing themselves to add value to exports. Brazil has led the way, partly because of growing local chocolate demand, followed by Malaysia and more recently by Africa, especially the Ivory Coast. It now grinds 20 percent of its crop and wants to raise the figure to 50 percent.

Origin processing creates another level of inventory in the shape of cocoa products. There is also a third inventory level. Industry in importing countries holds perhaps 4 to 6 weeks' supply, and they often trade substantially more.

Until recently, the International Cocoa Organization (ICCO) also held stocks of cocoa accumulated before its market-support buying operations were halted for good in 1988. Its holdings, however, were liquidated through regular monthly auctions between October 1993 and April 1998.

The processing of cocoa beans is complex. First, the ripe fruit or pods are cut from the trees, which grow to a height of 25 feet. The pods are split, and 20 to 40 seeds (beans) that look like almonds are removed. The beans are then fermented for 2 to 9 days. This kills the bean's germ and activates enzymes, which produces the unique flavor.

After fermentation, the beans are dried, bagged, and shipped to the processor. The processor cleans, blends, and roasts the beans.

After roasting, the thin shells, or hulls, of the beans are cracked and removed. The beans are now called *nibs*. The nibs (meat of the bean) contain approximately 54 percent cocoa butter. The nibs are crushed and ground to release the cocoa butter. The mixture of cocoa butter and finely ground nibs is called chocolate *liquor*. It can be used at this stage, stored, or further processed into baking chocolate, cocoa, milk chocolate, or sweet and semisweet chocolate. Drinking cocoa, by the way, contains 22 percent fat.

Demand Side

Cocoa is prized for its unique and tempting flavor, for which there is no substitute. Around 98 percent of all cocoa goes into chocolate and chocolate-flavored foodstuffs, such as beverages, biscuits, and ice cream, with most of the rest used by the cosmetics industry. Since its end products are luxury items, cocoa is consumed mainly in high-income countries, such as the United States and most European Union states, where changes in price have little impact on demand. Less mature markets that are more price-sensitive (e.g., Japan, Russia, and much of Eastern Europe) are growing in importance.

Price Determinants

While retail buying is reasonably stable, on the wholesale and futures markets, there is plenty of price activity. The cocoa market is very susceptible to the rumor mill, partly because the remoteness of some production areas makes hard information on crop size difficult to come by. Producers and some governments, namely the Ivory Coast, also tend to talk down output to talk up prices. In the 1990s, however, the problem has been reduced by better communication systems and by industry integration (helped by liberalization in producing countries). This has given users a rising stake in cocoa growing and shipment, increasing their confidence over supplies and reducing their stock requirements.

The familiar factor, weather, as with most crops, impacts price. Cocoa trees require a lot of rain. If it doesn't come, production is reduced. Too much rain brings crop diseases. A severe "harmattan" (a dry, dusty wind from the Sahara Desert) can severely damage the Ivory Coast crop.

Income and population help determine price as well. Increased wealth in a nation almost always leads to increased consumption demand.

At the same time, thanks to deregulation, governments today have much less influence over supplies and prices than they once had, and the ICCO's once strong market-regulatory powers have also gone. Today the ICCO-administered International Cocoa Agreement (to which most trading states, except Indonesia and the United States, belong) permits only the voluntary management of production to support prices. As with coffee and its voluntary regulatory body, output targets are invariably ignored. The trade pays no heed to the ICCO's management scheme, knowing that the ICCO may be abolished by October 2001 anyway.

Cocoa butter substitutes are other vegetable fats, which are being increasingly used in chocolate. Producers fear these substitutes will displace substantial volumes of cocoa. Industry, however, contends that they may encourage demand by allowing product innovation and improving storage properties.

Sugar is the other major ingredient in chocolate. One would expect the price of sugar to impact the price of cocoa. It doesn't, mainly because sugar candy is the major competitor of chocolate. When sugar candy prices go up, so does the price of chocolate candy, and vice versa.

Other price determinants include:

Transportation. Moving unprocessed beans out of the tropics is critical. Any disruption or threat of disruption runs prices up.

Strength of the dollar. A strong U.S. dollar tends to decrease the world price of cocoa.

Inventory levels. The three-tiered inventory situation keeps a substantial supply of cocoa in the market. This is the major stabilizing factor in the market.

Seasonality

Because of the long growing season and complex inventory system, there is very little seasonality. Most often the lows occur in the first quarter. Highs come in July and August. This is reflective of the main crop harvest, which takes place October through March.

Trader's Notes

This is a tough market to figure out for both the fundamentalist and the technical trader. The fundamentalist must rely on notoriously unreliable data. The technician must deal with relatively wide bid-ask spreads, high margins, and price movements that represent $10 per point. All in all, it is a fast-moving market that can easily whipsaw even the most experienced trader. Whenever possible, trade with a broker who has a substantial amount of experience.

OVERVIEW OF THE ORANGE JUICE MARKET

Oranges are grown in a variety of countries throughout the world, with Brazil and the United States being the leading producers. Mexico, Spain, China, and Italy are among the other leading producers. The United States was long the dominant producer and exporter of oranges and orange juice, but has been overtaken by Brazil in recent years. Brazil's estimated orange production in the 1997–1998 marketing year was about 19 million metric tons, or 31 percent of the world's production. That compared with about 13 million metric tons, or 21percent, produced by the United States. During the period from 1970–1971 to 1978–1979, the United States produced nearly 28 percent of the world's oranges, while Brazil's share was about 22 percent, according to figures from the USDA's Foreign Agriculture Statistics Services. The United States for the past several years has imported more orange juice than it exported, the amount depending on weather and production. Most of the imports come from Brazil.

Florida, with oranges under cultivation since the 1500s, is the leading U.S. producer, growing more than 70 percent of the U.S. crop. California, whose trees were planted about 1700, is the second largest U.S. producer, and Texas is third. Arizona also produces oranges.

Orange juice became a popular year-round breakfast drink with the development in 1947 of a process that freezes the juice without loss of flavor. The process overconcentrates the juice into a thick syrup and then adds more fresh orange juice and other flavorings prior to freezing. Thus, we have frozen concentrated orange juice (FCOJ).

Sugar is one of the key ingredients of FCOJ. Fruit buyers are concerned about "pounds solids" when they buy oranges for FCOJ. This refers to the amount of solids dissolved in the juice, sugar being the primary one. The orange crop becomes sweeter the longer it grows. Valencia oranges make the best juice because they have a high concentration of solids and the variety matures late.

Supply Side

Weather and disease are keys to production. Most of the early and mid-season U.S. crop is harvested in late January. The harvest period for late oranges ranges from mid-April to June. The early and mid-season crops are very vulnerable to frost. This can make for some very exciting roller-coaster rides on the price charts. During the first four crop years of the 1980s, Florida was hit with four early frosts in a row. Frost can be very damaging to the orange trees, as well as the fruit. Therefore, serious frost damage can impact future years.

Florida is the major U.S. producer of oranges for both eating and freezing. Because of the frost in the early 1980s, Florida's ability to be a reliable supplier was brought into question. Brazil's increased production could offset U.S. losses. The problem would come when both of the major producers experience reduced crops because of weather or disease.

Brazil's crop has increased significantly in the past few years as the government began providing its growers incentives and subsidies. São Paulo is Brazil's largest producer, with about 225 million trees (197.5 million bearing trees and 27.4 million nonbearing), but citrus canker has become a serious concern for growers in the São Paulo commercial citrus area, according to the USDA. Fundecitrus, the São Paulo State Fund for the Defense of Citriculure, has been taking an active role in the detection and eradication of citrus canker. Still, the USDA says several million trees could be eradicated in the next few years in an effort to control the disease.

Demand Side

Most commodities are affected by supply and demand, but this is not necessarily true with FCOJ. With orange juice, the supply side dominates the price equation. Historically, oranges were shipped fresh and squeezed into juice in the home or peeled and eaten. They were a seasonal treat. When they were not available, the consumer did without. Now FCOJ is always available in the freezer case. If it gets too expensive, the consumer may choose to do without or switch to a less expensive fruit, juice, or drink. In other words, the demand is elastic. It will respond to changes in price. If the price moves up sharply, demand decreases. A plentiful supply and lower prices will spark demand.

Besides using oranges for juice and eating fruit, oranges have some other uses. The peel can be candied, dried, or made into marmalade. An oil, pectin, can be squeezed from the peel. It is used as a flavoring or as a scent in perfumes. The pulp left over after commercial squeezings can be fed to livestock.

Seasonality

Like most crops, the price in the cash and futures markets tends to peak prior to harvest and decline afterward. For FCOJ, the highs traditionally come in November and the lows in June.

Price Determinants

Weather has a greater impact on the supply of oranges than on just about any other commodity. Winter freezes, from late November to mid-February, can wipe out the Florida crop and the trees. Because Brazil is in the Southern Hemisphere, winter occurs there during June, July, and August. Orange groves require warmth and moisture. A shortage of water during blooming can be devastating, and too much rain or irrigation can hurt as well. In addition, insects take their toll. Sudden heat waves can cause young fruit to prematurely drop. Even strong winds will hurt yields. Disease such as citrus canker and citrus chlorosis variegated can also destroy trees. This is a difficult crop to grow.

Because orange juice production is a supply-driven market, worldwide competition is a major factor. After Brazilian production overtook that of the United States during the past few years, Brazilian oranges are even being imported by Brazilian interests who operate processing plants in Florida. They process the Brazilian oranges and mix the juice with Florida juice. Analysts must track the total available crop and the number of newly producing trees coming into production. For reference, it takes about 5 years from the time an orange tree is planted until it begins to bear fruit.

FCOJ can be stored indefinitely, so inventory levels must be watched carefully. These inventories are held on several levels—the concentrate processors, brokers, warehousers, and major grocery chains.

The market for FCOJ has primarily been in the United States, but has been spreading to other developed countries, which can increase consumption and prices.

The ever-changing taste of consumers will also affect price. Recently, the amount of chilled, as opposed to frozen concentrate, juice has been steadily increasing. This trend requires watching.

Trader's Notes

Trading frozen orange juice is a lot like trading pork bellies. It is for traders who like to skydive on weekends. Sudden and significant price changes occur unexpectedly. You should be firm of heart and deep of pocket when trading this market.

OVERVIEW OF THE COTTON MARKET

Cotton is an ancient crop first cultivated in China over 5,000 years ago. It worked its way west via Persia and India over routes traveled by Alexander the Great. The first weaving techniques were introduced into Spain in the thirteenth century. From Spain, the science of making cotton spread to the Netherlands and to England, where it flourished in the seventeenth century. The first cotton mill in North America was established in Rhode Island in 1790.

It was good old Yankee ingenuity that really gave the industry a boost. In 1793, Eli Whitney invented the cotton gin. This machine alone increased productivity 50-fold. The gin removed seed from the fiber, so it could be woven into cloth. For the first time, enough fiber was available to supply a commercial textile industry.

Supply Side

On the supply side of the supply-demand equation (refer to the corn overview) are 75 countries growing cotton—about 85 million bales a year the past few years. Most use all their production internally. The dominant producers are China, the United States, India, Pakistan, and the Commonwealth of Independent States (the former Soviet Union). Turkey and Egypt are also major suppliers of raw cotton.

There are many different varieties of cotton, but the one that is traded internationally is called *upland*. Upland cotton is evaluated using three characteristics: grade, staple, and micronaire.

Grade is based on several factors, such as color, foreign matter, and preparation. Color refers to the whiteness or brilliance of the raw fiber. Low-grade cotton has a spotty color. Foreign matter is the amount of dirt, bark, leaf particles, and other impurities that combine with the cotton during harvesting. Preparation means the roughness and uniformity of the cotton fiber.

The second characteristic used to evaluate cotton is the length of the staple or fiber. Short staple cotton is below $13/16$ of an inch; medium to long is from $13/16$ of an inch to $1 3/32$ inches; long is from $1 1/8$ to $1 5/16$ inches; and extra-long staple is above $1 3/8$ inches. Upland cotton has medium to medium-long staples.

The last characteristic is called *mike*, which is short for micronaire. A scientific instrument measures the airflow through cotton to determine the "mike" rating. Immature and overly mature cottons have lower values than "perfectly" mature cotton.

Cotton requires a 180-day, frost-free growing season. Hot weather with evenly spaced rains is preferred. In recent years, irrigation has been substituted for natural rainfall.

Of the cotton grown in the United States, 14 states produce 98 percent, with Texas the leading grower and California second. The other major producing states are Alabama, Arkansas, Arizona, Georgia, Louisiana, Mississippi, Missouri, New Mexico, North Carolina, Oklahoma, South Carolina, and Tennessee.

Demand Side

The predominant use of cotton grown in the United States is in the manufacture of clothes. The remainder is used for household or industrial uses. This division allows for a fairly stable demand pattern.

Synthetic materials, with their low cost and resilience, became very popular and had a significant impact on cotton demand for many years. But the cotton industry fought back and recaptured much of the market share it lost to products made of rayon and polyester. In 1968, cotton had a 49 percent share of the total apparel market in the United States. By 1982, this had slipped to a low of 35 percent. Aggressive marketing and promotion campaigns by the cotton industry raised the market share to over 60 percent by 1990, moving to 68 percent by 1997, according to National Cotton Council statistics.

The demand side of the supply-demand equation is also impacted by the importation of textile and finished garments from the Far East. Competition from Korea and China, using cotton grown in that part of the world, reduces the demand for U.S. grown cotton.

Price Determinants

Cotton is a crop that is produced once a year. Although it is grown in 75 countries, most countries use all their production internally. Therefore, the cotton price analysts need only track the production of the five key producers mentioned earlier.

Additionally, while demand changes are very significant, they usually occur slowly and in somewhat predictable patterns. Supply changes, on the other hand, occur abruptly and without warning.

Not surprisingly, supply-demand factors start with weather. As with any crop, weather is critical, particularly during the growing season. For example, rain and cold temperatures can delay planting in the spring. Late-planted cotton can be caught by an early frost. A wet, cool fall can cause the cotton boll to rot. If rain washes the insecticide off the plants, insects, particularly boll weevils, boll worms, and thrips, will do plenty of damage. Too little moisture reduces yield; too much reduces fruiting and causes late maturity.

Government programs during the last 60 years have had as much impact on production (supply) as the weather has. Government protection of cotton began in 1929 with the Agricultural Marketing Act, which established loan rates. Later, price support programs priced the U.S. crop out of the world market, and cotton carryover grew to 17 million bales in the mid-1960s.

The USDA says that the continuation of planting flexibility established in the 1996 farm legislation should mean the upland cotton area will remain responsive to its own price, competing crop prices, and other market signals. Exports are forecast to increase an average of 2 percent annually through 2008/2009, after a small decline in 2001/2002. The 1996 Farm Act capped total expenditures for cotton user marketing certificates (Step 2 payments designed to keep U.S. upland cotton competitive) at $701 million during fiscal years 1996–2002, but funding was exhausted by the end of calendar year 1998. USDA projections assume that the program will not be capped for fiscal years 2003 and later. As a result, it says annual Step 2 expenditures near $150 million are assumed in baseline projections for crop years 2002/2003 through 2008/2009.

Fashion often dictates price. The demand for permanent press clothing hurt the demand for cotton for many years. This fad reached its bottom, and there is a greater demand than ever before for more "natural" fabrics, particularly jeans made from cotton. As noted earlier, cotton's percentage share of the total apparel market has rebounded from a low of 35 percent in 1982 to 68 percent in 1997.

Inventory and carryover is the amount of cotton available at any one time. It is a critical element that must also be taken into consideration. Cotton ginners, brokers, millers, and shippers all hold inventory, not to mention the Commodity Credit Corporation.

Seasonality is predictable. Prices usually reach lows in late fall during harvest. Highs normally come between May and July. The crop year officially begins August 1 of each year.

Trader's Notes

There are many types of cotton. When evaluating demand, make sure the need is for the type of cotton you plan to "buy" on the futures exchange. For example, on the New York Cotton Exchange, the contract calls for 100 bales (50,000 pounds) of "low-middling, 1-1/16 inch premium mike." You would hate to go long only to find out the market is demanding extra-long staple cotton.

METALS

OVERVIEW OF THE SILVER MARKET

Silver was first used by people sometime around 4000 B.C., which is slightly after people learned to use gold and copper. The earliest known mines of "native" silver (pure silver found in nugget form) were in Asia Minor.

The first use of silver was decorative, primarily jewelry and armor. Inscriptions found in the Royal Tombs of Chaldaea indicate that by the fourth millennium B.C., silver had become a medium of exchange. It was the ancient Greeks who popularized the use of minted silver coinage. Europe remained silver poor until Spanish and Portuguese explorers discovered vast deposits in the Americas during the sixteenth century.

Supply Side

Total world production ranges between 300 and 500 million troy ounces per year. The main producing countries are Australia, Canada, Mexico, Peru, the United States, and the Commonwealth of Independent States.

Most U.S. silver mines have played out, and the metal is now primarily produced as a by-product of the mining of base metals such as copper, zinc, and lead. Silver is also often found in association with gold ore. The fact that most silver is produced as a by-product makes production somewhat insensitive to demand. Increased demand for the base metals, on the other hand, can create oversupply situations for silver.

People have a habit of hoarding precious metals. This can distort the supply side of the supply-demand equation. When silver becomes very precious, hoarders will dump their silver, thus driving prices sharply lower. India best reflects the magnitude of this problem. It is estimated that Indians hold 5,000 million ounces of silver—approximately a 12½-year supply.

The French are also known as world-class silver hoarders. There are no accurate figures on how much silver is hidden away in France.

In addition, new and efficient technologies have been developed to recover silver from photographic solutions, thereby adding recycled silver to the supply side of the balance sheet.

Demand Side

The demand for silver as a medium of monetary exchange has all but dried up. Only about 7 percent of silver supplies are still manufactured into coins each year. Its traditional use in jewelry, silver place settings, and art objects still represents a major portion of annual consumption.

The really big users are the electrical and photographic industries. Silver has several very desirable physical characteristics. It's a better conductor of heat and electricity than copper. And some of its salts are light- and radiation-sensitive and form the active ingredient in almost all film emulsions. In photography, about half of the silver consumed is for x-ray plates.

Marketing of Silver

In London, the silver marketing capital of the world, there are two very distinct silver markets. The first is the bullion market. Three banks—HSBC Bank plc, Deutsche Bank A.G., and the Bank of Novia Scotia-ScotiaMocatta—hold a daily "fixing" meeting each morning to set the price they are willing to pay for silver. This "fixes" the cash or spot price and gives brokers around the world a benchmark price to trade on.

The other market, of course, is the futures market. The two major futures exchanges trading silver are the New York Commodities Exchange (COMEX) and the Chicago Board of Trade (CBOT). The Far Eastern silver markets, particularly Hong Kong, Singapore, and Tokyo, have been steadily gaining in importance. The London Metal Exchange also began trading a silver futures contract in 1999.

Fundamental Analysis

There are five key areas the investor in silver must analyze from a fundamental point of view.

First is industrial usage. Is the use of photographic film and emulsions expected to increase or decrease? The rapid growth of digital cameras and their use with the Internet threatens this market. Statistics show that in 1997 more than 2 million digital cameras were sold—this was the second consecutive year the new devices outsold the traditional 35-mm single-lens reflex cameras. The popularity of digital cameras is spreading from commercial use to the general public and is certain to have an adverse affect on the amount of silver used for photographic purposes. Other industrial uses of silver, such as an electrical conductor and as a catalyst, must be gauged as well.

The second area of concern is currency fluctuation. Although not a perfect hedge against inflation, silver prices reflect the values of stronger currencies.

Third, you need to evaluate the impact of the political situation. Unstable world conditions encourage the hoarding of silver and other precious metals. Some governments have often tried to "control" the price of silver through legislation or decree. Other governments, such as India, have attempted to restrict the export of this precious metal. Can you predict what political action is going to occur? What impact will the political changes have on silver prices?

Fourth, you must estimate production and recovery. Normally, more silver is consumed each year than is mined, but the supply remains plentiful.

Lastly, you must consider the unpredictable, such as the fact that major producers have been known to disrupt the market to gain a political advantage.

Technical Analysis

Two technical formations work well for silver. Major lows in the silver market are usually made in rounded bottoms. Rounded bottoms may take years to develop, as was the case from 1974 to 1978, or from 1968 to 1973.

After creating a rounded bottom, silver often makes a spectacular rally—frequently doubling or tripling from its previous high. Highs, on the other hand, occur in a matter of seconds. A reversal from a top is often a spectacular spike top with "island reversals" and other kinds of violent formations.

Seasonally, you should expect silver to create its lows during summer, and its highs are often made in January.

OVERVIEW OF THE GOLD MARKET

Like silver, gold came into common use around 4000 B.C. It was first found in nugget form and later mined. Although it has been in constant use since prehistoric time, 90 percent of the world's gold has been mined since 1848. More than one-third of the amount produced since the beginning of time has been mined in the last 30 years. The reason is simply the advances made in mining technology.

One of the unique characteristics of gold is its malleability. An ounce can be formed into wire over 1 mile in length. That's one of the reasons it has been a favorite metal of jewelers over the centuries.

However, from a supply-demand perspective, it is quite inelastic. This means that demand is somewhat insensitive to supply price. For example, if the supply drops, demand may not be greatly affected. Gold is not like food. With food, if supplies disappear, prices soar. If the gold supply decreases, consumers (particularly industrial users) simply go without or find a replacement, e.g., platinum, palladium, or silver.

Gold has some other supply-demand considerations that an investor must be prepared to evaluate. First, gold is usually used in applications that allow for reclamation. It's so valuable that steps are usually taken to plan the recovery of whatever gold is used. This is particularly true in industrial applications. Therefore, disappearance as we know it in other commodities, like soybeans, corn, cattle, copper, etc., is not a serious factor.

Supply Side

New gold comes from mining. South Africa is by far the leading producer, followed by the United States, China, the Commonwealth of Independent States (CIS), Australia, and Canada. The rest of the world trails far behind.

Hoarders distort the supply side of the supply-demand equation. Central banks maintain the largest stockpiles. For example, central banks in the top 15 industrial countries store over 85 times the world's total annual production. If just 1 percent of this supply comes to market in any one year, the annual supply of gold would double.

Gold is one of the most politically sensitive commodities, and unpredictable behavior by its major producers can affect prices. South Africa and the Commonwealth of Independent States are major producers, although the CIS output has slipped in the past few years. In 1996 it ranked behind both the United States and China. In the past, South Africa and the Commonwealth of Independent States have been somewhat unreliable suppliers that did not always bring their gold into the marketplace in an orderly manner. South Africa, however, became more politically and economically stable in the mid-to-late 1990s, after the end of apartheid and the establishment of a black-dominated government led by Nelson Mandela. Russia and some of the other CIS countries still are politically and economically unpredictable, and their influence in production has waned.

The Organization of Petroleum Exporting Countries (OPEC) members are another group of unstable gold hoarders. They release gold reserves based on the price of a barrel of oil. If petroleum prices drop, they must sell gold to pay debts. If petroleum prices rise, they'll buy gold to add to their hoards.

Individuals, particularly individuals in countries that have experienced serious monetary problems, have learned to hoard gold. Germany, for example, has experienced the total destruction of its currency four times in the last 100 years. France is not far behind. Citizens of the United States are supposed to have enormous stock stashed away. The problem for fundamental analysis is that no one knows for sure how much is hidden away and what it would take to bring it back into the marketplace.

Demand Side

Decorative uses, primarily jewelry and objects d'art, account for about 60 percent of demand. Other major uses include electronics, dentistry, coinage, medicine, and chemicals.

Unfortunately, for commodity analysts, demand doesn't project price since it is an inelastic commodity. Additionally, there are several substitutes (metals mentioned earlier) that can dampen a demand-driven market.

Marketing of Gold

Like silver, the gold bullion price is fixed each day in London. Five major brokers get together twice each trading day and set the price. The brokers are N.M. Rothschild & Sons Ltd., Deutsche Bank A.G., HSBC Bank plc, Bank of Nova Scotia-ScotiaMocatta, and Republic National Bank of New York. Other very important marketing centers for bullion are Zurich, Hong Kong, and Singapore. Chicago and New York City dominate the futures market in gold.

Fundamental Analysis

The problem involved in analyzing the price of gold is isolating the pressures that impact gold. Gold is a commodity that is used in a variety of ways, but its impact is wider because humans have a sentimental attraction to jewelry made from this metal. Governments use it for coinage or to pay foreign debt. It has a monetary value. Individuals respond to this by hoarding it to stave off the effects of inflation or to protect themselves in times of financial crisis.

Through their central banks, governments also control the vast majority of aboveground gold. Therefore, it becomes a tool of their foreign or domestic policies. President Roosevelt's "New Deal," in 1933, made the possession of gold bullion illegal and confiscated bullion held by U.S. citizens. Iran and Iraq sold gold to support their war. South Africa, before the end of apartheid, used gold to bribe other countries to lift sanctions imposed to protest the treatment of blacks.

During the late 1990s, with gold already far down the slope of a 10-year decline, European Union central banks pushed it even lower by selling gold reserves, partly to help their countries meet criteria for the European Monetary Union. Plans for the International Monetary Fund (IMF) to sell part of its gold reserves to fund debt relief for poor nations also pressured gold. Gold prices fell to below $260 an ounce in mid-1999. But in late 1999, the European Central Bank (ECB) and the central banks of 15 other countries said they would limit gold sales to 400 tons per year through 2004. Also, the IMF bowed to U.S. congressional pressure to abandon its plan to sell 10 million ounces of gold, opting instead to revalue up to 14 million ounces of gold at current market prices to fund the debt relief programs. The actions briefly pushed gold back to over $325 an ounce, although it later slipped again. The actions eliminate some of the political pressure on gold, if the ECB and the other countries stick to their pledge during the period.

Technical Analysis

Just as gold is one of the most popular of possessions, it is also a commodity on which analysts love to do price projections, because "everyone" follows gold.

Its seasonal pattern finds the high most often around February and the low in place around August. The reason for this is the migration of workers to and from their farms. Supplies from South Africa are reduced when they are out planting their fields in February (our winter—their summer). Supplies increase when they return to the mines in August (our summer—their winter).

The silver-to-gold ratio is a simple, technical trading system. You simply calculate the number of troy ounces of silver it takes to buy 1 ounce of gold. At present, the "normal" ratio is around 60 to 1. When it drops below 50 to 1, gold is too scarce compared with silver and should be bought. When above 70 to 1, buy silver. Gold markets often trend. The basic bar chart formation analysis can often be used successfully.

OVERVIEW OF THE COPPER MARKET

Copper, known as the "red metal" since antiquity, was first used by people for the manufacture of weapons, armor, and tools. Because of its malleability, people quickly learned to blend it with other metals to produce more rigid materials, such as bronze and brass. Since prerecorded history, copper has been one of the most widely used metals. Even today, copper is one of the most actively traded metals on an international basis.

Supply Side

Copper enters the supply stream from two directions: newly mined and reclaimed. Copper mining utilizes the open pit method. Large amounts of earth are dug and run through a three-step process of milling, smelting, and refining. The milling procedure crushes and grinds the earth dug from the open pits. It is then moved through a flotation device that separates the copper ore from the earth, resulting in a copper concentrate. Intense heat is applied to the copper concentrate in the smelting step. This produces a copper that is 99 percent pure. The last stage is refining. It is an electrolytic technique that removes just about all the remaining impurities, bringing the copper to a purity level of 99.9 percent. This is the most commonly traded grade on futures markets.

Newly mined copper primarily comes from four areas: the western slopes of the Andes mountains in Chile and Peru, the South African countries of Zaire and Zambia, the United States, and Canada. These countries account for approximately two-thirds of the world's mining production. In the United States, Arizona produces the most copper.

One of the most popular characteristics of copper is its ability to resist corrosion. This makes copper an ideal metal to recycle. The scrap or secondary production of copper has been an ever-increasing source and must be taken into account when doing fundamental price analysis.

Demand Side

Copper is an industrial metal. Therefore, the demand for copper comes primarily from developed countries. Its industrial uses stem from its ability to conduct heat and electricity, resistance to corrosion, strength, ductility, and malleability. Copper is often alloyed with tin and nickel.

The two largest consuming countries are the United States and Japan. Japan, however, is not a major producer. The electrical industry is the largest single user. Copper, because it conducts electricity well, is used as wiring and in electrical components of all sorts. The growth of the space and telecommunications industries in recent years has boosted usage even more. Extensive use of copper can also be found in the housing, automobile, and plumbing industries. In addition, a considerable amount of copper is used for jewelry and coinage.

Price Determinants

Since much of copper is mined in undeveloped countries and consumed in developed countries, it must be exported from its source to where it is needed. This means that foreign exchange rates and transportation play an important part in the price discovery process. Second, no single nation has a monopoly on either the mining or refining of copper. It is truly a worldwide commodity. This fosters competition, which impacts pricing strategies.

As mentioned earlier, copper is a commercial metal used heavily in construction, automobiles, and electrical appliances. For this reason, the supply-demand equation is sensitive to economic trends within the developed countries. If housing starts or new-car sales plunge, you can expect copper prices will follow as demand slackens. Actually, copper prices usually lead the way as users cut back on inventories.

Thus, during economic hard times, look to short the copper market, but be sure to evaluate the situation on a global basis. If not, you could be caught in a situation where prices stay firm because demand is still strong in some parts of the world.

When evaluating economic or business cycles, you need to pay particular attention to the strength or velocity of change. Demand for copper feeds on itself and becomes stronger and stronger as demand builds momentum.

Politics in both the source and consuming countries must be monitored closely. For example, strikes by mine workers can restrict supply and drive prices higher. Political unrest in undeveloped countries is common and can spill over into the copper mines or slow down the movement of copper to the consumer nations.

In the developed countries, political programs that promote housing, construction, or manufacturing of electrical components foster demand and usually translate into higher copper prices. Governments can also influence demand with their monetary policy. For example, programs that encourage development of industry and promote jobs usually have a favorable impact on prices. Governments also directly control the amount of copper used for coins. If they lower interest rates, it will often impact housing starts, which will eventually be felt in the price of copper. Finally, don't forget the defense industry, which is a major user.

Copper inventories on all levels can be a damper or spark to prices. Heavy inventories hold prices down; shortages instigate bull markets.

Seasonality

Copper does have a seasonal pattern related to its uses in the housing and automobile industries. These industries build inventories that cause copper prices to peak during February through April. The trough usually comes in late summer and early fall.

Trader's Notes

Because copper futures contracts have a long history, are heavily traded, and are known for making long trending moves, they are very popular among speculators. Copper futures trade somewhat similar to lumber, which is also a commercial commodity and is influenced by interest rates and housing starts.

Copper futures are traded on the COMEX division of the New York Mercantile Exchange. Cash copper is also traded on the London Metal Exchange.

ENERGY

AN OVERVIEW OF PETROLEUM AND PETROLEUM PRODUCTS

The petroleum market historically was a reasonably stable market with steady prices and a reliable distribution system until the early 1970s. Since then, a lot of changes have occurred. The primary disruptions began in 1973 and 1974 with the formation of OPEC and the oil embargo. Prices shot up; lines formed at gas stations.

The major significance of these developments was a shift of power away from the major oil companies (the Seven Sisters) and into the hands of the producers. OPEC has had its ups and downs in its attempts to be a unified force in the energy world, with its influence ebbing and waning. Big players, notably Saudi Arabia, have often ignored the agreed quotas. Some producing countries refused to join, hampering efforts by OPEC to keep supply down to the level it would like.

The sharp drop in crude oil prices in the late 1990s to below $10 a barrel galvanized OPEC to holding closer to its quotas to get supply back into line. Prices moved back up to more than $20 a barrel in 1999.

Chaos often reigns in the energy market, providing both super opportunities and high risk for investors. The Iranian crisis of 1978 and 1979 continued these trends, as did the Iraq-Iran War and the Iraq-Allied (Desert Storm) War of 1990. Even in times of relative price and supply stability, the ominous threat of disruptions hangs over the market because of the friction between the United States and some Arab countries and between Israel and most Arab countries, particularly in view of the continued close United States–Israeli ties. Israeli-Palestine peace accords in the late 1990s could lead to lessened tensions in the Middle East, but it only takes a spark to ignite the long-smoldering distrust in the region.

Supply versus Demand

Two of the largest producers of crude oil, the Commonwealth of Independent States and the United States, are also net importers. That gives control of supplies to the major exporters: Saudi Arabia, Iran, Iraq, Kuwait, Libya, Nigeria, and Algeria. This group of producers must carefully balance output and usage.

For a time, the producers believed usage would never be a problem. They could charge what they wanted and the world would pay, but high prices convinced even U.S. citizens that enough was enough. Eventually, in 1983, conservation efforts left consumption in the United States unchanged for the first time in its history. This led to an oversupply of crude oil and lower prices. The oil cartel weakened, and the point was made. Although U.S. oil imports declined from 1983 until they reached a low of 3.2 million barrels per day in 1986, they began a steady climb after that. By the end of 1998, the United States was importing 8.7 million barrels per day, a result of a booming economy.

Seasonality

Demand has another twist when it comes to petroleum. Gas for automobiles is most in demand in the summer, while demand for heating oil peaks in the winter. These two factors complement each other as far as demands for raw crude, refining, and storage capacity is concerned.

The basic process of a refinery is distillation. Crude oil is heated until it vaporizes. The vapor or gas is then cooled to a liquid form. This process separates ("cuts" or "fractions") raw crude into several petroleum products. Compounds in the raw crude vaporize at different temperatures; the lighter the compound, the lower temperature at which it vaporizes. The "fractions" that compose crude oil, in order from lighter to heavier, are butanes, gasolines, naphtha, kerosene, heating oil, and residual oil.

Two other critical considerations are the types of crude available to a refinery and the distillation process a refinery uses. First, there are sweet and sour crudes. The lower the sulfur (less than 0.5 percent by weight), the sweeter it is. Sour crude contains over 1 percent sulfur. This characteristic has become very important because of pollution standards. Density is another consideration. Low-density, or light, crude is more desirable because it produces more of the more valuable products, namely gasoline and jet fuel. The origin of the crude is also a critical factor. It accounts for such characteristics as viscosity; pour point; color, flash, and fine points; and metals content.

Second, every refinery is designed to efficiently process a certain type of crude. If the right crude is not available for the way the refinery is set up or for the end products needed, the price for the "right" crude may shoot up on the spot market while other crudes go begging for a home.

Price Determinants

Not unexpectedly, price determinants start with weather. Unseasonably warm or cold weather during the winter (heating oil season) can play havoc with projections. Conservation will continue to be another factor. How seriously are consumers reacting to pressure by the government and other bodies to conserve energy? Political threats of war, blockades, etc., send prices higher. Peace and cooperation among nations drives the price down. The solidarity of OPEC sends prices up, while squabbling leads to lower prices.

Plentiful stockpiles and pipeline supplies reduce prices; shortages send prices skyrocketing. Discovery of new reserves damages price prospects. High prices can open closed or inefficient wells. Crude oil and its by-products can be stored for reasonably long periods of time. One would expect the deferred contracts to evenly reflect the cost of storage and insurance, as is usually true in the grains. However, because of the seasonality of both gasoline and heating oil (the two main by-products), this is not true. Also, petroleum is a very regional business, with each area of the country having different demands.

Trader's Notes

The petroleum markets lend themselves to hedging. Oil companies need to hedge future production; refiners hedge their requirements for crude and production of gasoline and heating oil; jobbers buy contracts of gasoline futures to hedge their needs.

Intercontract (crude oil versus gasoline, crude versus heating oil, gasoline versus heating oil) and intracontract (buying 1 month and selling another) spreads are very popular. More sophisticated speculators arbitrage between the New York and London futures markets. The important thing for the investor to note is that these are usually very liquid markets.

STOCK INDEXES

OVERVIEW OF THE STOCK INDEX
FUTURES MARKETS

Stock indexes and their futures market counterparts proliferated during the bull market of the mid-1990s. The first index, the Value Line Composite Index (Value Line) futures contract, commenced trading on February 24, 1982, on the Kansas City Board of Trade. Several others followed shortly thereafter. They are the Standard & Poor's 500 Stock Index (S&P 500), the New York Stock Exchange Composite Index (Composite), and the Major Market Index (MMI) futures contracts. There are options on futures for the S&P 500 and the Composite Indexes.

Other indexes cropped up during the 1990s, reflecting the growth of technology and small-capitalization stocks. Large-company indexes include the Dow Jones Industrial Average (DJIA), the Russell 3000, the Schwab1000, the Standard & Poor's 500 Composite Stock Index, and the Wilshire 5000 (which contains about 7,000 stocks). Medium-company indexes are Standard & Poor's 400 Mid-Cap and the Wilshire 4500. Small-company indexes are the Russell 2000 and the S&P SmallCap 600.

Each of these indexes reflects a different type of stock portfolio. For example, the S&P 500 and the Composite represent a broadly based portfolio. The S&P 500 includes 500 stocks, while the Composite is composed of over 1,500 stocks. Both of these indexes are weighted by capitalization. The MMI mimics the Dow Jones Industrial Average, and the Value Line mirrors stocks with low capitalization. The MMI is price weighted, and the Value Line gives equal weighting to all stocks. The Russell 2000 contains the 2,000 smallest stocks in the Russell 3000. The Russell has gained a wide following, especially among fund managers.

Stock Market Risk

The index contracts and their options were developed to either manage or capitalize on the risks inherent in the stock market.

Basically two types of risk are associated with the stock market. The first type relates to the changes in the price level of the overall stock market. Is the stock market bullish (going up) or bearish (going down) overall? In which direction are the Dow and other indexes going?

The second type of risk relates to price changes of individual stock issues relative to the level of the overall stock market. The first type of risk is commonly called *market risk,* and the second, *stock-specific risk.*

You, as an investor, must look at individual stock prices as they compare with the overall market. This is called *volatility.* If a stock is highly volatile, its price level will swing up or down in a wider range than the overall market. Volatility is measured by use of "beta" coefficients. For example, if the price level of a given stock increases by 1.5 percent when the overall market goes up only 1 percent, this stock has a beta coefficient of 1.5 and is considered highly volatile. The opposite is also true. With stocks with low betas or low volatility, their price levels do not change as much as the overall market.

Stock portfolio managers want to be in stocks with high beta coefficients when a bull market is in progress. The price level of these stocks should outperform the averages or indexes. In bear markets, the portfolio managers want to be in low-beta stocks or out of the stock market completely.

Index Trading Strategies

The investor or portfolio manager can combine actually trading the stock market with the use of stock indexes and options trading. Let's say you expected the overall stock market to go up, but you are not sure what to expect from a specific stock or group of stocks you are holding. Remember, a specific stock does not necessarily move in the same direction as the overall market or with the same volatility. Therefore, you could hold onto the stock and purchase a stock index futures contract or option to take advantage of the expected upward move. If you're bearish, you could short the futures market or purchase a stock index put option.

This is hedging a stock or a portfolio. You can select the futures contract that most closely resembles your stock portfolio. Use the S&P 500 or Composite for broad-based portfolios, the Russell 2000 or Value Line for small stocks, and the MMI for portfolios similar to the Dow Jones Industrial Average.

Price Determinants

Naturally, you can speculate about the direction of the stock market through the use of stock index futures and options without owning any specific stocks. But like all other futures markets, you need to have an opinion about whether the market is going up or down and when.

There are at least two technical approaches to analyzing the stock market index futures contracts. The first utilizes the analysis of charts and chart formations, including several types of moving averages, algorithms, oscillators, and relative strength indicators. The second technical approach uses several stock market indicators, such as short interest, specialist short interest, advance-decline ratio, and odd-lot buying and selling.

Other stock market analysts use fundamentals, such as:

1. *Corporate profits.* Higher corporate profits usually equate to high stock prices and an increase in the indexes.
2. *Interest rates.* Higher interest rates usually mean lower corporate profits and lower index levels.
3. *Economic conditions.* Here's a catch-22. Better economic conditions lead to higher corporate profits and eventually higher interest rates. The indexes go up for a while and then down.
4. *Public expectation.* If the public is optimistic about the near-term future, the indexes usually go up. Pessimism drives them down.

Traders Notes

You'll notice that most of the volume and open interest in the stock market index contracts is in the nearby contract months. This indicates most traders are looking at the short-term situation and avoiding the long term, which is difficult to trade because the market is so emotionally charged.

DEBT MANAGEMENT

OVERVIEW OF INTEREST RATES

Simply put, interest rates are the cost of money. Just as you must pay (buy, rent, lease) to have the use of any other tangible product or service, you must pay a price to have the use of money. Also like any other product or commodity, the cost of money varies with changes in the supply-demand equation.

Interest rates impact every commodity traded on the futures market directly or indirectly. For example, low interest rates make it easier for farmers or manufacturers to expand. This gives us more corn, soybeans, cattle, etc. Abundant supplies drive down farm prices. When manufacturers expand because of low interest rates, their earnings increase. This enhances the value of their stock, and the futures contract in the S&P 500 moves higher, and so on.

Interest rate changes have a direct impact on the debt instruments traded on the exchanges. When interest rates go up, debt instruments go down, and vice versa. Thus, when you trade debt instruments, you are taking a position on whether you believe interest rates are going up or down. Debt instruments traded on the futures and options on futures exchange encompass Treasury bonds, bills, and notes.

Fundamental Factors

Understanding exactly where within an economic cycle the country stands is probably the single most important fundamental factor. Studies have verified the fact that interest rates follow the level of general economic activity. When the economy is expanding, the demand for (and therefore the price of) money increases. In periods of recession, the supply of money exceeds demand, causing interest rates to fall.

Herd psychology also must be taken into play. Once a period of expansion is well under way, the demand for money continues after the actual expansion has subsided. Momentum carries demand forward, as reflected in high interest rates. The same is true in the late stages of recessions. Interest continues to decline, even as expansion is beginning.

The fact that the transition in the economic cycle, from boom to bust and back again, precedes major changes in interest rates emphasizes the need to closely monitor the economy. The Department of Commerce issues three important indexes that should be watched. They are the Index of Leading Indicators, the Index of Coincident Indicators, and the Index of Lagging Indicators.

Interest rates must pick up momentum, meaning demand for money, before they make a major impact on the indexes. For this reason, they most closely follow the Index of Lagging Indicators, but for purposes of forecasting, you'll want to monitor the other two indexes because you need to wait 3 to 6 months for a trend change in the economy to be verified. For trading purposes, you use the old grade-school-race starting sequence: On your mark (check the Leading Index), get set (verify with the Coincident Index), go (trade the Lagging Index).

To find out more about the three indexes, check out a free website, the Dismal Scientist (*www.dismal.com*). It provides data on and analysis of the three indicators.

Bank Reserves

There is a strong, well-documented correlation between interest rate trends and the level of free or net borrowed bank reserves. When reserves go down, so do interest rates. A move from free or low net borrowed reserves to higher net borrowed reserves coincides with higher interest rates. Therefore, the reserve position of banks is an indicator of the supply-demand situation. The Bank Reserve Position Report is issued each Friday by the Federal Reserve.

The Fed

The Federal Reserve has three valves it can manipulate to control bank reserves and, in turn, interest rates. The first is the discount rate. When the discount rate is increased or decreased, the reserves of bank members are reduced or expanded, respectively.

The second valve is the reserve requirement, which is the percentage of various deposits that banks are required to hold in reserve. It, like the discount rate, is seldom used, except in emergencies.

The dominant tool used by the Federal Reserve is the open market option. This is the purchase or sale of government securities. If the Fed wants to drive interest rates down, it buys government securities from dealers. This injects funds into the system, increasing supply. If it wants to push interest rates up, it sells government securities, thereby draining funds from the system, reducing the supply of money in the marketplace.

Some interference or government control over the economy may be unavoidable in this day and age. But when this power is used to artificially control inflation, it only compounds the demand for the area under control. Eventually the economy is distorted more than if it were left to freely react to economic pressures.

Forecasting Price Trends

Tracking the economy and the Federal Reserve is your first step. The real challenge lies in determining correctly the impact on interest rates of these two forces. Will a certain action taken by the Federal Reserve to reduce or slow down interest rates throw the economy into a recession?

The United States, and the world economy for that matter, is like a battleship. It takes a good bit of ocean and a few hours to turn it around. It always has a lot of momentum. In other words, when you are dealing with interest rates, time and patience are important virtues.

Technical Analysis

Debt instrument futures are very popular among both institutional and individual traders. This has given rise to much research on the technical side. Particular attention has been paid to price chart formation analysis and cycles. You must study these two areas thoroughly.

FOREIGN CURRENCY

OVERVIEW OF THE FOREIGN CURRENCY FUTURES MARKETS

When the Smithsonian Agreement came apart in March 1973, it set all currencies floating freely. This action provided momentum to the futures markets that began in 1972 at the International Monetary Market (IMM), a division of the Chicago Mercantile Exchange. The IMM is still the world's largest currency futures market.

The initial markets traded were the British pound, the Canadian dollar, the West German mark, the Japanese yen, the Swiss franc, and the Mexican peso. Later additions have been the French franc, the Australian dollar, the South African rand, the New Zealand dollar, the Brazilian real, and the euro.

Futures contracts go through a physical delivery process in March, June, September, and December. Contracts all have the same amount and the same expiration and delivery time. When a contract is traded, a margin, or minimum payment that is set by the exchange, must be made. Unlike forward contracts that don't change in value, futures contracts do, and their value can shift minute by minute.

Skeptics of the Foreign Futures Exchange (Forex) markets didn't see any need for the futures contracts because there was already a well-established bank forward market for foreign currencies. However, the bank forward market had some drawbacks. First, access was limited to large banks and corporations with excellent credit. Small firms and retail speculators were barred. Second, only large denominations of $1 million and above were traded on the bank forward market. Additionally, the market was set up primarily for traders to take or make delivery. It's expensive and difficult to liquidate a position before expiration of the contract.

Since futures contracts negate all these drawbacks, they immediately found a place in the foreign currency market. Volume has steadily grown over the years.

The complexion of foreign exchange trading will change somewhat in 2002 with the full implementation of the European Union's monetary union and its single currency, the euro. The euro went into effect January 1, 1999, when 11 of the 15 European Union currencies had their parity rate set to 1 euro. The 11 currencies that originally went with the euro are the Belgian franc, German mark, Spanish peseta, French franc, Irish pound, Italian lira, Luxembourg franc, Dutch guilder, Austrian schilling, Portuguese escudo, and Finnish marka. The Danish opted out of the first round of the euro. Austria and Greece had not met all the criteria to become charter members of the single currency.

Britain, although a member of the European Union, did not join the single currency initially, so the pound continues as an individual currency. Although the Labor government elected in 1997 was more inclined to join the single currency, it has been cautious because of the strong feelings in the United Kingdom about scrapping the pound. Switzerland has opted to stay out of the European Union completely, so the Swiss franc continues to trade separately.

The euro immediately began trading as a currency and is being used in financial transactions between companies and countries. Actual circulation of the euro as a currency won't begin until January 1, 2002. At that point, the individual currencies will cease to exist.

These developments will take the German mark and the French franc out of currency futures trading arena, and the euro will become the key European Union player. Analysts are watching the euro trade to see if it eventually challenges the U.S. dollar as the world's dominant currency. A weak euro could, in the long term, enhance the Swiss franc's reputation as a "flight of quality" currency.

Under the European Monetary Union, the European Central Bank conducts monetary policy for the euro, but each individual country continues to conduct its own budgetary and taxation policies. Skeptics point to this split control as a recipe for trouble when countries grow at different rates. A country that is growing slowly will need lower interest rates to boost growth. A country that is growing rapidly may be facing inflation, which will require higher interest rates.

Arbitrage and Hedging

Developers of the foreign currency futures contracts made it easy for banks and other commercial users of the bank forward market to arbitrage between it and the futures market. In the beginning this increased volume when it was dearly needed. It also helped keep the price range of some of the thin futures currency markets in line with the more liquid bank forward market. In time, the banks took the lead and began arbitraging for their commercial clients, thus keeping additional profits for themselves.

Agricultural firms are another group of U.S. commercial firms that are major users of the foreign exchange futures markets. They need to hedge their foreign exchange exposure since the very large grain deals often take several months to complete.

Since the "commodity" discussed in this group is money, there isn't any real supply-demand equation in the classic sense. Granted, countries can increase or restrict the supply of their currency from time to time, but the value of or demand for a currency depends more on other factors.

Price Determinants

Foreign exchange rates, or the price of money, are commonly expressed in their relationship to the U.S. dollar. Foreign currencies are quoted on the futures market in the number of U.S. dollars that must be paid for 1 unit of the foreign currency. Therefore, to determine the value of another currency, the financial or economic situation of that currency must be compared with that of the United States. The impact of a variety of trends, factors, and events on the relationship of the currency being compared with the dollar must be assessed. Some of the most important influences on this relationship are balance of payments, interest rates, economic growth, inflation rates, and political conditions.

Balance of payments is a measure of the number of dollars flowing out of the United States compared with the flow of foreign currencies into the United States. Over the years, this concept has become more complex as economists have tried to measure different types of inflows and outflows. For example, merchandise, services (together these are the balance of trade), direct investments, stock issues, bank claims and liabilities, and government assets abroad each tell something different about the U.S. financial situation.

When more money flows out of the United States than flows in, there is a deficit position. A balance of payments surplus is the opposite. As a rule of thumb, a surplus causes the dollar to become stronger relative to foreign currencies (the dollar value of foreign currency declines) because there are fewer dollars in foreign countries. A deficit, on the other hand, causes the dollar to weaken compared with foreign currencies (the dollar value of foreign currency increases) because there are more dollars in foreign countries.

High interest rates in the United States compared with those in foreign countries usually attract capital. Money flows into the country. The dollar becomes stronger. Bankers call this worldwide pool of money that flows to the best deal as "hot money."

Economic growth has been a double-edged sword for the dollar. A strong U.S. economy has sometimes led to balance of payments deficits, thus weakening the dollar. At other times, a strong U.S. economy has been seen as an indication of political stability in an unstable world. This perception has led to a strong dollar.

High inflation rates in the United States make American products more expensive relative to foreign goods. This increases imports and decreases exports. A deficit and a weak dollar result. At other times, inflation has created higher interest rates, leading to an inflow of capital and a stronger dollar.

Awareness of political conditions is another must. If there is political instability in foreign countries, wise investors move their funds into the United States. This strengthens the dollar. The opposite can also be true.

The price determinants discussed must be carefully evaluated because the impact can be either positive or negative for the relationship between the dollar and the other currencies. You must learn to read the psychology of the market as the events occur.

Trader's Notes

The rapid growth of futures contracts in foreign currencies testifies to their usefulness and popularity, but some of these markets are still somewhat thin. This can be very dangerous. It is advisable to avoid trading Friday afternoon after the London markets close because of the lack of liquidity at this time.

Understanding Analysis

Key Concepts

- ◆ How Good Is Fundamental Analysis?
- ◆ How Is Technical Analysis Performed?
- ◆ Four Basic Approaches to Technical Analysis
- ◆ Four Structural Analysis Methods
- ◆ Character-of-Market Analysis

Now that you have a general feel for the futures markets and have determined that you are financially and psychologically suited to trade, you need to consider the area of price-trend forecasting. Futures trading requires you to make a simple decision of whether to go long or short. Do you think the price of whatever commodity you want to trade is headed higher or lower? If you can't do this, there's no point in considering an individual trading account.

There are basically three methods of forecasting price trends. You can use fundamental or technical analysis. Or you can use a combination of the two.

WHAT IS FUNDAMENTAL ANALYSIS?

Fundamental analysis is the study of basic, underlying factors that will affect the supply of and demand for and therefore the price of a futures contract. In theory, it is quite simple. When the supply of

F I G U R E   6.1

Supply-Demand Equation

- Existing stocks
- Plus production
- Less usage
- Equals supply

Fundamental analysis is based on an analysis of the comparative strength of the opposing forces of supply and demand. If supply exceeds demand, prices usually decline. If demand outstrips supply, prices usually rise.

a commodity becomes scarce, the price goes up. When it is plentiful, the price goes down. (See Figure 6.1.) Unfortunately, it doesn't always work this way. For example, some of the toughest factors to accurately quantify are those of supply and demand. How much of a given commodity is enough? Where is it, and is it in a usable form?

Agricultural commodities illustrate this point very well because most people are familiar with them and because they are very responsive to supply and demand factors. To make an accurate price projection for corn, for example, here's what you'd need to know for a given crop year: existing stocks (on-farm and commercial inventory), production (projected acres / yields), and usage (food, feed, and seed). This sounds much easier than it is.

First, keep in mind you're doing this on a global basis, and many of the countries from which you need vital information will be uncooperative. The developed countries may share only the information that suits their side of the supply-demand equation. If they expect to be corn buyers, they might provide inflated figures on the supply they have on hand or expect to produce. Their objective is to drive prices down. Undeveloped countries may do the same thing, or they may not have an established infrastructure to gather, process, and evaluate what information they have on their crop.

As you attempt to piece together all the facts on production and usage, you quickly come to the conclusion that much of the information is unreliable for a variety of reasons. With agricultural products, the weather is always a major uncertainty. Too much or too little rain, even over a short period of time, can drastically impact prices. Other groups of commodities are equally influenced by seemingly uncontrollable factors that are virtually impossible to predict. Consider what wide swings in political unrest or interest rates can do to the price of precious metals.

The point is simply that the accuracy of fundamental analysis often hinges on fast changing information, much of which is not easily obtained, nor can it always be accurately interpreted.

HOW DO YOU DO FUNDAMENTAL ANALYSIS?

For years, number crunchers have attempted to quantify supply and demand statistics. It's been like the search for the Holy Grail. Who wouldn't want a mathematical formula that can accurately forecast prices 3, 6, or 9 months into the future? For that matter who wouldn't want one that would be good for tomorrow's prices?

Statisticians have tried linear and nonlinear regression analysis, double exponential smoothing, probability and trigonometric curves, multivariable analysis, and just about every other technique they could think of. Hopes were raised with the advent of computers. The Wharton School of Business and Chase Manhattan Bank were two well-known leaders in the field of econometric modeling. Their models were sophisticated computer programs that attempted to account for just about every variable affecting price.

However, to date, fundamental analysis has not been particularly successful in day-to-day trading of the futures markets for three reasons: (1) Projections have been marred by unexpected events. (2) Variables never seem to be taken into consideration. One or more critical ones always seem to be missing (or misinterpreted) after the projections are made. (3) This type of analysis is long term in nature, while most futures trading tends to be short to medium term.

If you combine all this with the fact that fundamental analysis is not self-correcting, you can begin to get a feel for the problem. For example, if a fundamental analyst determines that $2.00 is a cheap price for corn and goes long, what happens when the price drops to $1.50? Should the loss be absorbed and buying continue? How does the analyst justify the position with what the market is doing?

IS FUNDAMENTAL ANALYSIS USELESS?

No, definitely not. Some CTAs have found it very effective. They often use a particular aspect, weather for example, to make projections. They are position traders who take long-term approaches to the market.

More often than not, the CTAs who use it do so by combining it with technical analysis. Fundamental analysis can provide the overview and the long-term trend. Technical analysis is used to signal the short-term entry and exit points. Since fundamental analysis deduces its conclusion from external or underlying factors influencing supply or demand, it is unique to each commodity.

WHAT IS TECHNICAL ANALYSIS?

Technical analysts confine their prognostication of future price trends solely on the analysis of price activity. The price of a futures contract, they contend, reflects the impact of every single bit of fundamental information known by anyone who can even remotely affect the price of the commodity. Every fact that is known about supply, demand, and, most importantly, the psychology of the public ends up on the price charts. Therefore, price action is the composite opinion of everyone involved in the markets.

That is why learning to analyze price action is so important to anyone trading stocks, futures, or options. The function of technical analysis is to determine through the analysis of price change the probable strength of demand compared with the pressure of supply on a futures contract at various price levels and then to predict the direction, length, and velocity of the next move.

HISTORY REPEATS ITSELF IN PATTERNS
AND FORMATION

In the commodity markets, history does repeat itself. Past price action can provide clues about future price action. On commodity price charts and indexes, price movements tend to repeat themselves with remarkable consistency.

You'll learn that some patterns or formations indicate that demand is greater than supply. Others suggest the reverse is true. And some imply that supply and demand will remain indefinitely in balance.

This occurs for two reasons. First, technical analysis can be a self-fulfilling prophecy. It is self-fulfilling because so many professionals use it. They all see the same patterns and often expect the same results. Therefore, if enough of them act the same way to the same chart signal, the signal fulfills its promise. This occurs regularly with the most common and widely known signals.

Second, the market is anticipatory, and you can see price movement first in the charts. For example, major buyers, like the Chinese, have been known to go long the futures market before they announce a big grain deal. They enter the futures market to cover their cash sale. Therefore, the first alert that something is about to happen often occurs on the futures price charts.

Entering the market causes a price movement before the fundamental facts are known. Technical analysts are alerted in advance, before the fundamental information is public. Supply and demand factors are still the prime movers, and yet technical analysis is the earliest indicator of movement.

If you use technical analysis, you don't have to understand or acquire all the fundamental information in the world in order to trade. The impact of all the activity affecting price comes to you in the form of price movement. If you don't understand what is causing the price movement, you can exit the market until you do.

IS IT FOOLPROOF?

There is no infallible system—technical or fundamental—for trading the futures markets. Chart signals, just like fundamental news, can be misleading. You don't always have to be right to enjoy trading futures and options, but you need to have structure in your approach to the markets. Technical analysis can give you that structure (see Figure 6.2.). Since technical analysis is probably the only forecasting technique an individual investor can utilize, it is important to know the most common tools and signals. Fundamental analysis, because of the enormous amount of information necessary and the enormous amount of time required to absorb all the fundamental factors, is usually too costly and time-consuming for individual investors.

There are basically four general approaches to technically analyzing commodity markets: (1) price charts, (2) trend following, (3) structural, and (4) character of market. The first two are the most widely used and recognized.

Price chart analysis involves finding chart formations or patterns that often repeat themselves, such as reversals, support-resistance areas, head and shoulders, continuing formations, and others.

FIGURE 6.2

10 Technical Analysis Trading Rules

1. When a trend is established, it is likely to continue.
2. The longer term the chart (15 minute, hourly, daily, weekly, monthly), the more reliable the trend line.
3. The greater the volume of trading when a trend in established, the greater its significance.
4. In uptrending markets, when prices move too far too fast, trading volume decreases and prices decline.
5. In downtrending markets, volume is higher when prices are declining than when they rally.
6. Markets tend to give warnings before major trend changes occur.
7. If a market is in an uptrend, volume usually drops just prior to it reversing its direction.
8. Volume usually increases in downtrending markets, just before a reversal of trend.
9. Before they plunge through their trend lines, markets tend to test them by making shallow penetrations. These dips are warnings of impending trend reversals.
10. The steeper the trend, the more unstable it is and the more likely a reversal of trend is imminent.

Trend-following types of analysis include trend lines and moving averages.

Structural analysis presumes the market itself moves in established, recognizable patterns—seasonal, cyclical, or wave patterns being the most common. Once the analyst can exactly locate the current position of the market, a prediction can be made on the next move or price objective.

Character-of-market analysis is more sophisticated, because it attempts to measure the quality of a price movement and then take a position that may be opposite the current trend. The other types of analysis try to spot existing trends or certain formations that are reliable harbingers of future price activity.

TECHNICAL ANALYSIS SIGNALS
AND CHART FORMATIONS

There are 18 basic technical analysis signals and chart formations that you should be aware of: trend lines, rounded bottoms, consolidations, tops, bottoms, support, resistance, retracements, reversals, head and shoulders, continuation formations, triangles, coils, boxes, flags, pennants, diamonds, and moving averages.

THE TREND LINE

The most common technical analysis tool is the trend line. Prices tend to follow straight lines. They almost cling to them. If they bounce off a line, they are drawn back to it. There are sound psychological reasons why prices trend.

A trend line is a line drawn between at least two points on a price chart. Uptrend lines (see Figure 6.3) should be drawn so they connect lows and are drawn below prices. Downtrend lines (see Figure 6.4) connect highs and are drawn above prices. Sideways trend lines (see Figure 6.5) are drawn below prices and connect lows.

FIGURE 6.3

Uptrend Formation

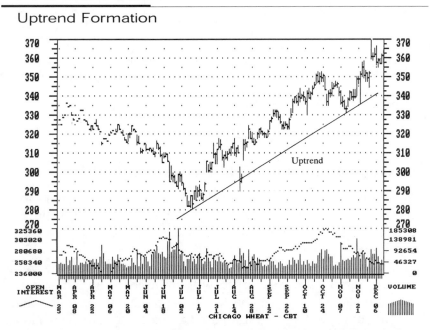

The uptrend formation is probably the most common and most followed of chart formations. Traders using this trend believe prices will continue to increase.

Chart courtesy of "Pocket Charts."

FIGURE 6.4

Downtrend Formation

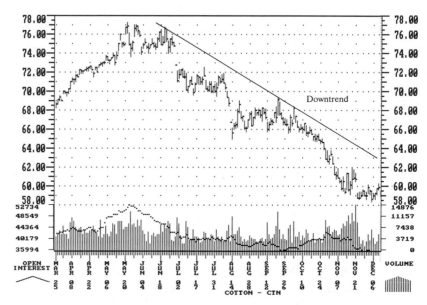

Up, down, and sideways trends are usually drawn by connecting highs or lows. Trends tend to continue until something upsets the supply-demand equation.

Chart courtesy of "Pocket Charts."

Why Do Prices Cling to Straight Lines?

It is simply human nature. A trader will resist paying more for a commodity than others are willing to pay unless there is some reason to believe it will continue to increase in price. The converse is equally true.

Therefore, if a price is going up, traders will watch the trend. As long as it moves higher, buyers will continue to buy. If it increases a little too fast, buyers hold back and the price returns to the trend line. The more buying (volume) taking place, the more confidence traders have that prices will continue to rise.

Everyone is more comfortable when others are behaving the same. This is referred to as *herd psychology*. Sometimes the herd psy-

FIGURE 6.5

Sideways Trend

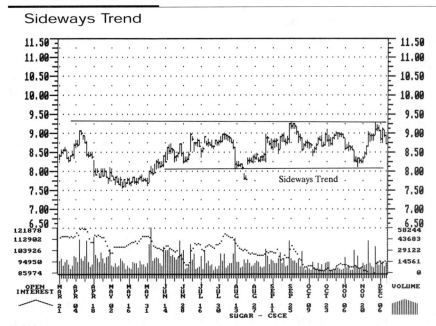

SUGAR – CSCE

Traders commonly say, "The trend is your friend." This simply means prices will continue in the established direction until there is a reason for change of direction.

Chart courtesy of "Pocket Charts."

chology can be quantified through the measurement of volume and open interest. Volume is the total number of contracts traded in a day. Open interest is the number of contracts outstanding at the end of a trading day.

Other human psychological tendencies also come into play. The inventory manager, who is responsible for buying a commodity for a company or a country, increases purchases as prices go up, out of fear that prices will be even higher in the future. This increases consumption.

The person who owns the commodity holds out for higher prices when prices are seen to be increasing. This reduces the supply. And the uptrend continues.

The Law of Price-Trend Inertia

Human resistance to change has a strong impact on trends. Nobody wants to be the first one to go against the crowd. This brings us to rule 1. When a commodity is found to be following a trend, it is likely to continue along on that trend. Spotting trends is simply a matter of drawing trend lines on price charts. The key to technical analysis is recognizing which trends are significant and reliable. Technical analysis is more of an art than a science.

Rule 2 says the longer the term of the chart, the more reliable the trend line. A trend line on a monthly price chart is more reliable and significant than one on a weekly chart. One on a weekly is better than one on a daily, and a daily means more than an hourly. The reason is that the longer something lasts, the more comfortable it seems, and the less likely we are to want to change it.

How Do You Confirm a Trend Is a Trend?

One of the answers is volume. The more trades behind a price move, the stronger the conviction there is in the marketplace of the trend. This is rule 3. The greater the volume, the greater the significance of a price trend.

Volume also tells you when traders think prices are moving too far or too fast. In these two situations, volume decreases and prices reverse. For example, in the normal uptrending market, when prices move too far above the trend line, volume will decrease until prices return to the trend line. Conversely, in a downtrend, the volume is usually greater when prices are falling than when they are rallying. These are rules 4 and 5.

Markets are like rattlesnakes. They make a noise before they bite. Each time an established trend line is penetrated, it's a warning that the market may reverse. This is rule 6.

Substantial changes in volume are another rattle from a market that it is about to reverse. Rule 7 notes that if the market is in an uptrend, volume usually decreases before a reversal. If it is a downtrending market, rule 8 notes that volume usually increases before it reverses. The reason is that prices can fall from their own weight, but they need constantly increasing buying activity to trend higher.

The first sign to look for when a market is changing direction is a violation of the trend line. A small dip below an uptrend doesn't necessarily mean the trend has changed, but it is a warning (rule 9).

Other Formations

There are several different types of trend lines besides the basic up, down, and sideways. There is the fan formation, for example (see Figure 6.6). It is a series of trend lines extending from the same point, but drawn at different angles.

The fan trend-line formation develops when an established trend line is broken, but the price continues to move in the same direction, forming a new trend line. This can happen two or three

FIGURE 6.6

Fan Formation

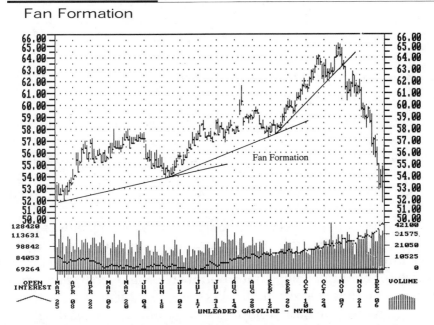

As prices reach a peak (high or low), the trend line becomes increasingly steeper. This is a warning to experienced traders that a trend change is imminent.

Chart courtesy of "Pocket Charts."

times, and rarely four or more times (rule 10). After the third, be very alert.

It also occurs when prices heat up. Each successive trend line becomes steeper and steeper as a market heads for a blow-off top.

The internal trend line is an interesting formation. It develops out of a broken uptrend line. After the uptrend is broken, the market retraces, and eventually the highs are attracted to the bottom of the old trend line. This is also an example of the "pullback" effect.

What Does All This Mean to a Trader?

Trend lines are your basic signals for whether you should be on the long or the short side of the markets. Additionally, they tell you how much conviction traders have in their positions. They warn you when investors are losing faith in their positions. They tell the contrary trader what the herd thinks about where prices are headed. The trend can be your friend—if you learn how to read it. Always analyze it in light of volume and open interest. (There's more on volume and open interest later in this chapter).

A CHARTIST'S DREAM FORMATION— THE ROUNDED BOTTOM

The chart formation known as the rounded bottom (see Figure 6.7) is a chartist's dream, because it is easy to recognize, it is reliable, and it alerts you to an upcoming long-term price move. Most important of all, this formation gives you time to make your decision. If you miss taking advantage of a rounded bottom, it is your own fault.

The formation starts with prices gradually moving down. They bottom. Then they gradually increase. Like any meaningful chart formation, there are some good psychological reasons behind it. A rounded bottom develops out of an increasing oversupply situation. As supplies of a commodity become plentiful, inventory managers (buyers) purchase from hand to mouth, believing the commodity will become less expensive tomorrow.

Volume on the exchanges for the commodity drops off, as traders wait to see if the movement is a major bear market or just a retracement where the market reacts to the main trend by retracing

FIGURE 6.7

Rounded Bottom

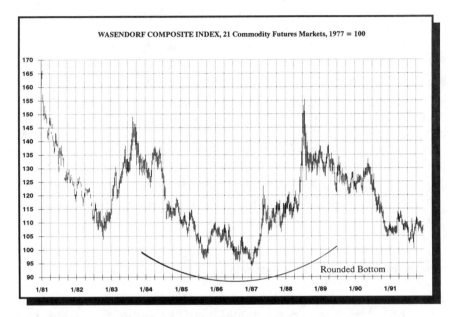

The rounded-bottom formation is a harbinger of a major uptrend in prices.
It often takes a long time in developing.

Chart courtesy of "Pocket Charts."

itself. The supply-demand equation becomes balanced, and a long, flat bottom develops.

Great Bull Markets Are Children of OverSupply!

Once the price stabilizes at a low price, the users of the commodity begin to take advantage and increase their usage. Demand builds. Inventory managers sense future price increases and add to the demand by laying away inventory.

Traders anticipate increased activity and begin bidding prices up at the exchanges. The volume of trades mirrors the price activity. A bull market often erupts from the rounded-bottom formation.

PERIODS OF CONSOLIDATION

A variation of the rounded formations is horizontal channels or flat formations. These occur when a commodity or index has developed a base for a major move in the future.

They appear on the price charts as long sideways patterns. Prices trade in a very narrow range. Volume is low because traders feel that the market has little potential. Speculators are bored by these markets. They become flat or stagnant.

This formation can develop at major tops, major bottoms, or intermediate formations, occurring somewhere between major highs and lows. This formation is often a harbinger of a major move, which could just as easily be up as down. Some people describe them as trading plateaus. The longs and the shorts are neutral until something positive or negative heats the market up. At that point, a major move often occurs.

SPIKED TOPS AND BOTTOMS

The spiked-top or spiked-bottom formation is as unpredictable as the rounded bottom is predictable. It strikes without warning. It is almost as if all the traders in a given market got together and decided to sell or buy at one time.

In the spiked-bottom formation (see Figure 6.8) the price of a commodity drops sharply and hits a point substantially below where the fall began. It then stops and begins moving up sharply. The turnaround usually is done in a single day of trading, although the decline can occur over a few days. After the bottom, the climb up continues for some time. You must draw a steep trend line along the downtrend portion of the formation. You cannot be sure the bottom is in place until this trend line is broken.

Take care that you don't get whipsawed. This occurs when you prematurely reverse your position and move from long to short or short to long before you are sure the trend has changed. This can happen with spiked moves. The market moves sharply down and then pauses, only to plunge even deeper.

The psychology behind spike formations is the same herd psychology that causes cattle to stampede. To begin with, the market is nervous about what to expect. Often it has recently experienced

FIGURE 6.8

Spiked-Bottom Formations

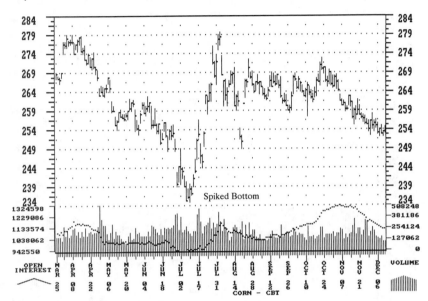

Spiked tops and bottoms can strike fear into the most experienced traders. They occur without warning and result in a major trend change.

Chart courtesy of "Pocket Charts."

some totally unexpected news. Everyone's confidence in analysis is at a low. No one really believes anyone knows what will happen next.

Then, out of nowhere, more very grim unexpected news may occur. Traders sell the news, panicking and rushing to get out of their longs. The market makes a spiked move downward while the market learns the true facts, which may be nowhere near as devastating as the news seemed to be. Traders begin buying the facts, and the market recovers.

Multiple Tops and Bottoms

Double and triple tops and bottoms are among the most common, yet most deceptive, of chart formations.

FIGURE 6.9

Double-Top Formation

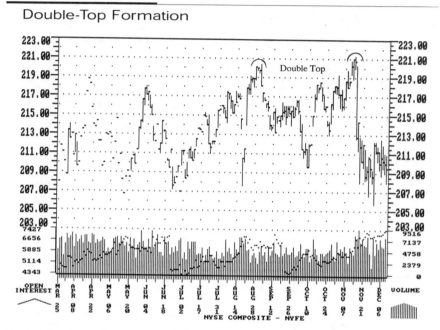

Double-top formations are sometimes referred to as "M" formations. They
signal a change in trend. Warning: They can become triple tops, which can
whipsaw traders.

Chart courtesy of "Pocket Charts."

The double top resembles the letter "M" (see Figure 6.9). Prices
rise sharply to a point, fall back about half as far, and rise again to
the previous point. Then they decline beyond the point where the
formation began. The double bottom looks like the letter "W" and
is the reverse of the double top.

These formations are deceptive, because it is very common for
commodities to trend up and down. Inexperienced chartists begin
seeing M and W formations on every chart. So many of these are
false signals.

As well, it is nearly impossible to definitely call a double top or
bottom until the reversal in trend has become pronounced and
prices have moved below the initial starting point. To confirm an M

or W formation, prices must fall or rise, respectively, beyond the vertex that is between the double top or bottom. By this time, the formation is complete, and a good deal of the move and opportunity has been missed.

Lastly, the move could be a triple top or bottom. If you act when it is only a double, you could be whipsawed.

The normal pattern for volume shows increases around the peaks. But again, this is not reliable. Studies have shown a lot of variation in volume.

SUPPORT AND RESISTANCE AREAS

Have you ever watched a commodity move up or down in what can be described as a stair-step movement? The commodity, for example, moves up 10 or 15 points, consolidates for a few days, and then moves up again.

Or have you ever observed a bull market move up to a certain point and then stop? Or watched a commodity retrace, after a bull move, to a level it had been previously trading?

These are often examples of support and resistance levels. (See Figure 6.10.) A support level is a price or price range at which you can expect increased demand for the commodity. For example, a commodity drops in price until it hits a point where traders or inventory managers (buyers for the users of that commodity) can't resist buying.

One way to detect this activity is by watching volume. As the price of a commodity decreases, it is common to see the volume decrease. There simply isn't any buying activity to bolster prices, so they fall by their own weight.

When the commodity reaches a level that is attractive to buyers, volume increases as they take advantage of the "bargains." Prices trade sideways or rebound slightly on the charts. This becomes a support level.

Resistance levels are just the opposite. They are price levels where you can expect a lot of selling. Prices reach a range where traders no longer see the potential for further increases. Prices consolidate or retrace to lower levels.

Changes in volume and open interest alert you to resistance levels. Therefore, if volume, open interest, and prices are all down,

FIGURE 6.10

Support and Resistance Levels

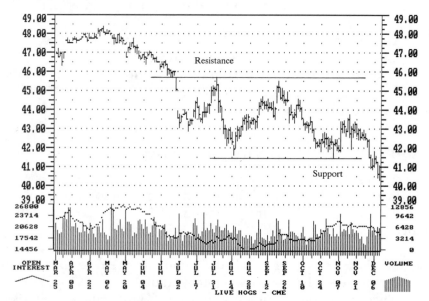

These are pricing levels where the majority of traders actively trading think prices have become too high (resistance) or too low (support). Therefore, price moves stall.

Chart courtesy of "Pocket Charts."

you know traders are closing out their long positions. For whatever reason, a resistance level is created on the price charts.

Serious technical traders study the long-range charts looking for these areas of support and resistance. They know that, as mentioned earlier, when it comes to technical analysis, history repeats itself.

By knowing where prices are likely to stall during a bull move or likely to find support in a decline, technicians time their trading. The information gives them clues about when to enter or exit markets, where to place protective stop orders, and what the size and length of anticipated moves will be.

Another interesting technical phenomenon you'll notice as you study charts is that previous resistance levels often become support levels, and vice versa. For example, a commodity breaks through a resistance level based on some bullish news. Once the move is exhausted, it retraces to find support at the level that previously had been the resistance level to the initial bull move.

RETRACEMENTS

A retracement (see Figure 6.11) is a market reaction to the main trend. If the main trend is up, the market may often decrease or retrace the ground it just covered.

Always keep in mind that there are good psychological reasons for every chart movement. When traders think a market has moved too far or too fast, many will take their profits and exit the markets.

F I G U R E   6.11

Retracements

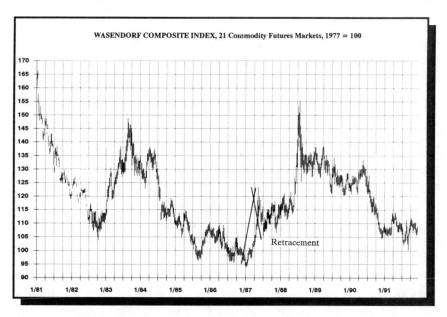

Prices move in uneven, stair-stepping patterns. It's common for them to move higher and then retrace before moving higher again.

Chart courtesy of "Pocket Charts."

Others short the market because they feel it is unstable. This causes a retracement.

But how much of a retracement will occur? How far down or up will the market go? Retracements often pull back or rally to areas of support or resistance, respectively. It is also common for retracements to occur in calculable mathematical proportions.

The first step is to calculate the distance from important highs to important lows. Next, you analyze how the particular market previously performed under similar circumstances.

What you learn is that most markets often have repetitive retracement patterns. Market analysts accept retracements of 33, 50, or 66 percent as most common. This means that a market that begins to retrace will probably retrace 33, 50, or 66 percent of an amount equal to the distance between the previous significant high and low.

Again, you use this information as a timing device, or to help you select a point where you will take your profits, or reenter the market, or buy or sell an option.

KEY REVERSALS, ISLAND REVERSALS, CONTINENT REVERSALS

Key reversals can occur at either market tops or bottoms (see Figure 6.12). They are very reliable indicators that the current market trend is likely to reverse for an undetermined period of time.

To understand how one takes shape on the charts, look for key reversals when a market is in a steep uptrend or downtrend. Next, see if the trading range widens. A new high or low is often made. The market closes near the high in the case of a top or near the low in the case of a bottom.

On the following day's trading or the key reversal day, prices move higher than the previous day's high and lower than the previous day's low, closing near the low of the day for a key reversal top. This reversal is more definitive if accompanied by high volume, sometimes a record high volume, and new contract or all-time highs. An opposite pattern occurs for key reversal bottoms, again on high volume.

An island reversal is similar to a key reversal, but usually involves a few more trading days and requires a gap at either side of

FIGURE   6.12

Key Reversal Formations

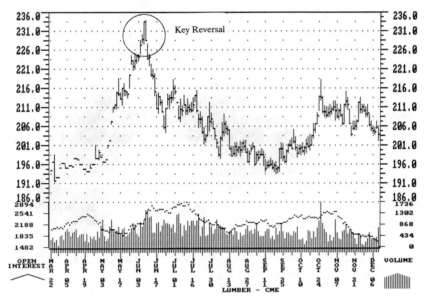

Key reversals can occur at the top or bottom of a market move. They signal a major change in the direction of the trend.

Chart courtesy of "Pocket Charts."

the island formation. Typically, the gaps are at approximately the same price level.

The continent reversal is identical to the island reversal except that it may take weeks or even months to form.

These chart signals alert you to the possibility of a trend change. You must analyze them in light of the entire situation for the commodity you are studying. Do not use them as your sole decision-making guide.

THE VERY RELIABLE HEAD-AND-SHOULDERS FORMATION

For several reasons, many technical analysts get excited when they see a head-and-shoulders chart formation developing. First, it is probably the best known chart formation. And since technical analysis can be a self-fulfilling discipline, the more traders who recognize it, the more likely its promise will be fulfilled. Even dyed-in-the-wool fundamental traders cringe at the thought of trading against a head-and-shoulders formation. They'll stand aside first.

Head-and-shoulders formations are among the best known because they stand out on the charts. Everyone sees them and tries to trade them. For these reasons, they have come to be known as one of the most reliable of formations. Novice technicians, as well as experts, are eager to take advantage of them. Not only are head-and-shoulder formations reliable as reversal indicators, but they also project a price objective.

A head-and-shoulders formation is a harbinger of a major reversal in the trend of the commodity or index being charted. This formation can be either a head and shoulders or an inverted (reverse) head and shoulders.

The head-and-shoulders formation signals the end of an uptrend. The inverted head-and-shoulders formation alerts traders to the end of a downtrend (see Figure 6.13).

The head-and-shoulders formation simply portrays three successive rallies and reactions. The second or middle rally reaches a point higher than the other two rallies. The formation looks like the silhouette of a person. The left shoulder is the first rally, the head is the second (middle), and the right shoulder is the third.

Volume Is the Key

As previously mentioned, the volume of trading must be watched closely. It is the key that tells you what the market is really thinking.

During the first rally and reaction represented by the left shoulder of the formation, volume expands materially on the rally and contracts noticeably on the reaction. The overall volume is considered heavy during the development of this shoulder.

During the second rally and reaction, which forms the head, volume is high on the rally phase. But the overall volume may be lower than the overall volume that occurred during the formation of the first shoulder.

When the right shoulder forms, the overall volume drops even lower. This third rally fails to reach the high established by the second (the head) rally and is a distinct sign of weakness.

F I G U R E   6.13

Inverted Head and Shoulders

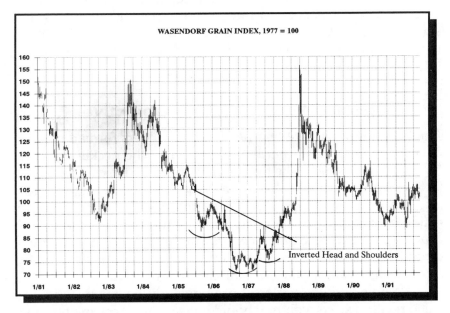

WASENDORF GRAIN INDEX, 1977 = 100

Inverted Head and Shoulders

The head-and-shoulders formations are considered by many chartists as one of the most reliable. Besides heralding a trend change, they often indicate the size of the next move.

Chart courtesy of "Pocket Charts."

As soon as the third rally fails, the technician draws a line connecting the lows created by the failure, or reaction, that occurred when the right shoulder and head were formed. A line drawn using these lows forms the neckline of the formation. It should be noted that no head-and-shoulders formation is considered complete or reliable until subsequent price action breaks the neckline.

Another unusual phenomenon often occurs at this point. It is called the *pullback* or *return* move. Once the neckline is broken, prices drop below the neckline (or above it in the case of an inverted head and shoulders) and then are drawn back up to the trend line (or down to it in the case of an inverted formation).

This characteristic of trend lines was discussed earlier. A broken uptrend line, after it has been penetrated by the bear move, often becomes a resistance area for future bull moves. Prices seem to be attracted to and cling to straight lines.

Technical traders, who are convinced a valid head-and-shoulders formation has been formed, use the pullback move as their signal to enter the market or add onto their position. If volume increases after prices bounce off the neckline, it confirms the fact that a major trend reversal has occurred.

How Do You Calculate Objectives?

The first price objective of a head-and-shoulders formation is calculated by measuring the distance between the neckline and the high (or low) made by the top (or bottom) of the head. Multiple objectives can be calculated by doubling or tripling this measurement.

Once the move begins, you must double-check and confirm the action by referring to other price-trend indicators. For example, in order for a trend reversal to continue to make a substantial move, other technical formations are likely to come into play and be fulfilled. Confirmation chart formations are also useful.

Volume and open interest provide additional clues. Once the trend reversal starts, volume should increase and open interest must be building in the direction the market is now trending. You also look to see what the large traders with reportable positions and the commercial hedgers are doing. This information should be available from your broker and is reported by the Commodity Futures Trading Commission.

You should highlight on your charts the areas where the move is most likely to encounter resistance. Then study the price action as these points are reached. Does the volume increase and does the price bust right through the resistance? Or do the price movement and volume slow down? This tells you if you should stay in the market and look for a second, third, or fourth objective, or take your profits and look for a new trading opportunity.

Head-and-shoulders formations can more closely resemble a Picasso than a Renoir. It's common for them to have two or three shoulders or even multiple heads. Sometimes the formations are angular, reminiscent of Picasso's cubist period. Seldom are they simple and perfectly formed.

Therefore, head-and-shoulders formations can be misleading,

especially when the right shoulder is formed. If it doesn't break the neckline, prices can continue sideways for a long time or even move in the unanticipated direction. Even when the neckline is broken and the formation is complete, the formation may still be highly reliable, but it could be a very expensive lesson if you bet the farm on the first objective always being reached.

CONTINUATION CHART FORMATIONS

As discussed earlier, the most common chart formation that indicates that a price trend will continue is the trend line. But what happens when a trend line is broken? Should you immediately reverse your position, close it out, and stand aside, or should you wait out the reversal until the market decides where it is headed?

Much of the decision depends on how the trend line is broken and the changes that take place in volume and open interest at that time. Also, you must consider how close the price is to major support and resistance levels.

Always remember that even the strongest trends do not roll on indefinitely without an interruption. It sometimes helps to think of them as long distance runners, who must occasionally back off to get their wind.

There is a very interesting financial reason for this. It's called profit taking. Following a sharp up or down move, some of the traders on the correct side of the move will want to cash in their position and pocket their profit.

There are other reasons as well. The move may enter a support or resistance level, causing traders to evaluate their positions. Or some fundamental news or a well-circulated rumor can cause a trend to stall or temporarily congest.

At these junctures, traders become uncertain and are not sure whether they are looking at a trend reversal or just a place where the move is pausing to catch its breath.

TRIANGLE OR COIL FORMATIONS

The triangle or coil formation develops when a trend hits a price level where the buying dries up (see Figure 6.14). The move stalls. Profit taking develops. The "bulls" second-guess themselves. The

F I G U R E   6.14

Coil Formation

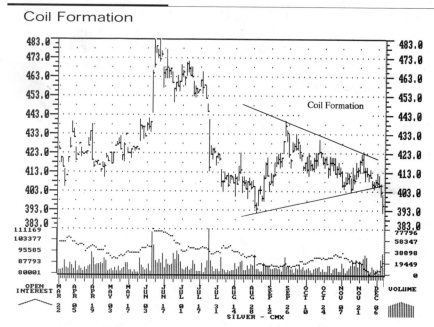

The coil formation indicates prices are going to make a major move.
Unfortunately, it is not always clear whether the breakout will be up or down.

Chart courtesy of "Pocket Charts."

market moves sideways. Each successive high is lower, and each
successive low is higher. A triangle is formed where the uptrend line
and the downtrend line meet.

Prices move into the apex of the triangle, which forces them to
make a move up or down. About 60 percent of the time prices continue in the direction they were going when they entered the triangle, thus continuing the trend.

Sophisticated technical analysts categorize triangles into four
groups: symmetrical, ascending, descending, and inverted triangles. This approach increases the reliability of the signals. The symmetrical triangle is the one just described above.

With the ascending triangle, the top line is horizontal, while the
bottom line slants to meet the top line. This formation suggests that
a supply of the commodity is available at the price level of the top

line, but there are no sellers below it. Prices are drawn up and finally break out to the upside. The descending triangle is just the opposite and is a harbinger of lower prices. The horizontal line, like the base of a right triangle, is on the bottom. The hypotenuse descends to meet the base, and prices break out to the downside. The inverted triangle looks somewhat like a funnel and represents a very nervous market. Prices can go either way out of this formation.

BOXES, FLAGS, PENNANTS, DIAMONDS

These chart formations are more reliable than the triangles. Their graphic names help you to spot them easily.

The box formation takes weeks or months to develop. Prices move sideways, with the highs and lows staying at the same levels, or in a channel. A vertical line drawn at both ends of the trading channel forms the box.

The box occurs when there is a tug-of-war going on between equally matched teams of bulls and bears. The breakout of the box is usually valid and usually goes in the direction prevalent at the time prices entered the box.

The flag formation (see Figure 6.15) is similar to the box, but the channel is on an angle. If the angle is down, it is an up flag because that is the way prices will be headed when they break out of the formation. A down flag has the channel angles headed up and prices will be going down. The flag formation looks like a parallelogram with the top and bottom on a 45-degree angle.

Some analysts claim that the tighter and neater the flag formation is, the more reliable it will be. Flags formed quickly are more dependable than slowly, sloppily formed ones. The length of the flagpole supporting the formation can also be an indication of how far the price trend will continue after it breaks out.

Pennants fly from "poles," like flags, but they look like symmetrical triangles. The up pennant forms out of bull moves and signals a continuation of the uptrend. Again, the tighter the pennant, the higher its level of reliability.

The diamond formation develops during a period of wide swings in price. It is an exciting time, with traders wildly bullish one minute and bearish the next. Prices seesaw back and forth with greater and greater swings on high volume. Then the excitement

F I G U R E   6.15

Flag Formation

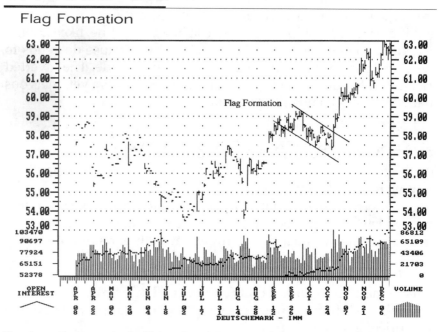

Flag formations can be bullish or bearish depending on the direction in which it is "flying." The flagpole gives clues to the length of the next price move.

Chart courtesy of "Pocket Charts."

ends and the prices taper off. Thus the diamond is formed. Diamond formations are hard to predict. They can just as easily alert you to a reversal of the price trend as a continuation of the trend.

As always, pay close attention to volume when analyzing the formations just described. It usually dips as the formation develops and then increases as the breakout occurs. These formations are not as reliable as the head-and-shoulder formations discussed earlier. Use them as guides only. Find confirmation from other sources.

PRICE SMOOTHING AND FILTERING TECHNIQUES

When a major trend takes hold of the market, all the commodities are usually affected. It's rare that an individual commodity can move in the opposite direction of a major trend.

That's why it is so important to have the trend at your back, moving your position in the desired direction. But commodity prices often make very jerky and erratic moves. Trends are not always clear-cut.

Changes in trends can be equally difficult to spot early. If you act too soon when you're anticipating a trend change or planning to take profits out of a position, you may miss a good deal of the move because you mistake minor corrections for major trend changes.

Technical traders who face choppy, sawtooth price charts have developed some techniques to overcome this roadblock. One of the methods they use is moving averages.

SIMPLE MOVING AVERAGES

Moving averages combine the price activity of a commodity over a period of time and smooth it out. For example, to calculate a 4-day moving average, you would:

1. Select the first 4 days' prices.
2. Total them.
3. Divide by 4.
4. Subtract the first day and add the fifth day.
5. Divide the new total by 4.
6. Subtract the second day and add the sixth day.
7. Divide the new total by 4.
8. Continue doing this with each day's price.

Refer to Figure 6.16 for an example of a 4-day moving average using the closing prices for 12 trading days of a corn contract. You can use the high, low, and open price, as well as the close. You must be consistent in your choice to keep the data meaningful.

Once the moving averages are calculated, you simply chart them on a graph. Some analysts like to chart them right on their daily commodity price charts so they can compare them with the actual price activity. In a downtrending market, the moving average usually remains above the current price. In an uptrend, it tends to stay below the current market price. The point at which the moving average crosses the actual price is a critical point.

Some technical analysts use moving averages to simply indi-

F I G U R E   6.16

Moving Averages

Day	Price	Total	4-Day Moving Average
1	282.25		
2	283.75		
3	280.25		
4	279.25	1,125.50	281.38
5	277.75	1,121.00	280.25
6	271.75	1,108.75	277.19
7	273.75	1,102.25	275.56
8	273.25	1,096.25	274.06
9	265.00	1,083.50	270.88
10	268.50	1,080.50	270.13
11	259.00	1,065.75	266.44
12	262.00	1,054.50	263.63

cate the trend. The 4-day moving average described above would provide the short-term trend. An analyst looking for a bigger picture might use a 200-day moving average to represent the long-term trend.

Other analysts use moving averages to generate specific buy and sell signals. It becomes a mini-trading system within itself. To do this, you need to chart two different moving averages. Common ones are the 4-day and the 9-day moving average.

The slower one, the 9 day, requires more days in its calculation and determines the long-term trend. The faster one, the 4 day, signals the short-term trend.

If you want to buy a market, both moving averages should be moving higher. Place buy orders in the price range between the averages. Place stops below the slower moving average. Wait for prices to dip into the zone below the slower moving average to buy.

If you want to sell a market, both moving averages should be moving down. Sell orders are placed in the price range between the averages. Stops are placed above the slower moving average.

Wait for the market price to rally into this zone. Sell short only when this occurs. When you're placing a long-term trade or trading options, you want to make sure both moving averages are headed in the same direction. You'll also want to use a long-term moving average, perhaps a 50- or 100-day moving average.

A WEIGHTED MOVING AVERAGE

Some analysts like to give more emphasis to the current price. They believe it helps them anticipate trend changes sooner.

To calculate a weighted average, you would:

1. Arrange the numbers to be averaged in chronological order, the most recent number last.
2. Multiply the oldest number by 1, the next by 2, the next by 3, and so on, until you reach the most recent.
3. Multiply the most recent by a factor that is the total number of entries. (If you are averaging 5 numbers, the most recent number will be multiplied by 5.)
4. Now, add all the results and divide by the sum of the multipliers. This will give you the weighted average. (See Figure 6.17.)

Notice that the weighted average is greater than a simple average because greater emphasis is placed on the most recent values

F I G U R E   6.17

Weighted Moving Average Table

Day	Price		Weighing Factor		Result
1	$2.52	×	1	=	$2.52
2	$2.57	×	2	=	$5.14
3	$2.56	×	3	=	$7.68
4	$2.60	×	4	=	$10.40
5	$2.61	×	5	=	$13.05
Totals	$12.86		15		$38.79

$$\text{Weighted moving average} = \frac{\$38.79}{15} = \$2.59$$

$$\text{Simple moving average} = \frac{\$12.86}{5} = \$2.57$$

in this rising market. No matter how you do it, moving averages are an excellent tool to use to confirm trends, but like all our trading techniques, they need to be tempered with experience and common sense.

STRUCTURAL ANALYSIS

The ancient Greek philosophers developed the concept of natural law. All the religions of the world reaffirm that some known or unknown force has implanted an order on the physical world. The great advances of science have been predicted on the concept that the laws of physics, chemistry, biology, geology, etc., can be understood. Man's mind seeks out structure in every activity.

Several very successful technical traders have developed theories about the market that begin with the assumption that the universe, in general, and the markets, in particular, work in very precise patterns. More importantly, these theorists believe that these patterns can be discovered and exploited for profit. Four of the most prominent theories are (1) seasonals, (2) cycles, (3) Elliott Waves, and (4) Gann numbers.

Seasonal patterns are the easiest to understand, especially if you consider the agricultural commodities. The seasonal price trends these commodities undergo reflect the regular annual changes that take place in their supply-demand equation. Think about a typical crop year. What will impact the planting schedule? How will weather affect the growing season? Will there be the usual abundant supply at harvest? Studies have shown that 70 percent of all seasonal tops occur between April and July for soybeans, but 80 percent of the time soybean prices bottom between August and November.

How can you use this information? If you know the seasonal patterns for the futures contracts you trade, you can use these patterns to confirm signals you get from other methods of analysis. Some traders will not trade against reliable seasonal patterns without having a very strong reason for doing so.

Seasonal patterns have been uncovered for virtually all futures markets. Learning the ones for the markets you trade is as basic as learning which chart formations are most reliable for those markets.

Cycles are similar to seasonal patterns, but they can be longer than 12 months or extremely short in duration. Cycles are built on the observed phenomenon that events have a tendency to repeat themselves at more or less regular intervals.

As mentioned earlier, much of life is governed by repeatable patterns or cycles. Since people invest in and control the markets, it seems fair to assume that the markets would also possess definable cycles. Understanding these cycles within the price trends of the markets is another key to successfully trading the markets.

Cycles measure the time between each high and low (peak and trough). By knowing the time span between each high and low and the previous high and low, you are in a better position to anticipate the next high or low. Time is often measured in calendar days, as opposed to trading days used by some systems. Calendar days are used for the simple reason that people and nature do not take weekends off—money continues to change hands and events affecting cycles continue.

A long-term cycle generally lasts a year or more, an intermediate cycle less than a year, and a short-term cycle a few weeks or days. As a general rule, allow approximately 10 percent leeway in the length of a cycle when establishing your expectation for the next top or bottom.

The wave principle was named after Ralph Elliott, who contended that the stock market tends to move in discernible and predictable patterns, reflecting the basic harmony of nature. These patterns or waves reoccur. Prices unfold in "five waves" of crowd psychology when moving in the direction (up or down) of the primary trend. Then they move against the trend in "three waves." The wave pattern reflects life's starts, stops, false starts, and reversals. Progress is made in a jerky, sawtooth pattern, rather than a smooth uptrend or downtrend. By isolating the exact position of the current price activity within the wave patterns, the trader can profit by anticipating the market's next move. Once your trading becomes synchronized with the wave pattern, you can successfully ride the economic waves of the market, or so the theory goes.

Gann numbers are based on a premise of W. D. Gann, the best known structural analyst. His book *How to Make Profits Trading Commodities*, published in 1942, was the first important treatise on this subject. He believed that precise mathematical patterns govern everything, particularly the commodity market. More importantly, he believed these patterns could be uncovered and exploited. Since his price predictions became legends in his own time and he claims to have made millions in the market, he seemingly discovered many patterns. Integral to his trading system are Fibonacci numbers, a throwback to natural law, and angles of price-trend movement. His numbering system uncannily alerts traders to highs, lows, support-resistance areas, and reversal points. His work must be studied by every serious trader.

CHARACTER-OF-MARKET ANALYSIS

With character-of-market analysis, the technician seeks what are known as "overbought" or "oversold" conditions. If the market is found to be overbought, it is sold. If it is found to be oversold, it is bought. This approach is a 180-degree turn from the trend-following approaches. This approach works best in choppy, zigzagging markets. If you use them in a long-trending market, you may get burned badly.

You need many tools on your technical analysis workbench. These are excellent ones to have when the market appears to be confused or erratic—but never rely on just one approach to analyzing the market. The psychology behind character-of-market analysis is simply that when a market becomes too top heavy, it falls. Or when everyone gives up on prices ever rising again, they will. It is a contrarian approach to technical analysis.

The trick is determining when a market is overbought or oversold. This can be done through general oscillator systems or the more sophisticated Williams' %R, and Wilder's relative strength index.

Oscillators are concerned with price changes over a period of time. Simple oscillators utilize the difference between two moving averages. The departure between them indicates overbought and oversold conditions. More complicated ones use the difference between daily prices. It can be the settlement, high-low, or opening price. Take a simple 5-day settlement price oscillator as an example. It is computed by subtracting the settlement price of the fourth-previous trading day from the current settlement price. If the settlement price has risen, you get a positive remainder. A negative remainder occurs if the price has fallen. If the remainder is exceptionally high or low, the analysts will consider the market overbought or oversold and take the opposite position. Analysts using oscillators usually use more complicated ones than this simple example, but the basic concept is the same.

Williams' %R, copyrighted in 1979 by Larry R. Williams, is an example of a more complex approach. A 5-day %R is computed as follows:

Subtract the settlement price of the latest trading day from the high price of the 5-day period. Then divide that difference (i.e., the "change") by the difference (i.e., the "range") in the high price and the low price of the 5-day period. Finally, multiply that result by 100. The range of %R is 0 to 100 percent.

According to Williams, when the value of %R enters the 90–100 percent range, the market is considered to be oversold. When the value enters the 0–10 percent range, the market is considered to be overbought.

Wilder's RSI, copyrighted in 1978 by J. Welles Wilder, Jr., is another example of this intricate approach to the market. The relative strength index is a system that measures the change in price over a period of time to determine overbought-oversold situations and can best be described using the following formula:

$$RSI = 100 - [100 / (1 + RS)]$$

where RS = Up Avg/Dn Avg
Up Avg = Up Sum/1
Dn Avg = Dn Avg/1
L = number of days in RSI

To calculate a 15-day RSI, the Up Sum is first computed by tabulating the positive changes in the settlement prices of successive trading days over the 15-day period and adding those changes. The Dn Sum is computed by tabulating the negative changes in settlement prices over the period and adding those changes. Then, the Up Avg is computed by dividing the Up Sum by 14, similarly for the Dn Avg. Next the Up Avg is divided by the Dn Avg to get the RS. And, finally, the RSI is computed by adding 1 to the RS, dividing this sum into 100, and subtracting that result from 100.

According to Wilder, when the RSI exceeds 70, the market is considered to be overbought. When the RSI is less than 30, the market is considered to be oversold. Clearly these are not calculations you can do on your fingers. These very complex mathematical calculations are available on computer software, allowing the average trader to exploit them. Many of today's electronic quotation systems include them as special features.

OTHER TYPES OF TECHNICAL TRADING SYSTEMS

There are many other technical trading systems besides those already described. Three most notable are (1) rate of price change, (2) countertrend, and (3) countercyclical systems.

The theory behind rate-of-price-change systems is simple. Mathematical formulas are devised which indicate to the trader when a market is about to change directions. Think of it as the momentum in a football game. As one team moves the ball down the field, it has the momentum. Yardage gained on each successful play is longer, and successful plays become more frequent. Then something happens, and the defense tightens. Gains per play become smaller and less frequent. Eventually, the defense holds, and the offense is forced to give up the ball. This activity is often accompanied by a switch in momentum.

Rate-of-price-change systems evaluate price changes on a periodic basis, usually on the day's closes. As the rate of change diminishes, the trader prepares to close out the current positions and open new ones on the opposite side of the market. In other words, if long positions are closed out, short positions are entered. In the options market, you would offset calls and open puts. In certain very orderly markets, these systems perform wonderfully. But like all systems, they are not loss-proof. For example, when the markets are highly volatile and choppy, these systems have problems.

The rate-of-price-change calculations can be used to develop a countertrend system. This is a system that attempts to buy at the low and sell at the high. Traders try to anticipate the next market move and hope to catch all major moves early or just before they begin. When using this type of system, you must use protective stop-loss orders. It's not like a trend-following system that eventually corrects itself by establishing an offsetting position. With a countertrending system, you are net long or net short until you close out your position. That's why stops are recommended.

There are several types of countertrend systems. The fading-minimum-move system is a typical example. A sell signal is triggered when the market rallies by a predetermined amount above the low point after the last countertrend buy was signaled. The reverse is true for buys. The size of the price change required to generate a signal can be either a percentage or a nominal figure arrived at through testing or analysis of past moves. The size also determines how sensitive the system is.

The countertrend system, like any other system, allows you to require confirming signals before a buy or sell signal is taken. It's common with countertrend systems to wait a day to make sure the trend has changed before placing a trade.

The use of oscillators is also common with countertrend systems. Oscillators, as mentioned before, are technical indicators that measure market momentum.

The popular RSI attempted to solve one of the big drawbacks of these tools. How much is too much? When does an oscillator indicate a change in trend—60 percent or 90 percent? Wilder's RSI pegs tops when its values are above 70 percent and lows when they penetrate 30 percent.

Countercyclical counting uses cycle analysis to develop a countertrending system. By plotting the anticipated highs or lows, entry and exit signals can be generated. You position yourself on the short side of the market when your cycle analysis indicates a top is due. You position yourself long if a low is anticipated. Stops are strongly recommended for this type of trading system.

Another approach to forecasting price trends is known as *contrarian investment strategy* or *buying into fear!* The phrase "buying into fear!" was coined by Bernard Baruch. He strongly believed that once you determined what most of the marketplace was going to do, you should do the exact opposite. This philosophy worked well for him.

Options are an excellent tool for the contrary trader. You can take a position opposite to what everyone else is doing and limit your risk of the cost of the premium plus the transaction costs (sales commission and exchange and NFA fees). Never forget as you trade futures that not only must you be right but you must be right at the right time! Buying options that do not expire for 60 to 90 days provides some time to "become" right.

Basically, this is the concept of going against the crowd—trading the opposite side of the market from the popular thinking of all traders as a group. Your first question might be, "Where can I get this kind of information?" A good place to start is the *Wall Street Journal*. Three important pieces of data are published daily on the Commodity Page: (1) estimated volume for the current trading day, (2) actual volume for the previous day, (3) and open interest. You'll also find the high, low, settlement, change, and lifetime high and low. It is very critical in estimating market sentiment to grasp what these numbers mean.

Another good source of contrarian information is the Consensus Index of Bullish Market Opinion (www.consensus-inc.com). The index provides indications of potential market directions. Contrary opinion would hold that when a predominant number of market analysts are bullish, it is quite likely that the market is approaching an overbought condition and that a reversal in trend may be imminent. The same theory would hold if a predominant number of market participants were bearish.

UNDERSTANDING VOLUME AND OPEN INTEREST

Volume and open interest figures benchmark the degree of activity and the amount of trader participation in the individual futures markets. As noted earlier, volume is the velocity of trading, and open interest measures the number of contracts held at the conclusion of a trading session.

Volume reported daily by the commodity exchanges and published in the *Wall Street Journal* indicates the number of contracts traded during that day, not the sum of the buyers and sellers. For every contract traded, there is one buyer and one seller. To determine the volume of trading, simply count either all the buyers or all the sellers. The number of contracts traded includes the creation of new contracts, the transfer of either the buy or the sell side of a contract, and the liquidation of a contract.

Open interest is a measure of the number of contracts outstanding at the completion of the trading day. Many transactions may occur in a given day without initiating any new contracts or eliminating existing contracts. Existing futures contracts may merely change hands. To understand open interest and volume, follow the example below:

Day 1: Trader A buys one contract.

Trader B sells one contract.

Trader C buys one contract.

Trader D sells one contract.

If these were the only transactions on the first day, the open interest would be two contracts. Volume is two contracts also.

Day 2: Trader E buys one contract.

Trader A sells to offset one contract.

If these were the only transactions taking place on the second day, the open interest would still be two contracts. Volume would be one contract. Trader A simply transferred the position to trader E.

Day 3: Trader F buys one contract.

Trader G sells one contract.

Trader B buys to offset one contract.

Trader C sells to offset one contract.

Trader E sells to offset one contract.

Trader D buys to offset one contract.

At the end of the third day, only one contract survives; the open interest is one, but volume is three contracts.

After the dust clears, open interest indicates the number of contracts that are held by participants in the market. Notice that for every buyer, there was a seller. The next step is to analyze the interrelationship of these statistics. Once you know how all the other traders are calling the market by their actual trading activity, you can determine what position you wish to take. (See Figure 6.18.)

For more clarification, take this situation. Everything—open interest, volume, and prices—is up, up, up. If you go with the crowd and purchase a call, your premium is high if the option is in-the-money or near-in-the-money. By the time the underlying future increases enough to bring your option to breakeven or a modest profit, the market has begun to retrace. Would you have had more success if you had purchased a put? You can buy them economically when everyone else is wildly bullish. Then you sit in ambush waiting for a retracement.

FIGURE 6.18

Interrelationship of Interest, Volume, and Prices

Open Interest	Volume	Prices	Interpretation
Up	Up	Up	Very bullish (strong participation and volume with higher prices)
Down	Down	Down	Slightly bullish (weak participation and volume with lower prices)
Up	Down	Up	Mildly bullish (strong participation but weak volume with higher prices)
Up	Down	Down	Mildly bearish (strong participation but weak volume with lower prices)
Up	Up	Down	Very bearish (strong participation and and volume with lower prices)
Down	Down	Up	Slightly bearish (weak participation and volume with higher prices)

Breaking into Futures Trading with Options

Key Concepts

- Using Options on Futures Contracts as a Risk Strategy
- Buying Options into a Bull Market
- Developing an Options Trading System
- Knowing the Dangers of Liquidity
- Recognizing the Four Major Types of Spreads, plus Straddles and Strangles
- Calculating the Premiums and Value of Options, Breakeven, and Delta Factors

Believe it or not, trading options on futures contracts is a good way to break into the world of futures trading. Trading options can help a new trader gain familiarity with the markets and the tools necessary for effective trading while limiting the financial risk to the price paid for the option.

USING OPTIONS ON FUTURES CONTRACTS AS A RISK STRATEGY

An option is the right, but not the obligation, to buy or sell an underlying futures contract at a specified price (called the strike price) during a specified period of time. Just like futures contracts, all options on futures are bought and sold at competitive auctions in the options pits on the floors of the futures exchanges. Also, just like futures contracts, at the end of each trading day all options transactions are accepted and cleared by the clearing association, assuring performance on all contract obligations. This frees buyers and sellers of any direct obligation to each other.

A *call* option conveys the right, but not the obligation, to buy a futures contract at a specific price during a specified time period. You would buy a call option if you expected prices of an underlying futures contract to rise.

A *put* option conveys the right, but not the obligation, to sell a futures contract at a specific price during a specified time period. You would buy a put option if you expected prices of an underlying contract to decline.

The *strike price* of an option is the price at which you may buy (in the case of a call option) or sell (in the case of a put option) the underlying futures contract. The various exchanges that offer options determine the strike prices for put and call options. Additional strike prices are added by the exchanges in accordance with futures price movements by applying a formula.

As futures prices rise or fall, options with higher or lower strike prices are introduced according to the formulas. The result is to create new options on the same futures contract. This allows option strategies and opportunities to reflect current market conditions.

Strike prices can be at-the-money, in-the-money, or out-of-the-money. At-the-money is an option with the strike price that is nearest to the current underlying futures price. In-the-money is a put option whose strike price is higher than the current underlying futures price, or a call option whose price is lower than the current underlying futures price. An out-of-the-money option is a put option whose strike price is lower than the current underlying futures price, or a call option whose strike price is higher than the current underlying futures price.

The length of time an option on futures runs until expiration varies, depending upon the underlying futures contract and the exchange upon which it is traded. You can trade some futures options a year or more before the options expire. It is important to note that the option month refers to the futures contract delivery month and not the month in which the option actually expires. Options expire before the underlying futures contract, often several weeks before.

For example, a call option on July soybean futures expires in late June. Options' expiration dates vary from commodity to commodity and exchange to exchange.

Premiums (the value of an option) vary according to the size of the option, the price of the underlying futures contract, the strike price of the option, the length of the option, and market conditions (volatility). Generally, out-of-the-money options with less time to expiration tend to cost less than options with more time to expiration and that are at- or in-the-money. The cost of premiums can range from a few hundred dollars to thousands of dollars.

The premiums on options can change from day to day, hour to hour, and minute to minute. It all depends on the price activity of the underlying futures contract. Also, it is important to note that options prices do not move in lockstep with the price of the underlying futures contract. For example, a 1-cent rise in the price of July soybeans does not mean the option on July soybeans rises by 1 cent. However, the premium on an option that is significantly in-the-money will tend to move in synchrony with the underlying price of the futures contract. The less time an option has remaining until expiration and the deeper it is out-of-the-money, the smaller the premium response is likely to be in relation to a change in the underlying futures price.

A trader can buy an option or sell (many times called *write*) an option. There are some big distinctions between the two, however. The options buyers—either puts or calls—have limited their financial risk to the price they paid for the option, including their broker fees. There should be no margin money required by the broker in the case of buying options. However, the options sellers (writers) have an unknown risk factor, just as do traders who trade the straight futures contracts. Options writers will likely have to post margins with their brokers.

Winning trades can happen before an option expires or after an option has expired and automatically becomes a winning position in the underlying futures contract. If an option is in-the-money on expiration day, it automatically converts into a winning straight futures contract position. However, most options buyers that have winning trades offset their positions before the option expires.

If you are an options buyer, you can take profits on a winning trade by simply telling your broker to offset your position. For example, if it is June 3 and you own a July soybean call option that is worth more than you paid for it (the premium is higher) and you want to take your profits, simply call your broker and instruct to sell.

The options writers (sellers) make their money by keeping the premium they receive from the options buyers—and hoping the options never get exercised (or are in-the-money) at the options' expiration. If the options they sold to the buyers are in-the-money at expiration, they have losing trades.

A beginning trader is wise to buy options as opposed to selling (writing) them. Most of the winning trades in options are made by the writers (who are usually professional traders)—and not by the speculative buyers. Still, writing options should only be considered by veteran traders with deeper pockets than the beginning trader has.

There are complicated options trading strategies about which entire books could be and have been written, but to better illustrate the advantages of a trader starting out using options on futures, a couple of conservative trading methods for beginners will suffice.

The first example involves a newer futures trader who has established a long or short position in a market, with one futures contract only, and has set tight stops. This is indeed a conservative method of trading. However, the fact that the trader placed a tight stop does not guarantee the position will offset (the order "filled") at that stop level. If an unforeseen event occurred to push prices right past the stop (in a price vacuum), the trader could lose much more money than planned by placing tight stops. In extreme cases, a locked-limit move against the trader's position could cost the trader a huge sum of money. These cases are uncommon, but they do happen. In any given month, looking across the commodity futures spectrum, you'll likely find a few markets that have made limit moves during that time frame.

The second example features a newer futures trader who has decided to start out trading on the Mid American Exchange, a subsidiary of the Chicago Board of Trade. On this exchange, individual futures contracts are much smaller in size, meaning less financial risk for each contract traded, than their counterparts at the Board of Trade. Still, the same rules apply as in the first example. Risk is less, but still an unknown.

With those two examples in mind, a newer trader may feel uneasy about the potential of losing big money trading futures. The trader is especially uneasy because the business is still being learned. This trader has read that a great way to learn about futures trading is to do it on paper first, but that's been done and it is time to test the waters with real money.

Buying a put or a call option that is out-of-the-money is a good, inexpensive way to wade into futures trading. The money the trader lays out to the broker for the option is all this trader has to worry about. No margin money. No margin calls. The trader can sleep well at night while still trading futures, learning the business, and honing market skills.

So why doesn't every beginning futures trader start out trading options? One reason is that the market may move in the right direction for the options trader, but because the trader's option is out-of-the-money, the premium (the price of the option) only rises slightly or not at all.

Compare the out-of-the-money futures options buyer (in this case, a call) with the straight futures contract trader in the same market. It is mid-May, and July soybean futures rise by 10 cents during the trading session. The straight July soybean futures contract trader has just made $500 ($50 per 1-cent rise in price). However, the July soybean option trader holding the call maybe makes a penny ($50). The options trader needs prices to move closer to being in-the-money, or to actually move into-the-money, before realizing the same profits as the straight futures trader. In some cases, an options trader can be right in forecasting the move (the trend) of the market, but wrong in timing the trade. The option could expire before it moves into-the-money.

What the options trader is doing is giving up some profit potential for the sake of limited risk and likely peace of mind. That's the trade-off in trading options versus straight futures.

What about the trader that still wants limited risk but doesn't want to buy options because it is more difficult to realize profits? There may be a happy medium for some. A trader can enter into a straight futures position and also buy an out-of-the-money option and have limited risk.

It's early May and a trader is bullish soybeans and wants to enter into a long position in the July futures contract. The price of July soybeans is currently $4.50 per bushel. The trader can enter into a long position in July soybean futures—and also buy a put option on July soybeans with a strike price of, say, $4.25. For the few hundred dollars that are paid for that put option, the overall risk of loss has been limited to $1,250. If the trader feels the $4.25 strike premium is too pricey, a $4.00 put may be opted, but the risk of loss has been increased to $2,500.

As you can see, there are profit-potential costs in reducing trading risk by using options, but for many fledgling futures traders, being safe is much more desirable than striking out with unknown trading risk.

BUYING OPTIONS INTO A BULL MARKET

By nature, most people come to commodity trading as bulls. It just feels more comfortable making money when prices are rising, rather than taking advantage of a declining market. An additional reason is that bull markets usually last longer than bear markets, which gives more time to trade them.

Options are an excellent investment tool to take advantage of an upcoming bull market. You can plan your trades enough in advance to be in the right market at the right time. Once a commodity with bull market tendencies is spotted, the trader begins to study the price charts looking for stage 2 or 3 where the long-term downtrend is broken, followed by a modest rally or a shallow uptrend.

These are the signals to get into a call that is in-the-money or near-in-the-money. You'll want one with as much time left on it as possible. At this point, you are acting contrary to what most traders are doing. They are still on the sidelines totally unaware of the developing situation.

You ride the bull market through stage 6. Again you want to be a contrarian and take your profits before the blow-off top. It's time to remember again that "bears win, bulls win, but hogs get slaughtered!"

Many traders, after successfully making profits in stages 3, 4, and 5, hold out to pick the top. This is a very dangerous strategy. As mentioned earlier, the market usually declines substantially faster than it rises. Those who wait are often disappointed. Options trading is risky business. You can easily lose your entire investment. The surest way to do that is to overstay a position or to try to pick tops or bottoms.

When the blow-off top begins, you again do the opposite of what most traders are trying to do. Instead of getting in the market long, you're looking for a put that is reasonably priced with enough time to take advantage of the impending bear market. Success in the commodity market often means thinking and doing the opposite of what most traders would do in the same situation. You buy your call before other traders have spotted the opportunity and sell the day you see a story about the price run-up of your commodity on the nightly news.

If you understand herd psychology, you'll be better prepared. A trader must be able to see reality for what it is in order to profitably trade reality. Traders get caught in a powerful mass delusion that causes them to lose control of their trading. The contrary trader must be prepared to recognize these situations and take advantage of them. Commodity trading is complex and vague. When CTAs, journalists, brokers, and newsletter writers get caught up in the image of what "everyone" thinks is happening, they can whip traders into a wild frenzy. This pulls the average investor in off the street. Everyone thinks the market will never stop.

You, as the contrary trader, recognize it as a blow-off top of a classical bull market. You need the discipline that comes with an understanding of the mass psychology to overcome this trap. Add to this the courage to stand up to your broker who says, "You want to buy a what? The market isn't even halfway to my first objective."

Contrarian traders study open interest and volume. Volume lets them know how active or how "hot" the markets are. The hotter they are, the more emotional they become, which gives strength to major moves. Open interest is even more important, especially if you can determine who is holding the positions.

One way to learn who's doing what is to study the daily reports supplied to the Commodity Futures Trading Commission. The CFTC requires clearing members of the exchanges, futures commission merchants, and brokers to report each trader's position on their books that, in any future month of a commodity, exceeds certain levels. These are the large traders usually with "strong hands" and good information sources.

Here are a few examples of the reporting levels by commodity:

Commodity Reportable Level

Corn	750,000 bushels
Silver	150 contracts
Treasury notes	500 contracts

Besides supplying the CFTC with the number of contracts, the reporting entities must also classify them as noncommercial or commercial. Commercial traders are hedgers as defined by the commission's regulation. These are usually companies, even countries, that are willing to take physical delivery of the commodity and use it in their business. An example would be a grain merchant who hedges an upcoming cash sale on the futures markets. Noncommercials include individual traders. Nonreportable positions are ones that are below the reporting limit.

This information is often published in commodity newsletters and other periodicals on a weekly or monthly basis. It is put into index or graph formats known within the industry as the bullish or bearish market opinion or consensus.

Traders must also study the data to determine if a market is overbought or oversold. They use the data as a guide to determine when to switch from the long to the short side, or vice versa. The problem the contrary investor faces is avoiding getting caught up in the illusions and mass hysteria that fast-moving and rapidly rising markets create. You need rules to follow to avoid this pitfall. For example, when they see the open interest numbers rapidly increasing in nonreportable positions (the small traders) and decreasing in reportable positions (the large traders), good contrarians may conclude that the "public" has a hold of the market. This means it may be time to begin picking an exit or reversal point.

Another important indicator of the general thinking of traders is the number of puts or calls for each option. If there are substantially more calls, most options traders are bullish. More puts indicate a bearish outlook. These numbers are found each trading day on the Commodity Page of the *Wall Street Journal*.

Since most people, including traders, are followers rather than leaders, by the time the majority get on board, it is time to switch sides of the market. An excellent example occurred when the stock market crashed on October 19, 1987. On Friday, October 16, there were 32,045 calls and 30,087 puts. On the day of the crash, there were

34,971 calls and 25,685 puts. The next day saw 35,183 calls and 24,327 puts. A week later there were still more calls than puts—38,346 versus 25,432.

The contrary trader knows the majority does not rule the commodity market. The best opportunities materialize when you resist following the crowd.

DEVELOPING AN OPTIONS TRADING SYSTEM

If you're planning to trade options rather than futures, the trading system you develop may need some extra refinements. The value, and therefore the price movement, of an option is related to the price movement of the underlying futures contract. If the price of the underlying futures trends upward, so will the price of the option in most circumstances. The same is true in bear markets.

However, options on futures are distinctly different from the underlying futures market. They have characteristics that sometimes cause their price movement to react differently from the futures on which they are based. You must keep these differences in mind when you attempt to relate the signals from a futures trading system to the anticipated price action of an option. And you cannot evaluate an options trading system exactly the same way you do a futures trading system.

SIMILARITIES AND DIFFERENCES

The special attributes of options bring their own set of problems to investing. The premium values for options are determined by a bid-offer open-outcry auction, just as futures prices are determined. Buyers and sellers of options get their lead from the futures markets.

Other important considerations, however, make options trading less responsive to those trading systems that are used successfully in futures trading. First, consider the delta factor. It is the value change of the premium price relative to the price change of the underlying futures market. Under optimum conditions the delta factor for an option will be 0.5, meaning that the value of the premium will move 50 percent of the value of the price change for the futures market.

If you are considering a trading system that has performed

well for futures markets, then you would have to make an adjustment to compensate for the delta factor. In other words, if your futures trading system anticipates a 50 percent increase in the price of the underlying futures contract and the delta was 0.5, you would look for a 25 percent increase in the price of the option.

It is typical for lower-cost premiums (i.e., out-of-the-money) to have low delta factors, thus reducing the positive effects of the high level of financial leverage provided by options. Actually, in-the-money options will provide the closest relationship between options and futures. They can have a delta approaching 1.

KNOWING THE DANGERS OF LIQUIDITY

The problem of slippage is compounded in the case of options. The reason is that for each individual commodity option, there are a large number of strike prices. For each strike price there are bids and offers for puts and bids and offers for calls. Also, actively traded options have less liquidity than actively traded futures. Therefore, you must plan for a wider disparity between the bid and offer prices.

To be assured of a fill, the premium of an option must trade at a price significantly less than the price offered. In other words, to be filled with an option at a premium of 10, it may be appropriate to only consider a fill if the premium drops to 8 when calculating hypothetical results.

In the case of nearly every option on futures markets, the expiration or declaration date precedes by a number of days the last trading day for the underlying futures markets. Since the option expires first, it may lose the benefit of the trading period within which the futures market most resembles the "real-world" cash market.

Before you can complete your trading plan, review some of the basic trading strategies. The most common is simply taking long or short positions in either the futures or options markets. If your analysis indicates that the futures contract you are interested in is trending, or going to trend, high, you go long. This means you contingently agree to deliver whatever the futures contract calls for on the date the contract expires at the price specified when your future order is filled. (See the Appendix.)

To illustrate, a June corn contract on the Chicago Board of Trade calls for the delivery of 5,000 bushels of No. 2 corn. The No. 2

grade specifies the quality (moisture content, cleanliness, etc.). Your fill price is $2 per bushel, or $10,000 total value for the contract.

As mentioned earlier, only a small percentage (2–3 percent) of contracts are actually taken to delivery. Most are offset by taking an equal and opposite position to the one already established.

Therefore, if you own (long) 5,000 bushels of corn at $2.00 per bushel and you sell it (go short to offset your long position) 30 days later at $2.50, you make 50 cents per bushel, or $2,500, for the 5,000-bushel contract, less brokerage commission and fees. If, on the other hand, the market goes against your position and you have to sell at $1.50, you lose 50 cents per bushel, or $2,500, plus the transaction costs. This is a sample of the risk and reward of futures trading.

You could have just as easily taken the opposite side of the trade described above if you felt corn prices were trending downward. In this case, you would have initially sold (gone short) a futures contract for corn and then later bought it back (offset). When you are short, you're contingently agreeing to accept delivery of a commodity at a given price by a given date. The lower prices go, the more profit you make when you "buy it back at a lower price" (offset).

OPTION STRATEGIES

Option trading strategies are basically similar to futures strategies, but a call option replaces a long future position and a put replaces a short. Investors who are new to the futures markets often start with options because the maximum risk can be defined in advance, while the risk of trading futures cannot be.

UNDERSTANDING BASIC OPTIONS CONCEPTS

The buyers (sometimes called *holders, takers,* or *longs*) of options have the right, but not the obligation, to receive a position in the underlying commodity futures contract at a predetermined price (strike price) on or before a specific date (expiration date). Unlike a futures contract, which requires the purchase or sale of a commodity if held to maturity, the buyers of options may elect to let the options expire without exercising the rights.

When an underlying commodity increases in value, the premium of the option on that commodity usually increases in value at the same time. Options traders, just like futures traders, can then close out their positions by taking equal and opposite positions. If the options have increased enough in value, the traders will make a profit. If not, they can close out their positions at breakeven or a loss.

The buyers of options even have a third option, which is to exercise the options. This means the buyers convert their options to futures contracts and assume the risk of holding the futures positions.

This defines the rights and opportunities of the buyers of an option. They pay a premium (plus commission and exchange fees) and can take one of the three actions described above. Their risk is limited to the total amount that they initially invest in the options, while the profit potential of the options and of the underlying commodity futures contract is unlimited.

PUTS AND CALLS

The two types of options are the put and the call. A call option gives the purchaser the right to acquire a long position in a futures contract at the strike price on or before the option's expiration date. Call premiums typically increase as the futures price increases, thus benefiting the call buyer. Calls can also be employed for protection against rising prices. If you call, you'll want to own the commodity in the future because it is increasing in value. You are basically calling something to you.

A put option gives the option purchaser the right to acquire a short position in a futures contract. Put options are the type that may be most useful in seeking protection against declining prices, because the premium of a put tends to increase in value as the futures price declines.

RIGHTS VERSUS WRITERS

The term *right* refers to one of the primary differences between futures and options. With futures, an obligation is created for both the buyers and the sellers. The buyers must be willing to take and the sellers must be willing to make delivery unless the positions are offset prior to delivery. In the case of options, unilateral obligation is placed on the "writers" (also referred to as *sellers, givers,* or *shorts*) of the options—that is, only the option writers are obligated to perform. The buyers of the options may exercise the options, but they may also decide to abandon them, letting the options expire. In the event the options are exercised, the option writers must deliver the underlying futures positions.

In return for assuming these obligations, the writers of the options receive payment of the premiums from the buyers. The premiums must be paid in full in cash when the options are purchased. The buyers are paying for specific rights. The sellers agree to grant those rights and are paid for assuming the risks of offering options.

To the writers, the premiums are the maximum profit available in the trade. However, if the value of the options rises, the writer may have to deliver futures positions, or cover their short sale at a higher price, thus incurring a loss. If the value of the options decreases, the short sales are profitable, but the value can only decrease to zero, thus placing a limit on profits. The intrinsic value of a call option declines to zero when the price of the underlying futures contract falls to the strike price or below.

COVERED AND UNCOVERED OPTIONS

As in the futures market, for every buyer there must be a seller. In options trading, option sellers (writers) must be prepared to enter appropriate futures positions opposite that of the option buyers, to accommodate buyers if the options are exercised. Option writers may be considered as "covered" or "uncovered." Call option writers are covered if they have long futures contract positions before writing calls. Put option writers are covered if they have short futures contract positions before writing puts. If either one of these covered options should be exercised, the writers would have the appropriate positions to deliver to the buyers of the options and would not have to acquire the position at the current, probably unfavorable, market prices.

Options that are not written against an existing position in underlying futures contracts are called *uncovered options*. If the adverse movement of the futures contract price is greater than the premium received, the writers of the contracts lose.

Therefore, you have four basic strategies to consider with options. You can buy calls, buy puts, sell calls, or sell puts. The novice trader should avoid selling calls or puts because of the unlimited risk. Buying calls or puts is a better choice since risk can be calculated exactly in advance.

OPTIONS PROVIDE STAYING POWER

Perhaps the most salient difference between options and futures is staying power, or the ability to withstand adverse market moves. With futures, both the buyer's and the seller's risk is theoretically unlimited, and both parties are in jeopardy of the market moving against their position. Options, on the other hand, have a defined risk. The premium and transaction costs represent the total amount the buyer has at risk.

If the options trader forfeits the options or lets them expire worthless, there is no further financial obligation. Due to this unique situation, the buyer is not required to provide margin or face the potential of margin calls regardless of where the underlying futures price moves during the life of the option. No matter how far the trade moves against the position, the buyer can hold the option in anticipation of an eventual turnaround in the market that will make the buyers position profitable.

THE PREMIUM

Who determines the amount of this payment? Options are traded in an auction-type environment (similar to futures) at a registered exchange with bids and offers made by an open outcry. There are, however, some guidelines for determining the option pricing models that mathematically calculate the theoretical value of an option. Computer software programs are also available.

The premium of an option is composed of its intrinsic value and its time value. *Intrinsic value* is the amount an option would be worth if it were to expire immediately. For example, if soybean futures were trading at $5.60 per bushel and your call option gave you the right to buy soybean futures at $5.25 per bushel, you would have an immediate profit of 35 cents per bushel and should be willing to pay at least 35 cents per bushel for that option. This call option with a strike price less than the market price is said to be in-the-money.

A put option is in-the-money when its strike price is above the market price. Using the example above, the right to sell soybean futures at $5.95 per bushel is worth an immediate 35-cents-per-bushel profit, and this 35 cents is the intrinsic value of this put option.

A call option with a strike price above the current market price is said to be out-of-the-money. The right to buy soybeans at $6.00 per bushel when they can be had on the open market for $5.60 per bushel is intrinsically worth nothing, but there may be a processor or soybean crusher (an inventory manager) who wants to assure himself the right to buy soybean futures at $6.00 in the event the market rallies higher than $5.60.

A future (or time) value may also be bid into the price of this option. There may be a producer who anticipates a sharp decline and wants to ensure selling soybean futures at $5.00 per bushel later even though they are at $5.60 per bushel now. When the strike price of a put is below the current market price, it is also out-of-the-money.

When the strike price of an option, put or call, is exactly at the current market price, it is said to be at-the-money. With soybean futures at $5.60 per bushel, a $5.60 option still has no intrinsic value. But there is a high probability that it will gain intrinsic value, given that only a small move in the market would be needed.

The second component that makes up the option premium is *time value.* Time value is somewhat less specific than intrinsic value. It is based entirely on the future expectations of price movements. By definition, time value is the amount of the premium that exceeds intrinsic value. However, this definition hardly seems complete. To understand time value, some factors that contribute to the creation of this value should be explained.

In general, the more time until expiration, the greater the value. Common sense would dictate that all else being equal, the right to buy something is worth more if you have a year to decide instead of only 6 weeks. The options buyer is asking the writer to preprice his product regardless of future events. The writer must be paid for this risk. Logically, a year's worth of risk costs more than 6 weeks' worth. (See Figure 7.1.)

OTHER PREMIUM PRICE DETERMINANTS

Option premiums are also affected by short-term interest rates; that is, higher rates may result in lower premiums. Options are competing with other instruments for the investment dollar. If the competition's rate of return is lower, options need not be priced as attractively, and premiums will be lower. It is further assumed that the required margin for options will be met using interest-bearing

F I G U R E   7.1

Time Value of Options

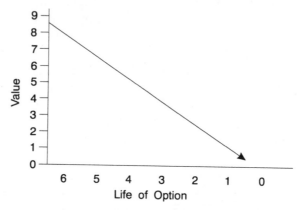

Options are wasting assets, because they eventually expire. Their time value continually deteriorates as they move toward their expiration date. To make money or conserve losses, you must offset or exercise options before they expire.

instruments so as not to lose efficiency in the use of investment funds.

Volatility is probably the most obvious and least understood influence on option prices. While there may be many mathematical explanations for volatility, common sense is the best rule. If soybean futures are at $5.60 per bushel, and will remain at that price for a year, there is little risk in selling a $6.00 call option. However, if soybean futures trade between $5.25 per bushel and $5.95 per bushel in the same week, there is significantly greater risk associated with the $6.00 call option.

Once again, the writer of the option must be paid for assuming the risk. The greater the likelihood that the option will trade through the strike price, thus increasing the chance of the buyer exercising the option, the higher the premium must be to accommodate the risk taken by the writer.

The common thread running through each of these components of time value is risk. Anything that increases the writer's risk will increase option premiums, regardless of the source of risk. Any time the amount of risk decreases, option premiums fall.

PRICE INTERRELATIONSHIPS
AND THE DELTA FACTOR

The delta factor is a measure of the change in the price of your option relative to a change in the price of the underlying futures contract. Let's say you have purchased a silver call because you expect the price of silver to rise. You know there is a relationship between what you paid for the option (the premium), the current price or premium being asked for that option, and the futures price of the contract on which you have an option (the underlying futures).

Can you expect a one-to-one relationship? If the futures price of silver increases 10 cents per ounce, will the premium of that option increase 10 cents?

The change in the option premium value is less than the change in the futures price, and that's where the delta factor comes in. Remember all the factors that impact the premium price: volatility of the markets, traders' expectations, the current price trends, the amount of time until expiration of the option, the number of calls versus puts, and whether the option is in-the-money or out-of-the-money. You'll learn through study of the options that the change in the options premium will represent only a fraction of the change in the price of the underlying commodity price. Logic dictates there should never be a higher demand for the option on a futures contract than there is for the futures contract itself.

HOW TO CALCULATE THE DELTA FACTOR

The delta factor is calculated by dividing the amount of price difference of your option by the amount of price difference in the underlying commodity. For example, if the price of your silver option increased by a nickel when the futures price of silver increased by a dime, you would have a delta factor of 0.50 (0.05 divided by 0.10 = 0.50). This means that you would expect your silver option to increase at half the rate of the futures.

A delta factor of 0.50 is common when an option is very close to being in-the-money. The delta factor should never exceed 1. Therefore, the higher the delta factor, the higher potential there is for profits as the underlying futures contract moves in price.

The opposite is also true. The higher the delta factor, the more expensive the option and the higher the loss can be for buyers. In futures and options trading, always consider the risk-reward ratio.

A low delta factor means that there is less of a cause-and-effect relationship between the option and its underlying futures contract. For example, a delta factor of 0.20 would mean that for every $1 increase in the value of futures contracts, the options premium would increase 20 cents.

HOW DO YOU USE AND TRADE DELTA FACTORS?

The delta factor is a gauge to help you anticipate what options to buy and when to sell (or offset) the options you own. To begin with, let's say you're looking at three or four different options. You're trying to decide which one to purchase.

You start calculating the delta factors every day or every other day for a week or so. If an option has a very low delta factor, below 0.25, it may be deep-out-of-the-money, or in some other way it has lost its relationship with the underlying market. You should probably cross it off your list—unless you have a good reason for playing a long shot.

As you track the delta factors of the other options, you may notice one becoming stronger than or outperforming the others in value. This is one reason for considering this option. However, it is definitely not the only reason. You must consider all the other elements that go into the calculation of the premium, which were mentioned earlier.

Later on, when you've held your option for a while and have decided to offset it, you'll want to look at the delta factor from a different perspective. Is it getting stronger or weaker? Knowing the trend of the delta factor of your option can sometimes help you make selling decisions.

THE DELTA FACTOR AS A PLANNING TOOL

The delta factor can also be used as a planning tool. For example, you're considering buying a soybean call. You think between now and the middle of February bean futures will increase by $2.00 per bushel.

When you calculate the delta factor of the two options you are considering, the first one is 0.50 and the second one is 0.60. This means that if your price projection of $2.00 is correct, the value of the first option will increase by $1.00 and the second by $1.20. If the second option costs only 10 cents per bushel more, it is probably a better bargain, all other factors being equal, than the less expensive option.

Always keep in mind that delta factors are not stable. They change whenever the price of the option premium and the price of the underlying futures change, which is almost constantly during trading hours. However, these prices usually move in tandem, except when the option approaches expiration causing its time value to decay rapidly.

You cannot calculate a delta factor once or twice and expect it to be valid days or weeks later, especially if your option is in a volatile market. Some traders calculate delta factors daily and then convert them to 3-, 4-, or 5-day moving averages. This smooths out the fluctuations, giving a better picture of the price activity.

SPREADING STRATEGIES

Spreading simply means trading both the long and short sides of a market at the same time. The spreader attempts to make a profit by anticipating the amount of change in the price movement between the two futures contracts or options. The price differential between the two markets is the spread.

There are various types of spreads. They can be described by market (exchange), commodity, or delivery month. You can trade "inter" or "intra" types of spreads or combinations of the two. *Inter* means between two different entities; *intra* means within the same entity. (See Figure 7.2.)

F I G U R E   7.2

Spread Types

Long corn/short wheat:	Intercommodity
Long CBOT wheat/short MN wheat:	Intermarket/exchange
Long July/short September:	Interdelivery
Short CBOT corn/long CBOT corn:	Intermarket/exchange
Short July corn/Long September corn:	Intracommodity

Spreads can also be described as bull or bear spreads. A bull spread is usually long the nearby delivery month and short a more distant delivery month. The expectation of the bull spreader is that if the price of the commodity rises, the effect will be felt strongest by the closest delivery month. The bear spreader has the opposite opinion: If prices are destined to decline, the nearby month will be affected more severely.

Also popular for grain futures traders are the crush spreads and new-crop–old-crop spreads. The former is executed within the soybean complex by spreading soybeans against their products, soybean meal and soybean oil. The term *crush* is derived from the ancient process of crushing soybeans under high pressure to extract the oil. Since the soybean processor purchases soybeans and sells the oil and meal, a crush spread would be long soybeans and short soybean oil and meal. A reverse crush spread would be short soybeans and long both soybean oil and meal.

A new-crop–old-crop spread may also be described as an interseasonal spread. This type of spread would have one "leg" in one of the delivery months available to market a crop that has already been harvested, and the other "leg" in a delivery month available to price the unharvested crop. This is a popular spread when opposing factors are affecting growing crops and crops in storage.

OPTION SPREADING

Spreading opportunities in options are far more numerous than in futures because spreading is available between a wide variety of strike prices and expiration dates besides market, commodity, and delivery/expiration date. An option spread is similar to a futures spread, consisting of a long and short position (a call and a put) in one option, with the call and put having either different strike prices or different expiration dates. Spreading can also be used by an investor to reduce the risk inherent in writing either a put or a call option.

VOLATILITY SPREADS

Volatility spreads are one of the simplest and most useful options spreads to learn and to use. The spread trader buys a put and a call at the same strike price. For example, let's say corn is trading at $2.52

per bushel. You buy a put and a call at a strike price near-the-money or in-the-money, at $2.50.

You do this with the expectation of the corn market becoming more volatile. For example, this situation can occur at the time of the release of an important crop report, such as Planting Intentions. You may not be sure if the report will be bearish or bullish, but you expect it to cause a lot of excitement and, therefore, volatility!

If this happens, the premium value of both your options could increase. Or if the market takes off north (bullish), your call becomes more valuable. If it goes south, your put premium goes into the money. Your net position should improve.

If the impact of the report is already in the market with prices and volatility unchanged, you lose. You must then decide whether to hold your spread in hopes of future volatility or to take your loss. A little added advantage of this spread is that the premium is usually lower than the sum of the premium costs of both a put and a call purchased separately. A put-call spread purchased at the same time at the same strike price is called a *special double,* which will be discussed as a separate strategy.

TIME OPTIONS

Another popular option spread is the time spread. It involves options with the same strike price but different expiration dates. The prime objective of a time spread is to take advantage of the tendency of the time value of an option to decline at a very rapid rate before finally disappearing just prior to expiration. Typically, a put or call with a nearer expiration date is sold (written), while a put or call with an expiration date that is more distant is purchased. The option sold and the option bought both have the same strike price.

The intent is to sell time. The more distant put or call loses its time value at a slower rate, which limits the risk of such a position by removing the potential for unlimited loss on sharp upside moves.

PRICE INFLUENCERS

The price of the underlying contract is the prime determinant of how much an option spread will profit. If the spread position is established by selling the nearby option and buying the more distant when both options are at-the-money, the spread will be profitable if the futures prices remain relatively constant. It will tend to lose money if the prices change.

The spread will be at its widest when the price of the futures contract is closest to the exercise price of the option. The spread will narrow as the price moves away from the exercise price in either direction.

BULL SPREADS

Option spreads that consist of options having the same expiration dates but different exercise prices are called *price spreads*. So, for example, if a study of the silver market indicates it is going higher, purchase a call.

Suppose March silver is $5.50 an ounce and a $5.00 strike price call has a 43-cent premium, or $2,150. That might be too much of a risk. However, even though silver has been somewhat lackluster over the past few months, it still seems to be headed higher. You are just not sure of the timing. On the other hand, you don't totally want to miss this opportunity. An alternative would be to write a call with a higher exercise price. In this case, the March $5.50 silver call could be sold for about 14 cents, or $700. The spread could be calculated as having a 29-cent debit. Such a spread is called a *bull spread*, and the risk in the position is limited to the amount of the original debit.

Risk limitation does not occur without giving up opportunity. If the risk is limited, so is the profit potential. The maximum profit in a price spread is computed by subtracting the original debit from the difference between the exercise prices of the two options.

In this example, the debit or net premium cost is 29 cents and the difference in the exercise price is 50 cents. You are risking 29 cents to make 50 cents. At the March expiration, a price above $5.50 would peg both options at their intrinsic value. If the price of silver dropped below $5.00, both options would expire worthless and the maximum loss would be 29 cents.

BULL SPREAD RULES

The rules concerning option bull spreads that you must keep in mind are as follows:

- A bull spread profits only when the spread widens.
- The maximum profit on the bull spread is the difference between the strike price and the debit (the amount of the cost of the long side exceeds the proceeds of the short side).
- The maximum loss is the debit, the net premium paid.

BEAR SPREADS

Basically, they are the opposite of bull spreads. Use them when you believe the market is about to plunge. If you project a declining silver market, you could sell (write) the lower strike price option, e.g., $5.00, and buy the higher, $5.50. At the time the options expire, any price below $5.00 would cause both calls to expire worthless, allowing you to retain the premium of the option you wrote.

The maximum loss would occur at any price over $5.50 at expiration. The options would be at their extrinsic value, having only time value. The rules for bear option spreads are as follows:

- A bear spread profits when the spread narrows.
- The maximum profit on a bear spread is the credit (the amount the proceeds from the short side exceed the cost of the long position).
- The maximum loss on a bear spread position is the difference between the strike price and the credit.

BULL TIME SPREADS

Just as you can trade bullish or bearish price spreads, you can trade bullish or bearish time spreads. A bull time spread would involve buying a deferred month and selling the nearby month.

If on the other hand you were bearish, a bear time spread would entail buying the nearby expiration month and selling a deferred expiration month. For example, buy a July silver call option and sell an October silver call option. The rules cited earlier apply to bull and bear time spreads, as well as bull and bear price spreads.

STRADDLE STRATEGIES

The straddle is another spread variation. It is similar to a spread in that you trade both sides of the market at the same time, but there is a difference. A straddle is a type of spread that entails the purchase of a put and a call (called a *long straddle*) or the sale of a put and a call (called a *short straddle*).

Bullish and bearish trading strategies are valuable tools when indications show where the market is headed. What do you do when it looks as if the market is going to take off, but you don't know in which direction? Or even more puzzling, how can you trade a trendless market?

The answer is the straddle. The long straddle, like the volatility spread discussed earlier, is a trading strategy to take advantage of dramatic market moves, even when we're not sure of the direction.

THE LONG STRADDLE

In its simplest form, the long straddle involves the purchase of a put and a call that share the same expiration date and strike price. To be successful, a big market move must occur before the options expire.

Use the corn market as an example. The primary growing region is the Midwest. Let's say that it has been in a drought for the past 2 years. By planting time, the subsoil moisture has not been replenished.

Last year the crop got by with a series of timely rains. Just enough rain occurred when it was desperately needed. The year before the farmers were not as lucky. What will happen this year?

The United States rarely has two down years of corn production in a row. Additionally, the price of corn is very sensitive. When supplies are scarce, the price skyrockets. When supplies are plentiful, the price plummets. When supplies are adequate, the price moves sideways.

This year one of two things will likely happen. Either there will be plenty of rain or there will be a drought. A full measure of rain will wash out prices. A drought will pop prices to new highs. How do you trade these fundamentals?

The price range could be anywhere from a low of $1.40 to a high of over $3.00 per bushel. Use a long straddle and buy a near-in-the-money put and call, at, say, $2.40. (See Figure 7.3.)

As you can see, the money is made with this strategy on the extremes. The more the market declines, the more valuable the put be-

F I G U R E   7.3

Results of Long Straddle

(In dollars)

Future Price	Call Price	Put Price	Total
1.40	(20.0)	80.0	60.0
1.60	(20.0)	60.0	40.0
1.80	(20.0)	40.0	20.0
2.00	(20.0)	20.0	0.00
2.20	(20.0)	0.00	(20.0)
2.40	(20.0)	(20.0)	(40.0) maximum profit
2.60	0.00	(20.0)	(20.0)
2.80	20.0	(20.0)	00.0
3.00	40.0	(20.0)	20.0
3.20	60.0	(20.0)	40.0
3.40	80.0	(20.0)	60.0

comes. The opposite is true of the call. At some point before expiration, the savvy trader would abandon one leg and exercise the other. The point is you're in good shape to take advantage of a bull or bear run without knowing which will occur!

You lose, of course, if the market trades trendless from the time you enter until expiration of the options. The maximum you lose is the two premiums paid for the put(s) and call(s) and the associated transaction cost. The upside is theoretically unlimited until the bull or bear market ends.

THE SHORT STRADDLE

The opposite trading strategy to the long straddle is the short straddle. Rather than going long a put and a call, you short or sell a put and a call. This is the ideal strategy to use when you think the market is going to be flat and lifeless for the duration of the options sold.

Let's use the same corn scenario described above, only now the rains will be normal, crop production will be normal, and the market will trend sideways until your options expire. Rather than buy a $2.40 call and put, sell them. (See Figure 7.4.)

You find the short straddle attractive because it allows you to

F I G U R E   7.4

Results of Short Straddle

(In dollars)

Future Price	Call Price	Put Price	Total
1.40	20.0	(80.0)	(60.0)
1.60	20.0	(60.0)	(40.0)
1.80	20.0	(40.0)	(20.0)
2.00	20.0	(20.0)	0.00
2.20	20.0	0.00	20.0
2.40	20.0	20.0	40.0 maximum profit
2.60	0.00	20.0	20.0
2.80	(20.0)	20.0	0.00
3.00	(40.0)	20.0	(20.0)
3.20	(60.0)	20.0	(40.0)
3.40	(80.0)	20.0	(60.0)

take advantage of the normal decline in an option's time value as it approaches expiration. In this case neither option is exercised, which means you retain the full premium on both sides. The danger is a serious price move, which could be very expensive.

As with all trading strategies, you begin with an analysis of the market. Always be prepared to adjust your position(s) whenever you discover that all or part of your underlying information has changed or is incorrect.

STRANGLING THE MARKET

The "strangle" is a type of straddle. It differs from the simple straddle in that both legs do not share a common strike price and are out-of-the-money. They are similar in the sense that you are trading both sides of the market and you can trade a long or a short strategy.

Another critical characteristic is different: the return curve. With the simple straddle, the maximum return was available at only one price point. With the strangle, the maximum return is available at several price points.

Strangles also differ from straddles when it comes to the usual position taken by traders. The short strangles are more commonly used, where you'll usually find straddlers on the long side.

WHY USE A SHORT STRANGLE?

The basic strategy is the same for the short strangle as it is for the short straddle or the volatility spread. You seek a market that you expect to trade flat until the expiration of the options. The strangle strategy becomes particularly attractive if there is a history of unexpected volatility in the market you plan to trade, or perhaps some seasonal patterns that might come into play. The short strangle, because of the reasons mentioned earlier, insulates you more from this kind of threat than does the short straddle or volatility spread.

The short strangle finds favor with traders over the short straddle because it further reduces risk. To begin with, you are trading different strike prices, and they are out-of-the-money. Therefore, the underlying futures contract must move farther than with a short straddle, which has the same strike price and is in-the-money or near-in-the-money, before someone will exercise one of the options you wrote.

As with most futures strategies, less risk means less reward. This is true here since the premium for out-of-the-money options is comparatively lower.

Suppose the bond market will be stable for the next 6 to 9 months. Therefore, you enter a short strangle by selling an out-of-the-money call at 74 and an out-of-the-money put at 72. The underlying futures contract is trading near 73:00. To simplify this example, let's say both options have the same premium, $1,500. The premium you receive would then be $3,000, less any transaction costs. (See Figure 7.5.)

Notice how the maximum income to be gained has increased from one price point on the straddle table to three price points for this strangle, from the 72 put to the 74 call strike prices. Between these two points, both options are still out-of-the-money. When both options expire out-of-the-money, you retain the full premium. This, of course, is the maximum profit you could expect. If one of the legs of the strangle expires in-the-money, then your profits diminish proportionally.

Futures prices can, at least theoretically, increase indefinitely and can decrease to zero. When prices move dramatically against one leg of the strangle, the option represented by that leg is likely to be exercised. This means you'd be assigned an equal and opposite

F I G U R E 7.5

The Strangle

Future Price	Call Price	Put Price	Combined Total
66	1,500	(4,500)	(3,000)
68	1,500	(2,500)	(1,000)
69	1,500	(1,500)	0
70	1,500	(500)	1,000
72	1,500	1,500	3,000
73	1,500	1,500	3,000
74	1,500	1,500	3,000
76	(500)	1,500	1,000
77	(1,500)	1,500	0
78	(2,500)	1,500	(1,000)
80	(4,500)	1,500	(3,000)

position in the futures market. For example, if you are short a put, you will receive a long futures position if the option is exercised. Since the market is moving against you, it could quickly become expensive.

CALCULATING BREAKEVEN

For this reason, strangle strategists often calculate their breakeven point. It is slightly different depending on the direction of the market. For example, if prices go over the call strike price, it is likely the short will be exercised. It is only when the loss exceeds the net premium received that you become a net loser. You can define the breakeven point by adding the call strike price to the net credit (premium received). Our 74 call strike plus the $3,000 premium, or 3:00, adds up to a 77:00 as breakeven.

The downside breakeven is determined by subtracting the premium from the put's strike price. Once this price is exceeded, you begin to lose money. In the example, you would reduce the 72 put by 3:00, which comes to 69:00.

THE LONG STRANGLE

Most of this section was devoted to the short strangle as opposed to the long strangle because the long strategy should rarely be used.

Everything mentioned about the short strangle is true for the long—
only in reverse.

THE LONG SYNTHETIC

Synthetic means "artificial" or "not genuine." A synthetic element or
material takes the place of one that naturally occurs. The most common example might be the invention of synthetic rubber and nylon
developed during World War II when rubber and silk were un-
available in the United States.

In options trading, you can use a strategy that utilizes options
only, but creates the same effect as trading the underlying futures
contract. The strategy is called the *synthetic long* or *short.*

You create a synthetic long futures position through the purchase of a call option and the sale of a put option, where the two legs
of this position share a common strike price and expiration date. Just
as the name implies (long), you must be strongly bullish on the direction you expect the market to head.

Suppose you do an analysis of the stock market. Your conclusion is that the Dow is headed much higher. You think nothing can
stop it. Instead of taking a position in an underlying futures, like the
Standard & Poor's 500, you opt to trade a synthetic long. This means
you will buy a call and sell a put. For this example, the S&P 500 is
trading at 350. Assume, for simplicity's sake, that the call and the
put are in-the-money. It costs you 2 index points to buy the call, and
you are paid 2 index points for selling the put. Therefore, you break
even, less the transaction costs.

You decide to hold the synthetic long position until expiration.
If prices shoot up as you forecasted, the call gains value and the
short expires worthless. You win on both by closing out or exercising the call and collecting the premium on the unexercised put.

What happens if prices drop? In this case, you lose double.
Your call expires worthless, causing you to lose the premium you
paid, and the trader to whom you sold the short exercises it. You are
required to deliver a short futures position that is in-the-money.

The third possibility is that the market moves sideways. Here
you break even, less transaction costs. You keep the 2-point premium you received for selling the put and lose the 2-point premium
you paid for the call. Keep in mind that the transaction costs are

doubled on this strategy, compared with just taking a futures position in the underlying futures. (See Figure 7.6.)

Now, both options do not have to be at the same strike price. If
the call is in-the-money and the put is not, you have a deficit since
the premium you receive for the put will not cover the call. On the
other hand, if the put is in-the-money and the call is not, you'll have
a credit. The only problem with this is that the underlying futures will
have to move farther in order for your call to start making money.

FIGURE 7.6

Synthetics Options Position

S&P Index	P/L Call	P/L Put	Combined	Futures
356	4	2	6	6
354	2	2	4	4
352	0	2	2	2
350	(2)	2	0	0
348	(2)	0	(2)	(2)
346	(2)	(2)	(4)	(4)
344	(2)	(4)	(6)	(8)
342	(2)	(6)	(8)	(8)

These figures illustrate how the synthetic options position (row 3) mirrors the
performance of a straight position (row 5) in the futures market. Negative numbers are in parentheses.

WHY USE THIS STRATEGY?

At this point you may well be telling yourself that this strategy
doesn't make sense—an outright futures position would be more
logical, and the only thing this strategy does is double the amount
of commissions that must be paid. If this is true, why would anyone
even consider it?

You can use the long synthetic strategy to convert a long call or
short put options position to a futures position with the same advantages and risk. Consider that you already have purchased a call
option. After a time you decide the market is well supported, and
you want to optimize your position by gaining the short put premium. Your resulting position would be a synthetic long.

THE SYNTHETIC SHORT

You can trade a synthetic short just as you could a synthetic long. For the synthetic short, you buy the put and sell the call. Again, you should use the same strike price and expiration date. This strategy mimics taking a straight short position in the futures market.

The same risks mentioned for the long are experienced if the market goes against you. In this case, you are looking for a bearish price move. If prices go up instead of down, your call will be exercised and your put will expire worthless.

As in the futures market, you must always do your prognostications first. If you call the market correctly, you win the brass ring. If you are wrong, you pay the piper.

CHAPTER 8

Developing Your Own Trading System

Key Concepts

- ◆ Developing a Trading System Discipline
- ◆ Maintaining a Money Management Discipline
- ◆ Monitoring Personal Discipline
- ◆ Managing Information
- ◆ Staying Abreast of New Technology
- ◆ Looking Ahead for Future Trading

Perhaps the biggest single mistake investors make when they begin to analyze the market is that they fail to put together a trading system. An analysis procedure is not a trading system. Most traders are attracted to technical analysis because they use or are exposed to a technique, such as moving averages or chart formation analysis, that works. They then want to apply this specific technique to every situation.

DEVELOPING YOUR OWN TRADING SYSTEM

All technical tools described have been used to successfully trade the futures markets at one time or another, but there are many, many technical approaches. A partial list might include astrological, complementary angles, Harahus pentagon, Japanese candlesticks, parabolic, point and figure, price bar congestion, speed resistance lines, stochastics, and swing charts.

However, neither a single technical analysis tool nor a combination of analysis tools makes up a trading system. Analysis is only a part of a trading system—often a small part! True trading systems are composed of three major components. The first and most important is a money management technique. The second is the analysis of the market, and the third is a market input-output mechanism.

Consider the following guidelines for selecting an analysis system.

1. Choose an analysis procedure, or better yet, a series of analysis procedures, in which you have a high level of confidence.
2. Pick a system that is qualifiable and quantifiable. It must be specific and tell you to go long or short and at what price.
3. Be sure your procedures are able to withstand serious, historical testing. You must be able to use historical market data and to run simulations that can be done quite easily on today's personal computer systems.
4. Choose optimizable analysis procedures. This will help avoid using yesterday's factors for tomorrow's markets. Optimizing is a fine-tuning procedure. It does not mean abandonment of analysis principles. Optimizing adjusts your analysis procedures based on a change in market conditions, such as a major change in market volatility, not just a change in your opinion.
5. Make sure the analysis procedure tells you when to get into a trade and when to get out.

Computer-based systems work better than systems that are difficult to computerize. Computers take much of the opinion out of decision making and allow more accuracy in determining historical track records and hypothetical performance.

DANGERS OF LIQUIDITY

As you test trading systems, the accuracy of your hypothetical results will depend a great deal on how closely your projected entry and exit prices resemble reality. When testing futures market trading systems, it is common to add an extra cost factor of $100 per trade to cover slippage and brokerage commissions. The degree of slippage depends on liquidity and the spread difference between bid and ask prices.

For grains such as soybeans, where high liquidity typically exists, slippage for an individual trade may only be a quarter of a cent per bushel or $12.50 per 5,000-bushel contract. But in less actively traded markets, such as orange juice, slippage may be as much as $200.

MATCHING MONEY MANAGEMENT WITH ANALYSIS

Money management is a primary concern. You can't trade successfully if your system constantly drains your trading account of equity. Successful traders talk about the necessity of surviving the rough, choppy markets so that they are in a position to profit when the market smoothly trends up or down. To succeed, you must first survive.

Surviving simply means preservation of risk capital. You must be able both financially and psychologically to withstand some losing trades. You should cut your losses quickly and let your winners run. The trading system you select or develop should have a definite procedure for protecting positions with stops or "bailout" points.

Money management may well be more critical than the analysis facet of the trading system. Even the best analysis procedure is seldom more than 50 percent right. Good money management preserves your chips when the analysis is wrong. It should provide readouts of risk-to-reward ratios.

Know your trading limits. If you can select the correct amount of money to trade that suits your emotional makeup, you can reduce the negative influence of greed. At the same time, you need to invest enough to make the risk taking involved in the futures markets worth your while.

It's common for beginning traders to overtrade. They often select markets that are cosmetically exciting and require large margins. Gold and silver are popular choices. Equally common are the nervous Nellies who invest too little. They have not fully accepted the concept of futures trading. If traders only stick one toe in the water, investing 1 or 2 percent of their risk capital, a doubling of their money makes little impact.

There are a number of formulas for selecting the proper risk capital that should be devoted to high-risk investment opportunities. The following formula has proved to be effective.

First, determine your net liquid assets (NLA). NLA include assets that are cash or can be converted to cash within 24 hours. These are savings accounts, CDs, common stocks, etc. They would not include real estate, life insurance policies, IRAs, etc.

Once the NLA have been determined, no more than 10 percent of this capital should be earmarked for high-risk situations. For example, if an individual has net liquid assets of $50,000, the amount of investment capital will be 10 percent, or $5,000. This is the smallest investment recommended to a beginning commodity trader.

Some informal studies have indicated that the larger the amount of investment capital placed in commodity trading, the greater the chance for success. The rough percentages are as follows:

With $5,000 in a commodity trading account, the probability for success after 1 year is approximately 1 out of 10. With $10,000, it is 2 out of 10. With $20,000, it is 3 out of 10. With $50,000, it is 50–50. With $100,000, it is 6 of 10. Notice that the odds are stacked against the trader with less than $50,000 in an individual commodity trading account. This certainly heightens the importance of good money management techniques.

The success ratio improves for two reasons as the investment capital available increases. The first is diversification. The more money in an account, the more markets you can test. The more markets you are in, the more likely you'll be in a market that makes the big moves.

The second reason is staying power. If you have a very small amount to invest, you may only have enough equity for one or two trades. The odds get better of hitting a winner when you have enough money to make 15, 25, or 60 trades.

W. D. GANN MONEY MANAGEMENT ADVICE

W. D. Gann is one of history's most noted Wall Street successes. During his commodity and stock trading years in the early part of this century, he supposedly amassed tens of millions of dollars while documenting his trading techniques in a market newsletter and numerous books.

He summarized his money management techniques for stock trading into 24 rules. In the following pages, these 24 rules have been revised to apply to commodity trading.

1. *Determine the proper amount of capital to use.* Divide the amount of risk capital that you are devoting to the commodities markets into 10 equal parts and never risk more than one-tenth of this risk capital on any one trade.
2. *Use stop-loss orders.* Always protect a trade with a protective stop.
3. *Never overtrade.* One often makes this mistake after reaping a considerable profit from a recent trade. Overtrading also occurs when a trader tries to recoup losses.
4. *Never let profit run into a loss.* Once you have a profit, raise your stop-loss order so that you will not lose capital on the trade.
5. *Never buck the trend.* It is particularly important to know the trend of the market before you buy or sell.
6. *If you don't know why you are in a trade or are not confident of the market's direction, it is best to abandon your position.* Never enter a trade when you are in doubt.
7. *Trade only liquid markets.* Those are the active commodities traded. There are plenty of good, viable commodity markets you can trade that offer profit without your having to go into left field and trying to trade the markets that are thinly traded and dominated by commercial or local interests.
8. *Diversify your risk.* Trade commodities from various groupings (grains, meats, metals, financials, food and fiber) to balance your account. Try to avoid tying up all your trading capital in one commodity or commodity grouping.
9. *Trade only with market orders.* Fixing a buying or selling price can be dangerous and should only be used when you have a specific purpose in entering a limited price on your order.

10. *Don't close out your trades unless you have good reason.* Following the trade with a stop-loss order will protect your profits but will not allow you to exit the market on a whim. Let the market tell you what should be done. If you are wrong, let the market kick you out by hitting your stop.

11. *As you produce profits, place these profits into a surplus account to be used only in an emergency.* This will help you to avoid becoming egotistical about your commodity trading and will discipline you to stay on the original track that you have set out for yourself.

12. *Never enter commodity trading for tax purposes alone.*

13. *Never average a loss.* If you have a loss in the market, do not increase the size of your position to lower your average loss. This is one of the worst mistakes a trader can make.

14. *Do not lose patience in your positions.* Don't exit the market simply because you have lost patience or because you are anxious from waiting. (This is particularly true for options traders.)

15. *Avoid taking small profits and large losses.*

16. *Never cancel a stop-loss order after you have placed it.*

17. *Avoid churning your account.* Avoid getting in and out of the market too often. Position your trades and stick with them.

18. *Don't be a one-way trader.* Be willing to sell short just as often as you are willing to buy. Let your object be to keep with the trend and make a profit.

19. *Don't buy because you think the commodity is oversold or too low, and don't sell just because the price seems too high.*

20. *It is dangerous to pyramid at the wrong time.* The best time to pyramid is when the commodity has broken resistance levels and has become active. Treat a pyramided position as a totally new position. If you would not buy if you didn't already have a position, then you should not be pyramiding the position. Remember that at the bottom of all the great pyramids, there's a dead pharaoh.

21. *It is best to pyramid on the buy side if the open interest has dipped, and it is best to pyramid on the sell side after the open interest has risen.*

22. *Never spread off a loss.* If you are in a loss position, get out. Do not spread the position and compound your error.

23. *Never change your position in the market without good reason.*

24. *Avoid increasing your trading after a long period of success or a period of profitable trades.*

Besides money, another type of asset is just as vital. Only you can manage "yourself" and function as a disciplined investor. To review, follow all the money management rules. Money at risk is, of course, a very serious source of stress. If those rules are violated, following the other ones described below will not do you much good. Experiencing losses in the futures market is not failure. It's the normal course of business. Don't run your mind through the wringer on every trade. Once you make up your mind on a position, stay with it unless you uncover some overwhelming reasons to abort the trade. Closely related is the ability to live with your trading decisions. You must accept full responsibility for them. At the same time you're accepting responsibility for your actions, you cannot marry positions. Stay impersonal. Be prepared to cut losing positions early through the use of stops. When you feel the market is dragging you down, walk away for a while. Take a trading vacation.

Take pride in yourself and your trading skills, but control your reaction to success and stay humble. Pride often induces over, trading, which can result in serious financial damage. Maintain the maximum amount of self-discipline. Set concrete rules for yourself and stick to them. Master yourself. Start a trade journal and include remarks about your behavior. Then work at correcting any flaws. You must work against natural instincts to be stubborn, emotional, and inflexible. Find your character flaws and overcome them. Always be open and responsive to changes in the marketplace, particularly changes in the basic facts on which your decisions have been made. When necessary, change your mind and reverse your position. Eliminate all distractions. Never trade when you are physically or mentally not up to it or under stress from non-trade-related pressures.

In summary, there are three areas of discipline every successful trader must master: (1) trading system discipline, (2) money management discipline, and (3) personal discipline.

Discipline is training intended to produce a specific character or pattern of behavior, or, more simply, controlled behavior. To be successful, it is important to train to do something as nearly perfectly as possible.

Most traders lose what they gain through lack of commitment. Written goals, written plans, follow-up procedures—all are fine, but without wholehearted commitment they mean little.

Studies seem to indicate there are a wide variety of systems that can make money in the markets. All trading systems have a few functions in common. They give specific trade entry and exit signals, along with some type of a timing mechanism. Your function is to take the appropriate action. Discipline keeps you focused. Discipline also makes sure you do your homework updating the system regularly, reviewing it, and following the signals.

Money management is covered in W. D. Gann's 24 money management rules. However, you need to be sure that you adopt rules applicable to your trading style. You need to put them in writing and keep them in front of you.

The last area refers to personal performance. You must discipline your emotions—particularly your pride, greed, hope, and fear. These are the emotions that lead you back to your old losing ways.

HOW DO YOU STAY ON TRACK?

From here, you must develop specific strategies to accomplish your mission. For example, following rules can be made easier if you set a firm schedule. Update and review charts daily by 7:00 p.m. every trading day. Discuss markets with broker at 8:00 p.m. each night. Think about possible trading opportunities overnight and call broker in the morning to place orders. Update data and journal before leaving for work. Check the market at noon.

You must back up your schedule with checklists, so nothing gets overlooked. It helps to match your homework with your personality. If you are not the type to do a lot of detailed number crunching each night, you need a simple system that doesn't require it. If you just don't have any time, you shouldn't be trading. Successful futures trading requires a lot of work. If you aren't up to it, consider an alternative approach to the markets, like a discretionary, guided, or managed account.

Homework includes the recognition of change and adaptation to it. Social and economic scholars have often observed that change is drawn toward improvement, and the stronger the potential improvement, the more rapid the change. This Darwinism applied to economic considerations is usually played out in the marketplace.

Over the last couple of decades of the twentieth century, the rapid development of electronic trading has provided greater efficiency, market transparency, and speed to a wide variety of investors. The "vacuum" of demand has drawn financial firms to create Internet and other direct electronic methods of trading to many different types of markets.

Rapidly expanding applications of the Internet are attracting innovation and inspiring new ways of doing old processes. Certainly, if one defines an efficient market to be one in which the greatest diversity of participation in the creation of a price and this participation is inspired by a greater transparency of information, then the Internet and other electronic means of trading are revolutionizing the way investors trade markets.

Until the past decade, futures trading was limited to the open-outcry system practiced in the trading pits of the futures exchanges around the world. Traders stood in the pits on the exchange floors in Chicago, New York, London, and other cities, frantically waving their arms and shouting out their bids and offers. When the trading hours ended, the action was over until the next day. However, the creation of Globex, an electronic trading system, by the Chicago Mercantile Exchange in partnership with Reuters, the British news agency and vendor, changed the complexion of the futures industry.

Globex spawned other electronic trading systems at other exchanges, arousing the fears of exchange members who felt their seats would be cheapened and their advantage in the trading pits would be weakened. Partially because of those fears, electronic trading on the futures markets still hasn't reached the point it has in the equity markets, where individual traders can deal directly through their online broker. Nonetheless, electronic trading has changed dynamically the way the futures markets are traded, and the change will be even greater during the next few years.

Despite the opposition, many futures market participants think the days of the open outcry are numbered, mainly because the economics of electronic trading will prevail eventually. Created in 1971, Nasdaq was the first electronic equity exchange. Since then, other stock exchanges around the world have either switched to electronic trading or set up electronic systems when they were formed.

So far in the United States, electronic trading has been relegated to after-hours operations. In Europe it's a different story. Futures contracts on such exchanges as the LIFFE in London and MATIF in Paris have switched to electronic trading, wiping out some open-outcry floor pits.

Yes, Globex was the catalyst for electronic trading, shaking up the traditional trading community and providing a glimpse of what was to come, but it was launched in the late 1980s, pre-Internet, pre-technological revolution. It was only an April shower before the deluge. The Internet was coming. The Internet and other online systems that have been spawned by the technological revolution of the past two decades have turned the investing world upside down. Although the bids and offers are still sung out loud and clear in the pits of the futures exchanges, the wolf lurks nearby—computers in the trading firms' offices.

The real impact has come in the amount of information now available to a futures trader. Unlike the stock market where a trader can register with an online broker and execute his or her trades directly online, futures trading online is still restricted to order entry.

MANAGING INFORMATION

Futures traders, you may recall, can be defined as hedgers, speculators, and professional traders. Hedgers are mostly farmers, grain elevators operators, processors, packing plants—those who either grow or use the product. They use the futures markets for price protection, selling contracts to offset the material they are holding. Speculators are the traders who take up that hedge, buying or selling in the hope of making a profit. Professional traders may trade for others, or be employed by a large brokerage firm, bank, or other institution.

Traditionally, hedgers and professional traders have been seen as having an advantage over the speculator, because they have access to more resources and information. The Internet has leveled the playing field between professional traders and hedgers and the typical speculator. Information is available via the Internet at little or no cost that was once available only to the broker or professional trader at a high cost. Delayed price quotes and real-time news are now offered free on many websites. Such websites as www. vtuniversity.com, www.smotass.com, and http:// apollo.netservers. com /~waldemar / f_main.html can provide a wealth of other sites offering futures materials.

Your trading plan, which includes your objectives and trading system, is your road map. All trading systems demand information. You must feed them their daily ration of prices, open interest, volume, or whatever they utilize. It is critical that this information be accurate, timely, readily available, and reasonably priced. If not, your system cannot function over the long term.

The computer axiom "garbage in, garbage out" applies to trading systems as well. If you don't input clean, accurate data, you can't expect reliable output.

ONLINE CLASSES OF DATA

Futures (or stocks for that matter) price information is usually separated into three classes based on how and when you receive it. You can be online and receive "real-time" prices. These are prices that are transmitted directly from the exchanges. They are sometimes called *tick-by-tick* prices.

To receive the online pricing, you have to pay a fee to the exchanges, as well as the monthly charge to your vendor. This service, depending on the bells and whistles included in the system, can run several hundred dollars per month. This price doesn't always include the equipment, usually a personal computer.

Additionally, you'll need a communications link. This could be a satellite dish, dedicated telephone line, FM radio antenna, cable TV, or similar arrangement. Keep in mind that as long as the markets you are following are trading, your equipment is tied up.

A less expensive variation of online services can be found in the form of the 15-minute delayed price quotation services. These cost less because you no longer have to pay the exchange fees, which can run from under $10 to over $100 per month per exchange. If you supply your own equipment, usually a TV set, these types of service can run less than $50 per month for individual investors.

With online services, you also need to consider if and for how long you are going to capture the data coming across the screen. Retaining the prices requires computer memory. Some systems are set up to capture and store data for the life of 30, 50, or 100 contracts. They send the price to memory every 5 minutes or every 15 minutes. Often you have a choice. Naturally, the more frequently you save data, the faster the computer's memory is filled up.

The data saved can then be used to perform technical analysis. Most current price quotation systems include very sophisticated studies as part of their packages. When shopping for a system, find one that includes software with the appropriate analytic tools needed for the type of trading system you plan on trading. Several trading systems are available that might fit your needs.

CALL-UP INFORMATION

Let's say you can't plant yourself in front of a monitor during trading hours, but your system requires you to review each day's trading, tick by tick. You could utilize a call-up or dial-up service. These are computer service bureaus that sell you access to their database to retrieve whatever pricing data you want. Some will allow you to select market by market, while others offer packages of 10, 20, 35, or 50 markets.

All you do, usually after 5:00 p.m. EST, is connect your computer through a modem and telephone line to their computer. You punch in your identification code and download the information you've agreed to purchase. You're then billed on a monthly basis. The Internet also makes it easy to call up databases and retrieve such information.

Once you have the day's data, you can study the information at your leisure. You can combine the data with previously collected data to get the longer-term view or run your favorite technical analysis studies.

HISTORICAL DATA

The least expensive pricing information is historical data. You can acquire these data on diskettes, or you can download them to your system. With historical data, you can go back to when a contract or a market first began trading. System developers use this type of data for evaluation purposes. They can use the data to hypothesize how well a trading program performs over a wide variety of market conditions.

WHERE ARE THE DATA AVAILABLE?

Keep in mind that not all the services are reliable. Further, the chances for errors, human and mechanical, are compounded when the data are input from the pit to a computer, are repeatedly uplinked and downlinked via satellites, are uploaded and downloaded to computers, and finally are delivered to the users in a variety of formats.

You have two basic sources: the full-service vendor and the specialists. Your choice probably evolves around your use of data.

If you're just interested in keeping track of what's going on, you might select a very general service. Yahoo, for example, provides some free financial information, as does AOL and other portals. Some of the vendors and wire services such as BridgeNews, Dow Jones, Reuters, and Bloomberg provide some free information on their websites, but again, you have to pay for the more valuable material. Both prices and news may be limited and delayed unless you subscribe. In addition to futures prices, these services provide stock quotes, news, weather, and even entertainment. There are specialized websites such as Pro Farmer and DTN / AgDayta, although their free information is limited.

As mentioned previously, there has been a proliferation of Internet websites with futures information, much of it free, although the more valuable sites usually require a subscription. The futures and stock exchanges have a wealth of free information on their websites, including delayed quotes. Some exchanges are even offering free real-time quotes in select markets. Check your exchange website to see what is available.

You can locate vendors and other information purveyors through magazines such as *Futures*, which has an annual reference volume, or on an Internet web directory. A search using the keywords *futures* or *futures news information* will turn up valuable information.

KEEPING ABREAST OF TECHNOLOGY

It is not enough that you develop the disciplines for trading futures and managing information from the investor perspective. You must also know what is taking place internally in the industry itself. That means you must watch what the exchanges themselves are doing to play catch-up and what other pieces of the puzzle will be impacted from the massive changes now taking place. Be prepared to stop thinking national markets and start thinking global markets.

EXCHANGES

More and more firms are now offering two levels of order routing. One will go directly to the the floor and the other through the trading desk. Some brokerage firms won't let customers enter more complicated orders such as options or spreads online because of the chance of confusion.

Firms use the Internet to transmit orders in a variety of ways.

They may link into the Trade Order Processing System (TOPS). This is a joint order-management system operated by the Chicago Board of Trade and the Chicago Mercantile Exchange. TOPS takes orders directly to the floors of the major exchanges and sends order confirmation and fill information back to the trader.

The CME also has Universal Broker Stations (CUBSII) in the pits. They not only receive orders on a screen, but organize the order deck for the floor broker. Other brokers link directly into the Globex system for immediate electronic order matching without using a floor broker in designated markets.

Other brokerage firms want to keep control over their orders, so they don't use TOPS or one of the other exchange systems. Instead, they have developed their own electronic systems to send orders straight to their floor staff.

One sign that electronic trading is here to stay is the emphasis the major exchanges have placed on after-hours trading. The benchmark after-hours trading medium is Globex (a division of the Chicago Mercantile Exchange). The first "after-hours" futures trading on Globex occurred in June 1992. Via Globex, the online trader can trade such futures and options markets as the S&P 500, Eurodollars, Japanese yen, Canadian dollar, Swiss franc, and many other currencies, as well as the French CAC 40 stock index on the MATIF Exchange in Paris.

The Chicago Board of Trade's Project A allows the online trader to day-trade corn, soybeans, and wheat, as well as trade U.S. Treasury bonds, one of the most popular futures contracts in the world.

Other U.S. futures exchanges, for example, NYMEX (the ACCESS system), also provide after-hours trading in futures markets such as crude oil, heating oil, unleaded gasoline, and natural gas.

To obtain contract specifications on after-hours futures markets, as well as the times those markets trade, consult the exchanges' websites: www.cbot.com, www.cme.com, www.nymex.com, www.liffe.com, and www.matif.com

If you do trade after hours, you have to be aware of the liquidity in a market. Make sure it is adequate enough to ensure a good fill. You also can trade markets that are not open after hours, but you won't get a fill until the open-outcry session starts the next trading day. Volatility is typically less during after-hours trading, but not always. Try some basic trades when beginning. Save the more complicated trades for later, or go the route of the conventional broker.

BROKERS

There is certainly no shortage of brokerages offering online futures trading opportunities. As with all e-trading, you will have to determine which firms are reputable and responsive to consumer needs.

To find an electronic trading broker via the web, simply use your favorite Internet search engine and type in the words *electronic futures trading* or some related string. Or check the websites mentioned earlier that have collected dozens of futures websites that provide trading information.

The better electronic brokerages should allow the futures trader to create and transmit orders directly to the floors of the major exchanges, or to after-hours processing centers. Order confirmations and fills as well as cancellations are automatically routed to your PC via the Internet in a timely manner. Be aware that some brokerages route the trader's electronic order to a phone clerk, who then processes the order in a conventional way. This should not usually be a worry, however, as this process still occurs quickly.

Learn what fees are standard and which supplementary services are fee-based with the broker you choose. Online trading commissions per round-turn futures trade range from $15 to the low $30s, not including NFA fees, exchange fees, and wire transfer fees.

Transferring funds electronically should not be a big concern. Reputable brokerage firms have safeguards in place for your protection during this process and for your account overall. However, it doesn't hurt to ask up front how security issues are handled.

LOOKING AHEAD FOR FUTURES TRADING

Where do the futures markets go from here? The likely development of online trading will look something like this:

One Screen All Markets

The futures market represents only a part of the investment picture. Rapid innovations in the field of online trading are likely to create greater efficiency in the trading of diverse markets. At this moment the most active use of online trading in the futures market is the trading of stock index futures, particularly the "e-markets," e.g., the e-mini S&P, the e-mini Nasdaq, and the Dax on the Eurex.

There is a rapidly increasing demand for the use of electronic trading of stock index futures with the electronic stock markets. It is quite likely that by the time this book is published, at least a few firms will be offering both stock market trading and futures trading on the same screen. This is the first step. There will be a natural evolution of a trading screen that allows the investor to trade stocks, bonds, futures, currencies, funds, and even derivatives of these markets on a single screen. To accomplish this, a number of fundamental changes will need to occur in the very infrastructure of the investment community.

Regulatory Compliance of the Future

The Internet has torn down national borders. An individual sitting at a computer screen in Germany can easily access Internet websites in the United States, Asia, and virtually anywhere else in the world. This vast access to information whets the appetite for the potential of trading any number of foreign markets. The demand for such trading will inspire investment firms to make their products available worldwide. Yet a potential problem develops when the regulation of one sovereign state prohibits its citizens from accessing another market, such as the prohibition by the CFTC for U.S. investors to trade London options during the late seventies and early eighties.

The difference in safeguards and compliance procedures between exchanges and nations can lead to an unlevel playing field between marketplaces. Clearly, the regulatory bodies of the world will be required to unify their efforts, thereby creating a uniform application of regulations. Otherwise, investors will be rapidly drawn to the markets with greater flexibility. The freedom of the Internet inspires a free world market.

Back-Office Procedures of the Future

The back office of investment firms provides the function of accounting for and balancing of investor transactions. The back-office software of years past simply will not work in the electronic environment. A couple of obvious examples are the T+3 settlement procedures of the U.S. stock market and the once-a-day posting of futures trades. T+3 settlement means that the actual settlement of stock trades occurs 3 days after the trading date. These 3 days in the past were used to provide for the physical handling of the stock certificates. When electronic trading allows a trader to be in and out of a stock several times in the same day, T+3 is not only meaningless but also cumbersome.

Single-day posting is actually a dangerous procedure when applied to electronic markets, particularly if the market is traded 24 hours a day. Single-day posting actually threatens the integrity of the market by failing to provide a real-time accounting of investor positions. Back offices are being forced to account for all investor transactions on a real-time mark-to-the-market basis.

Single- and Multiple-Currency Accounting

An investor in Japan may have positions in the U.S. stock market and the German gutures markets. The online trading system of the future will need to provide accounting to this Japanese investor in the currency of the investor's choice. In the absence of a single world currency, investors will want the option to choose what currency or currencies their investment is marked to and indeed have the flexibility to change the currency of record at their option.

Real-time portfolio analysis will be the hallmark of the future on time investing. In response to the capability to trade all markets worldwide on one screen in the currency of the investor's choice, new applications of portfolio analysis will be developed. Investors will be able to view a real-time portfolio risk analysis and even make fine adjustments in the application of modern portfolio theory.

In short, electronic trading of the future will give investors greater control over their investments, greater transparency in the marketplace, and near infinite diversity.

A System Must Be a System

The three components of a trading system described above must complement one another—they must work toward a single goal. Your analysis, for example, cannot violate good money management principles. The data input must suit the analysis component. In addition, you must be able to flex your system into the world of e-trading.

CHAPTER 9

Using Advanced Trading Strategies

Key Concepts

- ♦ The Function of the Arbitrageur
- ♦ Trading Futures and Options as a Team
- ♦ Hedging on the Futures Market
- ♦ Learning the Value of Trading Night Markets
- ♦ Mastering the Fine Art of Day Trading

From time to time, special opportunities arise in the markets. You need special trading strategies to take advantage of them. As an added benefit, you may even be able to shelter yourself from some of the risks associated with futures trading by using one of these strategies, but there are always some financial risks associated with trading futures.

THE ARBITRAGE STRATEGY

Arbitrage is the simultaneous purchase of cash commodities or futures in one market against the sale of cash commodities or futures in the same or a different market to profit from a difference in price. There is a similarity between arbitrage and spreading. The key word is *against*. You purchase one position against another. These positions offset each other. Therefore, the risk, compared with the risk of holding either position outright, is less. If one side, or "leg," goes up, the other side normally compensates by declining.

Profits are made from the changes that occur between the two positions. Your risk is not that one of the legs substantially moves against you. It is that no movement at all occurs. When this happens, the trade generally produces little or no profit—yet you are obligated to pay the transaction costs. Since you trade both sides of the market, the commissions and other fees can be twice that for a regular (one-sided) trade. On the other hand, margins can be less, thereby providing greater leverage.

USING OPTIONS TO "ARB"

The trader who uses arbitrage is called an *arbitrageur.* The objective of this type of options trade is to find options trading outside fair market values. If an option is overpriced, naturally you sell it. Conversely if an option is underpriced, you buy it. But to be an arbitrageur, you do more. If you buy, you sell a similar position to offset the risk. And if you sell, you buy at the same time.

An arbitrageur spots a corn call that is substantially underpriced and buys it. This is essentially a bullish move, but to avoid the risk of holding a net long position the arbitrageur would take a short position to balance the risk. The profit becomes the amount at which the corn call is mispriced. In time, the call moves from an underpriced position to fair market value. That move is where the arbitrageur makes money. The opposite works as well. An arbitrageur may short an overpriced call, taking a bearish stance, but at the same time offsets the risk of a bull move by entering an offsetting position on the other side of the market.

MARKET PURPOSE

Arbitrageurs serve as price policemen. They make sure that any price that gets out of line gets back in line. Arbitrageurs do this by constantly searching for commodities that are overvalued or undervalued. Then they pounce! Their market activity bids up the prices that are too low and pushes down those that have become too high. Since these arbitrage transactions are for most practical purposes without serious risk, the return is usually low. Little pain, little gain. But arbitrageurs accept the low return because they have little at risk.

Theoretically, anyone who has access to the markets can make these types of trades. But this is true only in theory. There are two problems. The first is the transaction costs. The return must exceed the cost of the two commissions and the other fees associated with the positions. Often the profit margin cannot withstand normal transaction costs. Usually, the only ones that can make money in this game are trading companies or floor traders. They may have their own seats on the exchanges and may trade in such large volume that their per-transaction costs are low enough to make a profit on these trades. For example, precious metals dealers may arbitrage gold and silver; security dealers actively arbitrage the Treasury bond futures or option markets.

The second problem is the ability to spot accurately those contracts that are overpriced or underpriced. To do this, you must have a reliable pricing model and be in position to act extremely fast. As with the problem involving transaction costs, the professional trader within a specific commodity complex has an edge. The important point for you to understand is how arbitrage works to keep commodity prices at or near their fair market value. Without arbitrageurs, you could be subjected to unexplained price moves within the various market complexes.

FUTURES AND OPTIONS TOGETHER

Another strategy to consider is to trade futures against profitable options positions. Imagine that the silver markets (spot, futures, options) have bottomed. It looks as if silver will begin to stair-step higher over the next few months. Experience says that it won't move up on a flat 45-degree angle. It will likely advance, retrace, advance, retrace, and so on, as do most developing bull markets.

What are the alternatives? Go alternately long and short the futures markets trying to catch the moves? Or try the same thing with puts and calls? You could take a long position in either futures or options and hold it for as long as you dare or until it becomes profitable enough. You could also trade futures against options. One way to do this is to buy a call in-the-money or near-the-money. As the market moves higher, the call increases in value. When the upward price trend hits an area of resistance and gives a signal that it may retrace, you take a short position in the futures.

The key to successfully using this strategy is being ready to take one of three actions:

1. You must offset your short at breakeven or near breakeven if the retracement doesn't materialize. You might want to consider a tight stop, depending on the volatility factor at the time of the trade. This action produces a profit on the short futures trade, and you still have the call option intact. If silver prices continue to increase after the retracement, the option becomes more profitable. If they don't, you don't have your futures profit to offset the cost of the option premium.

2. You must be poised to offset your short when your retracement objective has been reached, 50 percent, for example, in profits on the futures position. You continue to hold the call option. You either break even or lose a small amount on the futures side of the trade, perhaps the cost of the futures commission and a few cents per contract on the silver. You still have your profit in the call option.

3. You must be prepared to exercise your call option if the market violently moves limit up against your short position. It either breaks even or loses a small amount on the futures side of the trade, perhaps the cost of the futures commission and a few cents per contract on the silver. You still have your profit in the call option. The last action forces you to exercise your call option to offset the short futures position. This puts you out of the market. However, the price at which you bought the call was a lower price than the price at which you went short. The difference is your profit. This may or may not offset the commissions and fees paid to take these positions, depending on how much of a bull move occurred before you went short.

This strategy is actually creating a spread position. The approach is to use a call for the long side and a futures contract for the short. The spread, by its very nature, helps manage the risk; it puts you on both sides of the market at the same time. If the market runs away in either direction, the unprofitable leg is lifted and the profitable leg is held.

You need to be concerned if the market advances to the point where you think it will retrace and you put on the short, only to see the market trade sideways for a considerable period of time. If this occurs, you could exercise your call option, offsetting the short. The hope is that the profit already accumulated in the call position would be enough to pay both commissions and fees with a little left over.

PUT AND CALL TEAM TRADING

Puts and calls can work well together. A put can be used to hedge or lock in a profit on a call, and vice versa. If an investor has a put and a call in the same market and the market drops, the put is exercised in order to protect the call's profit. It is far more important that the put does not interfere with the call's ability to further profit from a continuation of a bull move. The cost of this protection, without jeopardizing future profits, is still only the premium cost, commission, and fees.

As a comparison, a futures long position profit can be locked in by using a short in another contract month which moves in a one-to-one linear relationship. When using futures to hedge futures (an intracommodity spread), the premium cost of the option is saved, but no additional profits are possible, regardless of how high or low the future ultimately trades. This strategy, as discussed earlier, creates a neutral trading position, one in which you are holding equal and opposite positions in the same futures market.

A second advantage of the option-hedging concept is the use of a call to hedge a profitable put position. Should the market rise, the call can be profitably exercised. But even more important, if the bearish move continues unabated, additional profits can be generated from the put. The cost of this hedge is simply the premium cost and the transaction costs.

THE SPECIAL DOUBLE

A unique idea available to options traders is the *special double option*, sometimes referred to as a *double option*. This is a combination of a put option and a call option at a fixed strike price for future delivery at any time prior to the expiration date. The premium cost of a double is usually close to, but slightly less than, the sum of the premium costs of both a put and a call purchased separately.

The only stipulation of the double option is that only one side of the double can be exercised, but both sides can be traded as many times as desired. All the trading techniques discussed earlier with regard to puts and calls will work equally well with either or both sides of the double, specifically the use of an option to hedge another option, options as hedges on futures positions, and options in lieu of stop orders. The only restriction is that only one side may ultimately be declared or exercised.

Naturally, all the advantages of regular puts and calls are available to the double options trader. These advantages include minimum and calculable risk exposure, tremendous leverage, unlimited profit potential, and freedom from margin calls. The double has one additional advantage that places it in a special category far and above other strategies. The "one big extra" frees the holder from dependence on market direction predictions. The double option, being the combination of both a put and a call, can be profitable regardless of whether the market advances or declines. You may often find it easier to determine a market's volatility rather than the direction it is headed. To use this strategy, you need to be confident of a major increase in market volatility. If not, both your put and call are likely to expire worthless.

To illustrate, you notice your favorite commodity beginning to trade in a tight coil or triangle formation. The coil gets tighter and tighter. You know the commodity is poised for a breakout. But will it go up or down? You're not really sure. All you know for sure is that it can't trade much longer without committing itself. This is the opportunity you're looking for to trade a double. You position yourself on both sides of the market. When the breakout occurs, you close out the losing side and ride the winning side to the next point of resistance, where you decide to take your profits or not. Like any trading strategy, it is not without risks. For example, the breakout could fizzle. You could end up holding two worthless options. The key is correctly evaluating the degree of volatility.

If, instead, you had purchased a put only, you would be predicting the market was heading lower, except where the put is used in lieu of a stop to protect a new long position or to hedge a profitable long position. The put buyer is anticipating a substantial drop in price. Simultaneously, the speculator who purchases a naked call without the expectation of immediately being short is anticipating a bull move.

The buyer of a double is looking for a major increase in volatility, but is not sure if the market will react bullishly or bearishly. Either way, the value of either the put or the call will increase. If the move is strong enough, it will offset all transaction costs and generate a profit.

HEDGING

The National Futures Association's *Glossary of Futures Terms* defines hedging as follows: hedging is the initiation of a position in a futures market that is intended as a temporary substitute for the sale or purchase of the actual commodity. The sale of the futures contracts in anticipation of the future sale of cash commodities as a protection against possible price declines or the purchase of futures purchases of cash commodities as a protection against the possibility of increasing costs. Most traders hedge between cash and futures as a form of price protection.

As a trader, you need to be aware of the concept of hedging because hedgers can have a major impact on prices. Also, bona fide hedgers hold commodities with strong hands—giving you an indication of where a market may be headed. If a farmer has 100,000 bushels of corn stored, the farmer is de facto long corn. The farmer actually has possession of the crop. If the farmer thinks corn prices are going to go down, one of three things can be done:

1. The corn can be sold on the open market before the price goes down.
2. Twenty 5,000-bushel short futures positions can be taken in the corn market. In this case 100,000 bushels of corn are being sold on the market. This makes the farmer neutral—100,000 bushels of cash corn are owned, and 100,000 bushels have been promised for delivery at a given price.
3. The third alternative would be to buy 20 put options. When and if it is decided to exercise these options, the farmer would be neutral—both long (cash) and short (futures) 100,000 bushels of corn.

When facing these alternatives, the farmer must evaluate his or her personal convictions and planning time frame. If corn prices are going to plummet indefinitely, shouldn't the corn just be sold?

Wouldn't it be better to pass the risk of storage and spoilage to the elevator or grain merchant?

If the profit margin (the difference between the cost of production and the current futures price) is acceptable, it might be best to execute a simple hedge: Short the 20 futures positions and deliver the corn when the contract expires.

If the conviction regarding price is not ironclad and there is no strong reason to believe corn is going down, put options should be considered. They give the protection needed with more flexibility and less cost.

The cost of the puts depends on how near they are to being in-the-money. The trader may choose to buy 20 "cheap" out-of-the-money options just for protection in case of a crashing bear market. The trader might buy several in-the-money put options with the hope of making some money when the price dip occurs and yet still have the protection of knowing they could be exercised if there is a serious price deterioration.

This same strategy can be used to protect a futures positions as well. Let's use a silver example. You go long silver in the futures market, rather than buying a call option. Basically, what you are doing is reversing your futures and options positions.

As expected, silver makes a major bull move. Your futures position gains just over $1 per ounce, which brings you to an area of very strong resistance. You are confident that the price will go higher, but you feel you should protect your gains.

What should you do? You could close out your long position and take profits. This is the most conservative approach. When you think the bull move is about to resume, you could reestablish your long position. This now becomes a risk-laden speculative trade. If the market corrects right after you get back in, you get whipsawed and end up giving back all the profits before the next bull leg was made.

A more prudent approach might be to establish a put as a hedge against your profitable futures position. If you bought a put at-the-money, you could ride it down during the correction and sell it at a profit when the bull move begins. It would protect your futures profits in case the next bull move never materialized. By exercising the option, you'd close out your futures position at the price level where you had a $1-plus gain. From this, you'd subtract the cost of the premium, commissions, and fees.

If your confidence level was very high that the bull move was going to resume after the retracement, you could calculate exactly what put to buy to break even on your futures position. This put would be out-of-the-money, and therefore the premium would be lower. You could think of this as a deductible insurance policy.

It is cheaper because you don't have full coverage. However, you do have protection if you are completely wrong and have a trading accident that totals your position! In the case where silver prices retreat substantially, your out-of-the-money put gains value as it becomes an in-the-money put.

PUTS AS STOP-LOSS ORDERS

Another way of thinking about this strategy is that the put is, in actuality, a stop-loss order for your futures position, but it has more advantages than a simple stop-loss order. First, an option provides protection at a guaranteed price. You're not at the mercy of the stop-loss order fill.

Second, you have more flexibility in deciding when to exercise your option. A stop-loss order is activated when its price is hit, and usually it becomes a market order. With an option, you can study the market longer before you pick the time you want to exercise it. You have more thinking time.

Lastly, the option gives protection from whipsawing markets. If, for example, your stop order is close to the market and the market makes a brief retracement before continuing its move, your stop could be hit. This would close out your position and your gains. The use of an option gives you more time to assess the situation before you have to act.

DO YOU WANT TO ADD THE NIGHT MARKETS TO YOUR TRADING STRATEGY?

The following anecdote offers one of the strongest reasons why any currency or stock index trader should give serious thought to the night markets. In late February 1989, the Nikkei 225 (the Japanese equivalent of our S&P futures contract) saw a tightening of the spread between U.S. and Japanese interest rates. Our rates moved higher as did theirs, but theirs moved at a faster pace. This caused their bond and stock market to tumble. The Nikkei 225 eventually found support at the 33,200 level. Another example occurred in November 1989 when the Berlin Wall was breached. The deutsche mark began a strong bull move that evening.

The point is simply that half the world is working and trading while U.S. markets are closed. In the example of the Nikkei 225, the yen gapped lower the next day. An 80–90-point gap, up or down, is not unusual for the yen. With the Berlin Wall news, the D-mark went up steadily for weeks. Trends (major moves) often begin and end while our markets are closed.

This could be very expensive for you. Let's say you are trading a currency and something dramatic occurs after the market closes in the United States. You don't have to spend a sleepless night waiting to enter or exit the market in the morning. All you need to do is get in touch with your broker and adjust your position at the evening session.

WHAT MARKETS ARE AVAILABLE?

Besides the Nikkei 225, which is traded on the Singapore Exchange from 6:00 to 9:30 p.m. and 10:30 p.m. to 1:00 a.m. (U.S. Central Standard Time), you can trade gold, silver D-marks, Swiss francs, Japanese yen, British pounds, and Australian dollars on the Forex. These trade from 2:00 p.m. to 7:00 a.m. U.S. CST. Don't forget the evening session on the Chicago Board of Trade. You can trade T-bonds and T-notes. The hours are 6:00 to 9:30 p.m. U.S. CST.

Electronic trading platforms provided by the various exchanges now make a number of contracts available for after-hours trade in the afternoon, evening, and overnight periods. Traders can be involved now in foreign exchange, financial instruments, energy, and agricultural and other commodity products via electronic trading. All the major U.S. exchanges—the Chicago Board of Trade, the Chicago Mercantile Exchange, the New York Mercantile Exchange (NYMEX)—have after-hours trading on many of their contracts. They also have links with other international exchanges such as the London International Financial Futures Exchange (LIFFE), the Marche a Terme International de France (MATIF), the Eurex of Frankfort, the Singapore Commodity Exchange, and the Singapore International Monetary Exchange (SIMEX). You can trade both domestic and foreign contracts through these after-hours electronic platforms.

Whenever you are trading foreign markets, do not neglect to take into consideration the ever-changing relationship between the currencies. The tick value of the Nikkei, for example, changes daily depending on the trading activity in the yen. This means that it is prudent to use stops. Stops are twice as important for the night markets!

What about fills, liquidity, and margins? These are not substantially different at night. Fills are just as fast, sometimes even a little faster, at night. The margin for the Nikkei is often less than for the S&P. Liquidity is not usually a problem, but that doesn't mean it won't be at some time. Check with your broker.

DAY TRADING

One last alternative strategy to consider is day trading. This simply means entering and exiting a position during the same trading session. You don't carry any positions overnight or into the next trading session. You get in and out of trades within a single trading session.

Why have traders been cautioned to avoid this type of trading? That rationale probably goes back to the old bucket shops of the 1920s and 1930s. These were the times before electronic transfer of price quotes (telegraph messages being the exception). In those days, the response time between the trader in the trading parlor and the pits was considerable. You couldn't get tick-by-tick quotes, nor could you telephone a trading desk on the floor. Now you can do both.

The more important question is why should you even consider it at all. The profit motive is valid. You should day-trade only if you think you can make money. But there are other reasons as well. In one sense, you reduce risk by not carrying positions overnight. Events can happen overnight which cause markets to move violently on the following day's open. That's life in the pits. Day traders are unaffected. Another plus for day trading is that it usually requires lower margins. This makes your money work even more efficiently.

When you are a bona fide day trader, you can simplify your

analysis. Fundamental factors are mostly meaningless. You can forget about them. All the technical approaches geared to determining long- or intermediate-term trends are irrelevant. You only need short-term analysis. When the markets open each day, you start out with a clean slate. Yesterday's problems no longer exist.

The biggest benefit of day trading is the discipline it forces on you. The entire trading cycle—research, trade selection, entry-exit point determination, execution—takes place in a matter of hours. More importantly, you go through this routine every day, over and over. You have to become organized. There is no time to procrastinate.

Despite all these positive factors to day trading, the drawback may be enough to stop you. Before you call your broker, consider the amount of commission generated. You could be trading one lot and have three or four trades in a single session. Also, you need a good source for tick-by-tick price activity. This could easily run $300 or $400 per month, including exchange fees. Then there is the time involved. You should be in front of your quote screen whenever you are in the market. This could be several hours per trading day. If all this weren't enough, there's the normal high risk associated with futures trading. To give you a better idea of how all this meshes together, Paul Lovegren, a senior futures trader, shares his rules for day trading the S&P 500. The fact that he has a written set of rules immediately available reinforces the importance of discipline.

1. Select a market with sufficient volume to permit day trading, the S&P in this case.
2. The market selected must have enough daily volatility to offer profit opportunities.
3. Cover your downside risk. A put and a call are held permanently for each unit to be day-traded. This is insurance against limit-up or limit-down days. These options positions can be exercised to exit any position in which you become trapped.
4. Roll options positions when they begin to approach expiration, so you don't suffer total loss due to time decay.
5. Always have a strategy planning session with your broker well before you start trading. During this session, agree on what you both expect the trading range will be

for the day. Then decide exactly what you plan to do—
for example, get in at the opening, wait until a specific
support or resistance level is reached, and react to a given
price formation.

6. When your expectations are totally incorrect, avoid that
   session and start planning for the next one.

7. Always trade with trailing stops and continually adjust
   them as necessary.

8. Don't enter the market late in the trading session, after
   3:30 EST (U.S. Eastern Standard Time) on the S&P, because the market is thin and volatile.

9. Have a definite system to identify the short-term trends
   and your entry and exit points.

10. Be psychologically prepared to reverse your position
    when the trend moves against your position or a pivot
    point is hit.

11. Have a cutoff point for profits and losses. (For example,
    Paul quits after he makes $1,000 per position during a
    session. This keeps him from overtrading. He also quits
    after he has two or three losers in a row.)

12. Know your breakeven to the penny, including commis-
    sions.

13. Use quote equipment, or be sure your broker has quote
    equipment, that allows you to access a wide variety of
    studies, like 5-minute RSI, stochastics, premium calcula-
    tions, moving average bands, trend lines, directional
    movement, equivolume, Japanese candlesticks, etc.

14. Be geared to making decisions immediately. If the market
    goes against you, get out. If your entry point is hit, get in.

CHAPTER 10

Giving Trading Discretion to Someone Else

Key Concepts

- ◆ Using Modern Portfolio Theory to Structure an Investment Portfolio
- ◆ How Various Types of Discretionary Authority Can Be Used to Reach Your Trading Objectives
- ◆ Step-by-Step Procedures for the Evaluation of Any Type or Class of Investments, with an Emphasis on Managed Futures Programs

Research studies by several experts indicate that a diversified portfolio with a futures position added may have more balance and stability and even increased return. The pioneers of this approach were such notable financial theoreticians as Harry Markowitz, John K. Lintner, and William R. Sharpe. Many of their ideas and research evolved into what is currently known as *modem portfolio theory* (MPT). MPT can be simply stated as "don't put all your eggs in one basket." They also developed sophisticated methods of structuring and evaluating the performance of portfolios.

MODEM PORTFOLIO THEORY

Both active money managers and academicians subscribe to this theory. The essence of the theory is that it is the duty and obligation of the prudent investor to seek combinations of assets that yield the maximum return with the lowest associated risk. The key phrase is *combinations of assets*.

With this as their goal, and access to virtually unlimited computer time, several renowned business schools began to crunch numbers. They loaded their mainframe with historical data detailing the performance of all major classes of assets: stocks, bonds, real estate, commodities, cash equivalents, etc. Then they played "what-if" games. They arranged and rearranged their experimental portfolios. They constantly changed the asset mix and evaluated it against historical returns generated over the last 10 years, last 20 years, etc.

NEGATIVE CORRELATION

They developed some extremely useful information, and they popularized the concept of balancing a portfolio with negatively correlated assets. This simply means that when a certain asset class goes up due to a given set of economic circumstances, other asset classes go down or remain the same.

Now this may not sound like much, but it is. If you can quantify the positive or negative reaction of various investment opportunities to given sets of economic data, you can begin to build sample portfolios that can withstand various types of adverse conditions.

What's the single most serious, long-term disease that your net worth faces? Most investors will probably say inflation. Many economists attempted to develop a portfolio resistant to inflation.

The most prominent researcher of the group was a professor from Harvard University, Dr. John Lintner. He used data from July 1979 through 1982, comparing 15 futures portfolio managers and 8 public futures funds to stock and bond portfolios. At Boston University, Zvi Bodie and Victor Rosansky took a longer-term view, 1950 through 1976. Jack Barbonel, Phil Lipsky, and John Zumbrunn studied the period of 1960–1982, while Scott Irwin and B. Wade Brorsen (Purdue University) analyzed data for 1963–1983.

A common conclusion of this number crunching was that the stock market and the futures market are negatively correlated. This becomes particularly critical during periods of inflation. Inflation pushes prices and interest rates higher. The cost of doing business increases while sales decrease—stock prices suffer and the market drops.

At the same time, inflation pushes prices higher. Futures investors profit from bull markets, particularly in the physical commodities. Inventory managers, fearing higher prices, buy more, which fuels the fires of inflation.

The recommendation resulting from much of the work on the subject was to spread your risk by reducing volatility while at the same time enjoying an increase in the return from your total investment package. A common theme was to put from 5 to 15 percent of your investment portfolio in futures.

While many investors showed interest in doing this, most were not willing or able to make the commitment necessary to trade a futures account directly. For this and other reasons, investors have sought the help of various professional (and even nonprofessional) traders to assist them. This is accomplished by signing over to the trader, called a *third-party controller*, the authority to trade the account. The authority used is usually a limited power of attorney.

TYPES OF DISCRETIONARY ACCOUNTS

There are a wide variety of trading approaches that can give your associated person (broker) or a third-party adviser varying degrees of freedom to act in your behalf in your futures trading account. For example, you can give your broker just price or timing discretion in a trade. This allows your broker to decide at what price level or time to enter your order in the market. This type of discretionary authority does not require giving power of attorney. But it must be to your (the customer's) benefit, not at the broker's convenience.

For example, you are very busy or will be out of touch during a particular day, but you want to place some trades. You discuss the situation with your broker the night before. You decide on the futures market, month, quantity, side (long or short, put or call), and strike price in the case of options that you wish to trade. You let your broker pick the time or the specific target price or range. Situations like this occur when you want to get a feel for the day's market before you commit. You might tell your broker to go ahead and place your order if the market opens higher tomorrow. This would be a time-only discretion order.

Or you might want to wait for a certain trading range. You instruct your broker to enter the market if the commodity you want to trade hits a certain price. "Buy me 5 December S&Ps if it trades over 322." When you use price-only discretion, you should limit your broker to a trading range.

There is another type of discretionary trading that also does not require you to sign a limited power of attorney. This is called a *guided account*. With a guided account, a third party, who must be registered with the NFA as a CTA, suggests all trades. The CTA explains the thinking. You, the client, must accept or reject the trades.

Another possibility is turning over your account to a third party who isn't required to have a formal disclosure document. To do this, you'll be asked to sign a limited power of attorney and a written statement explaining why this third-party account controller is not required by the CFTC to provide you with a disclosure document. There are four reasons a disclosure document is not required by an account controller:

1. If the controller advised less than 15 people over the last 12 months and does not generally hold himself or herself out to the public as a CTA

2. If the controller is a dealer, broker, processor, or seller in the cash market for the commodity to be traded or provides advice incidental to the conduct of the normal cash market business

3. If the person is properly registered in another capacity and whose advice is solely incidental to the normal conduct of business

4. If the person is a relative of the person doing the trading

Other than these four exceptions, all third-party advisers are required by the Commodity Futures Trading Commission to provide their clients with a formal disclosure document. Additionally, clients must sign a written acknowledgment that they have read and they understand the disclosure document. The purpose of the disclosure document is to make you aware of all the pertinent facts, i.e., the amount of risk involved, explanation of the trading system, fee schedule, past performance, etc.

Be aware that your broker may be exempted from the disclosure document requirement based on exception 3 listed above. An individual broker who is not registered as a CTA would be considered someone who is "properly registered in another capacity and whose advice is solely incidental to the normal conduct of business." The section about the advice being incidental means that a broker cannot trade all, or the majority, of accounts on a discretionary basis. Brokers also must have 2 years of experience in handling accounts before they are allowed to take discretion in other people's accounts.

Brokers who don't have 2 years' experience and want to take discretion in accounts can do one of two things. First, they can petition the NFA for a waiver of this requirement. (The NFA seldom honors such requests.) The other option is to register as a CTA. If a broker takes this route, a disclosure document must be prepared. In it, the broker's experience must be revealed. Therefore, it behooves you to read all disclosure documents carefully before investing. Being registered as a CTA doesn't mean that the person can trade profitably or even ably.

Other than the discretionary options mentioned, you can elect to invest in a managed account program. There are basically two types: individual and limited partnerships. With an individually managed account, the CTA takes complete control of trading your account and trades it. The size of the portfolio or the diversification possible depends upon the amount you put in the program. While some CTAs will trade amounts as low as $5,000, most require $50,000 or more. Many are asking $100,000 to $200,000, so the accounts have some staying power and can spread the risk over 10 to 15 markets.

Your other choice is a limited partnership, which may be either public or private. The basic difference between the two is the size, meaning the amount of money that can be raised by the commodity pool operator (CPO) and the number of investors that can participate. Private offerings are somewhat more restricted by the CFTC than public.

NEARLY $44 BILLION

Limited partnerships have become popular in the last decade. The amount under management was estimated at $43.9 billion at the end of 1998, according to the *Managed Accounts Report* newsletter. This growth has likely occurred because of some benefits intrinsic to this form of investment. For example, an individual can invest as little as $5,000 and receive the following:

> *Diversification into a wide variety of markets, far more than one could accomplish with most individual futures portfolios.* This gives your account more stability, putting it in a better position to take advantage of major moves.
>
> *Leading CTAs to manage your account.* You might not normally have access to this caliber of traders.
>
> *Lower than normal commission rates.* Most funds, because of their enormous volume, trade at or near discount rates.
>
> *Freedom from margin calls.* The fund or the limited partnership is responsible for all margin calls.
>
> *Defined risk.* Your initial investment is usually all you are obligated for, but be sure to carefully read the particular prospectus for the investment you are considering.
>
> *Interest income.* You gain interest income from funds held in Treasury bills by the fund or limited partnership.
>
> *No restrictions or upside potential.* Remember, many of the CTAs that manage these types of investments have very impressive trading histories, which will be detailed in the disclosure document.

WORD TO THE WISE!

It is extremely important to read, study, and understand the disclosure document or prospectus for any fund or limited partnership you are considering. It explains your rights, risks, and obligations. Be sure to understand what you are signing and the risks involved.

When you begin to do your research on an investment opportunity, the first thing you usually hear about is its past rate of return (ROR) or its expected ROR. Brokers of all classes of assets hype this number. If a product has a high ROR, it is supposed to overcome all other obstacles.

ROR is important, but it is not the number one indicator. The key issue is risk management. This is especially true of any investment involving the futures markets.

Consider this situation. You invest in a limited partnership (LP). The first month your LP has a 50 percent drawdown of equity. Month 2 it appreciates 50 percent. Are you back to breakeven? No, you are still behind. To recover from a 50 percent loss, you need a 100 percent gain. If the fund began with $1,000,000 and lost $500,000, a 50 percent gain brings it to $750,000. Only doubling its remaining equity can make it whole again (see Figure 10.1). Study the table in Figure 10.1 to get an insight into the effect that loss of equity has on an LP.

As you can see, the greater the loss, the greater the effort it takes to recover. Recovery from a substantial drawdown could take months, if recovery is even possible.

FIGURE   10.1

Loss-Recovery Table

% Loss	% Needed for BE
5	5.26
20	25.00
30	42.86
40	66.67
50	100.00
70	233.33
90	900.00
100	Impossible

RISK MANAGEMENT RANKS NUMBER 1

CTAs are no different from anyone else. If they try too hard and succumb to the pressure involved in recouping from a severe setback, they fail. For this reason, the first qualifications to look for in any CTA who is going to manage your money are management skills and experience. You want to know what downside volatility can be expected on average. How deep are the drawdowns of equity? How frequent? What was the maximum consecutive drawdown, and how long did it take to recover? In trading futures, there will always be months where you lose money. But if you can't quickly recover, you dig a hole that is near impossible to climb out of.

CONSISTENCY RANKS NUMBER 2

You should get a queasy feeling when you see a limited partnership that rocks up and down. Up 32 percent one month, down 26 percent, up 22 percent, down 17 percent, up 19 percent, down 13 percent. It may be making money, but it seems too anxious to enjoy it.

What you want is consistency. The last thing you need is to get a statement from your broker telling you your investment zagged twice in a row when it should have zigged. Steady and reasonable gains are more comforting than wild, uncontrolled energy.

How do you measure consistency? You chart out the monthly gains and losses of the CTAs you are considering. Are the monthly and annual gains impressive? Are the losses controlled and reasonable? A loss of 10 to 15 percent is not a problem if it is quickly recovered. But wide swings can leave you in a state of uncertainty.

NOW . . . ROR!

Once you're satisfied the investment vehicle you are evaluating manages risk and performs consistently, you begin to pay more attention to its rate of return. Keep in mind that the ROR means nothing until you're satisfied with steps 1 and 2.

The importance of ROR only comes into focus when you consider what you must give up or are expected to withstand to receive it. This is called the *efficient frontier*. It is the amount of risk, measured in standard deviation, that can be expected to obtain a given amount of reward, measured by the mean (average) return. Most of us draw a line regarding how much risk we can or will accept for any expected reward.

HOW TO MEASURE VOLATILITY?

One of the easiest methods to determine the amount of the volatility you'll be facing is to draw a simple bar chart. On a blank piece of paper, draw a straight line across the middle of the page. Let this represent zero percent change in the monthly rate of return. Now, plot a bar for the positive rates of return above the line and the negative months below. You find these figures in most disclosure documents on the "Performance Summary Page." Study the chart you create. How wide are the swings from positive to negative? How often are there consecutive drawdowns of equity? How deep are the drawdowns?

Another important aspect is the length of the study. You will need to know how the CTA(s) performs in bull and bear markets. Some traders and systems do better in one or the other. Certain trend-following systems, for example, do better in bull markets because they last longer than bear markets. Once trends are established, the trend followers jump aboard and ride them for all they're worth. You can't always do this with bear markets. Markets can turn around, and the moves are over before some trend-following systems can take advantage of them.

Markets moving sideways or in channels up or down present unique problems. Trend-following systems are virtually useless here. Discretionary traders who pick and choose each trade tend to do better in these markets.

You can also plot the CTA's month-to-month performance, using the Value Added Monthly Index (VAMI) table from the disclosure document on a chart with a long-term commodity market index. The index used should match as closely as possible the portfolio the CTA trades. For example, if the trader deals primarily with the physical markets, use an index such as the Wasendorf Composite Index. If the portfolio is only meats, metals, or grains, use one of its subindexes. Long-range charts are ideal for the purpose. If the CTA is into all commodities, including gold, you might want to use the Commodity Research Bureau (CRB) Index.

This combination of the CTA's performance and the composite index value of the futures markets provides an important insight into how the trader handles the upsides and downsides of the market. You want to know if the performance drops substantially when there is an abrupt change of direction of the market. Or does the trading system quickly adjust? Ideally, the line representing the track record increases each month, no matter if the index is going up or down.

The Commodity Futures Trading Commission requires the VAMI to be calculated for each CTA's track record that is printed in a disclosure document. The CFTC reviews all disclosure documents prior to the time they can be offered to the public. Its review does not in any way equate to an endorsement. It examines the documents to see that its regulations are heeded—not to evaluate the chances of the offering generating a profit!

The CFTC is the investors' watchdog. It tries to root out disclosure documents that may mislead the public. This is the thinking behind the VAMI. It is required by the CFTC so an investor can easily compare one offering against another over a given period of time.

The CFTC requires the CTA to re-index the VAMI to $1,000 at the beginning of each year. Therefore, you may want to calculate your own cumulative VAMI for track records over longer periods of time.

As you evaluate past performance, always keep in mind that it is not a reliable forecaster of future performance. That's why you want to look at as long a period as possible—3 years, 5 years, or longer. The period of time should include bear and bull moves. Again, that's why you chart the VAMI against a commodity price index.

All VAMIs are calculated using the same formula, as prescribed by the CFTC. The formula is

VAMI for Period Z

Z = (1 + rate of return of period Z) × VAMI for prior period

Therefore, the VAMI for any particular period increases or decreases based on the rate of return for that period. Calculating the number can become complicated when there are a lot of monthly additions and withdrawals. If all the withdrawals take place at the beginning of the period and all the additions at the end, they can skew the rate of return to the downside. The opposite is equally true. It is hoped that over a reasonably long period of time this evens out.

THE SHARP RATIO

The Sharp ratio is another way of evaluating trading programs. It is a method of determining the rate of return of an investment, after making an allowance for risk. You do this by subtracting the current rate of return available from what is generally considered a risk-free investment, such as Treasury bills, from the average annual ROR of the investment you are considering. This quantity is used as the numerator. The denominator is found by dividing the standard deviation of the average annual ROR of the investment into the remainder of the subtraction operation.

The product of the division generates the Sharp ratio, which can be used to evaluate one investment opportunity against another. It doesn't matter if they are in the same class of investments or not. You can calculate the Sharp ratio on a monthly or annual basis, depending on the data and time available. Do this on a monthly basis and then graph the data points of the various investments being evaluated. You should be looking for a Sharp ratio that is very consistent and increasing.

STERLING RATIO

Another evaluation tool is the Sterling ratio. It is a measure of the risk-adjusted return you might expect from an investment. Define it as the return you should reap for each unit of risk you are willing to accept. The more risk you take, the more you should receive for living with that risk.

With the Sterling ratio (SR), the higher it is, the better. A ratio of 2 is theoretically twice as attractive as a ratio of 1. The formula for the Sterling ratio is

$$SR = \frac{\text{average annual return for the last 3 calendar years}}{\text{largest average cumulative losses for the last 3 calendar years} + 10\%}$$

Notice that the average annual return for the last 3 calendar years is evaluated. Divide this figure by the largest average cumulative loss for each of the last 3 calendar years plus 10 percent. This extra 10 percent is added to the average cumulative losses because quarterly and monthly returns tend to underestimate the actual maximum loss periods.

A comparison of two commodity trading advisers might look like this. The first one has an average annual return for the last 3 calendar years of 30 percent. The average cumulative loss for the 3-year period is 20 percent. The second CTA has the same return, but losses are lower, 15 percent. What are their Sterling ratios?

	CTA 1	CTA 2
Return	30%	30%
Loss	20%	15%
SR	1.00	1.20

The calculation of the SR for CTA 1 would be: 30 divided by the sum of 20 plus 10 (or 30). The SR for CTA 2 is 30 divided by the sum of 15 plus 10 (or 25). From this analysis, CTA 2 appears to be 20 percent better than CTA 1.

Look Beyond the Ratio

You must pay particular attention to drawdowns and when they occur. If analyzing two CTAs with the same returns and losses as used in our example, adviser 2 looked good. However, the CTA's track record in the disclosure document may show CTA 2 had an average loss of 15 percent per year, but it was 30 percent over a 6-month period—October, November, December, January, February, and March. The "calendar" year splits the 30 percent loss into two 15 percent losses.

Now, a couple of things usually happen when a CTA loses money for 6 months straight. First, some investors lose faith and jump ship. This, combined with the losses, reduces the CTA's equity base. The lower the equity, the harder it is for the CTA to recover (see Figure 10.1). Second, when a CTA is losing money and clients, personal confidence suffers.

Using calendar years as part of this formula seriously flaws the results, but this is not the only problem.

In another hypothetical situation, CTA 1 has an average annual return of 30 percent and a maximum average cumulative drawdown of 20 percent. CTA 2 has the same. Therefore, the Sterling ratio is the same for both, namely 1. That makes them equal—right?

Which CTA would you be most interested in if the average loss of the CTAs were as follows: CTA 1 has an even loss of 20 percent each year; CTA 2's average drawdown of 20 percent is composed of 10, 20, and 30 percent. Both average 20 percent, but CTA 2's losses are increasing each year. CTA 1's losses are fairly consistent. What if CTA 2's losses are 0, 20, and 40 percent, or 0, 0, and 60 percent? Volatility like this can mean trouble—a fact that is not reflected in the Sterling ratio.

Where Did 10 Percent Come From?

There are also problems with the arbitrary 10 percent added to the losses. If you add 10 percent to an average loss of 15 percent, you increase it by 67 percent. If you add it to an average loss of 35 percent, you only increase it 29 percent. This, of course, substantially changes the Sterling ratio.

	CTA 1	CTA 2
Return	25%	50%
Loss	15%	35%
SR	1.00	1.11

CTA 2 is more volatile and yet has a better Sterling ratio. It appears to us that the more consistent traders are penalized by the arbitrary 10 percent assessment to the loss column.

When your broker begins to brag about the Sterling ratio of the CTA, take the time to go beyond the ratio. Find out how it is put together. How stable and consistent is the CTA? That's what counts.

CTA BATTING AVERAGES

Since there are some problems with the Sterling ratio, an alternative is needed. One devised by Nick Vintila, a commodity pool operator, overcomes some of the shortcomings of the Sterling ratio. It's called the CTA batting average. Its formulas are

$$\text{Long-term batting average} = \frac{\text{compounded annual ROR}}{\text{greatest cumulative drawdown ever experienced by the CTA}}$$

$$\text{Short-term batting average} = \frac{\text{compounded ROR over the last 36 months}}{\text{greatest drawdown experienced by the CTA over the last 36 months}}$$

What Are the Differences?

There are several important differences between the CTA batting average (BA) and the Sterling ratio. To begin with, the BA utilizes a present-value–future-value calculation in the numerator rather than a simple average. In our opinion, this much more accurately reflects the ROR.

The denominators of these equations are even more important. In the SR, you use the maximum average drawdown. It is based on a calendar year. This can be very misleading if a drawdown continues over more than one calendar year, as was pointed out earlier.

With the BA, the greatest cumulative drawdown for the last 36 months, or the entire track record, is used. This may seem somewhat unforgiving, but it illustrates a worst-case scenario. If this drawdown occurred more than 36 months ago, it doesn't affect the short-term batting average. Then the long-and short-term batting averages can be compared. Has a CTA improved or regressed? Having two views is also an important feature not available with the SR.

The BA also provides a new view each month. The numbers used are rolling constantly. You don't have to wait for the end of the year to recalculate the ratios. This allows you to do two important ongoing analyses. (1) You are alerted sooner to uptrends or downtrends in performance. This gives you time to react. (2) You can evaluate your CTA's performance in given market conditions shortly after they occur. If a major bull or bear market develops, how is your CTA performing? Can the CTA trade a trendless market? By recalculating the BA on a monthly basis and charting it on an index that reflects the CTA's portfolio, you'll know. You may want to switch location of your funds between CTAs depending on the long-term trend of the market.

Note also that the BA does away with the arbitrary 10 percent added to the denominator of the Sterling ratio. This does not discriminate against conservative and consistent CTAs.

With the BA approach, a CTA with large drawdowns cannot hide them in an average. For example, let's go back to the CTA with 0, 0, and 60 percent drawdowns over a 3-year period. Using the Sterling ratio, these averaged to 20 percent. With the BA, you would use the 60 percent loss.

When evaluating CTA track records, accumulation of losses is a key concept. The more equity lost, the more difficult it is for the CTA to recover.

Another aspect about the BA approach is being able to see if the CTA's performance is affected by changes made in the trading system used or in the amount of money under management. CTAs will often tell you that they "fixed" their system. By studying performance on a rolling basis, you can substantiate these claims.

How does a CTA's trading react to a big influx of equity? Comparing the results of the BA with the additions to equity on a month-by-month basis answers that question. Performance often drops when large amounts of equity are added if the CTA's back room and/or system isn't up to the challenge.

IT PAYS TO BE A LITTLE PARANOID

This old saying in the futures business simply means there is no perfect method of determining who will outperform whom in the futures market. You must use all the tools available to you and make your own decision. And there are more ways than one to calculate the return on investment. The various approaches produce different answers. The real ROR question is often not what the return computes to, but how it was calculated. To evaluate the performance of a commodity trading adviser, take the CTA's disclosure document and calculate the following VAMI figures:

Period	VAMI Value	% Increase
End of 1988	$2,928	
End of 1989	$8,766	299.38
End of 1990	$8,882	1.32
End of 1991	$12,828	44.43

A $1,000 unit invested in this particular CTA increased in value from the inception of the fund to $2,928 at the end of 1988. The next year was a big year for the CTA, with an increase of almost 300 percent. The year 1990 turned out to be rather flat, and 1991 brought an increase of over 40 percent.

Now, how should the overall return for the 3 years in question be calculated? The simplest method is to add the returns for the 3 years together and divide by 3:

299.38% + 1.32% + 44.43% = 345.13%/3 = 115.04%

This would give us an average annual return of just over 115 percent.

Option 2 would be to first calculate the total amount of gain. You would do this by subtracting the initial amount from the ending amount, or $12,828 less $2,928. The remainder is $9,900. You would then divide this remainder by the beginning amount—$9,900 divided by $2,928. The result is 338.11 percent over the 3-year period. On a per-year basis, it is 112.70 percent, which is 338.11 percent divided by 3.

What happens if a more sophisticated technique is used? You decide to do some time-value analysis. You want to determine the compounded annual rate of return. With the present value of $2,928 and the future value of $12,828, you decide to calculate the ROR over 3 periods, representing the years. This produces a figure of 63.63 percent as the compounded annual rate of return.

If you wanted to do this same calculation on a monthly basis, you would use 36 periods, rather than 3. This would generate a monthly compounded return of 4.19 percent. To annualize the monthly return, you would multiply it by 12, resulting in a figure of 50.27 percent.

This gives us four different ROR figures, using the four formulas. Once you select a method for a specific class of investment, always use the same one. If a broker provides some RORs to you, make sure you find out which method was used to calculate them. If necessary, you may have to recalculate the figures so they are consistent with your other data.

For evaluating a CTA, method 3 may provide the best measurement. Once you have an annual compounded ROR for the CTAs you are considering, you can evaluate them against an index of other CTAS. Figures on the performance of public and private funds can be obtained from the *Managed Accounts Report* newsletter or *Futures Magazine.* This provides an insight into how an individual CTA compares with other CTAs. It is similar to evaluating the performance of your stock portfolio with the S&P 500 Index.

THE IMPACT OF ADDITIONS AND WITHDRAWALS

The annual rates of return just discussed are the composite of 12 monthly trading periods. You need to take a closer look at how these periods are put together in order to have confidence in the ROR figures you calculate.

As mentioned earlier, one of the stickiest tasks any accountant or statistician has is accounting for additions and withdrawals when calculating performance. This is because of the timing of these transactions. Let's say an account receives an additional $10,000 of equity on June 15. Should it be included for the entire month, half, or not at all? What if the addition comes in on the first or the thirtieth?

You face the same problem with withdrawals. Money coming out of an account on the first of the month may make more of an impact on that month's return than a withdrawal on the last business day of the month. The commodity trading advisers will theorize that if they had the money all month, the return would be higher.

The point is simply this: When you attempt to calculate a ROR, you divide the gain or loss by the amount of equity. Much depends on how the denominator (or amount of equity) is determined. If you assume in your calculations that the funds always come in at the beginning of the month and always leave at the end, you'll skew the ROR to the downside. The opposite is also true.

Historically, here's how the Commodity Futures Trading Commission has done it. The monthly ROR is determined by dividing the net monthly performances (gain or loss) by beginning equity. For example, let's say a commodity pool operator has a fund of $1 million. Three CTAs are given $300,000 each, and $100,000 is held back in reserve. The CTAs use the $300,000 as their beginning equity for the first month.

If CTA 1 generates $18,000 in profits the first month, the ROR would be $18,000 divided by $300,000, or 6 percent. This changes his beginning equity for the second month to $318,000. If $5,000 is gained for the second month, the ROR would be 1.6 percent ($5,000/$318,000).

Losses are calculated the same way. Let's say in the third month the CTA takes a $6,000 loss. The beginning equity for the month is now $323,000, which is divided into the loss of $6,000. Therefore, the monthly ROR is a negative 1.8 percent.

This method works well, especially for small accounts that have very few additions or withdrawals. But once you get into a situation where there are a lot of large movements of money in and out, these ROR figures can become less meaningful. They can become very distorted, especially when the changes in total equity exceed 15 to 20 percent in a given month.

The entire process can become even more distorted when you're evaluating composite performances. This could be the track record of all the accounts traded by one CTA or the composite trading records of several CTAs advising a single fund. The reason is simply the large number of additions and withdrawals that it would probably include in multiple and long-term track records. To overcome this problem, the CFTC now requires additions and withdrawals to be time-weighted over the period of time the CTA has access to the funds.

AN ALTERNATIVE METHOD

With Nick Vintila's alternative method, you would base your monthly performance calculations on a $1,000 unit. If you opened a $60,000 managed account, you would have 60 units of $1,000.

Therefore, if your account was worth $64,000 at the end of the first month, barring any additions or withdrawals, each unit would be worth $1,066.66. This is an increase of 6.66 percent for the month. A loss is determined the same way, always calculated on a per-unit basis.

What about withdrawals? Let's say you needed to withdraw $16,000 after month 1. You would divide that amount by the unit value to figure how many units you were withdrawing. It would be $16,000 divided by $1,066.66, or 15 units. You now have 45 units with the same value of $1,066.66 each, or $48,000, which is $64,000 less the $16,000.

In the next month, you make $3,000. You add this to the beginning value of $48,000 and divide by the 45 remaining units ($51,000/45) for a unit value of $1,133. Next, you subtract the original $1,000 and divide by 1,000 to convert to a percentage. The return is therefore 13.33 percent for this month.

The most important consideration is that you deal only with funds in your account. This provides more validity and makes it easier to compare one CTA with another.

A MILKING STOOL

Solid investment programs are built like old-fashioned milking stools. The three legs are rate of return, risk control as measured by volatility, and consistency of performance.

Having considered the first two, what about the third? Why care about consistency? Can't a high enough ROR overcome all other obstacles to success? Actually, a high rate of return often covers up the true picture. You need to analyze the ROR figure to determine when the gains were generated.

Consider two CTAs who have posted RORs of 300 percent over a 3-year period of time. CTA 1 had an ROR of 100 percent each year, while the second CTA gained 300 percent in one of the years and broke even the other two.

Now, if you just happened to be investing with CTA 2 during this "hot" 12-month period, you'd be extremely happy—an ROR of 300 percent! However, what if your timing wasn't so perfect? Would you rather have had your money with CTA 1 for any 12 months during the 36-month period? It almost comes down to choosing between trying to be very lucky or learning how to discover advisers who produce consistent returns.

TIME-INTERVAL ANALYSIS

Another statistical technique, suggested by Nick Vintila, is called *time-interval analysis* (TIA). A CTA's track record is broken down into time intervals of 3-, 6-, 9-, 12-, 18-, and 24-month periods. TIA takes the position that calendar years are not any more important than any other 12-month periods. If you open an account in March and by the following April it's losing money, it's not any consolation that the CTA performed well from January to December. TIA gives you a higher number of observations at which to look compared with having only calendar performance statistics.

Therefore, you quickly team two things: the CTA's volatility and consistency. If you run TIA over 3-, 6-, 9-, 12-, 18-, and 24-month periods, it tells you immediately if the CTA has been more consistent when given 12 months, instead of 1 or 3 months to trade.

If a CTA has a 12-month ask record, you could calculate ten 3-month time intervals, seven 6-month time intervals four 9-month time intervals, and one 12-month time interval (see Figure 10.2).

Each time interval is determined by rolling one month forward and dropping the last month, similar to moving averages. The ROR is calculated based on the VAMI. Next, you take the results of the various time intervals and create bar charts. The midpoint of the charts is zero ROR. All intervals with positive RORs are charted above the midline and all negative intervals below. This technique provides a very graphic picture regarding a CTA's consistency.

Pay particular attention to the 12-, 18-, or 24-month interval futures. You're trying to find out how consistent the ROR is over long periods of time. The hope is that this period of time would include both bull and bear market moves, plus periods where the market moves sideways or is choppy.

Ideally, the ROR will be consistent no matter what the market

FIGURE 10.2

Time-Interval Analysis over 12 Months

Time Intervals	3 Months	6 Months	9 Months	12 Months
1				
2				
3	1			
4	2			
5	3			
6	4	1		
7	5	2		
8	6	3		
9	7	4	1	
10	8	5	2	
11	9	6	3	
12	10	7	4	1

is doing. By doing this analysis, you'll find out exactly when the money was made and over what period of time, i.e., at the beginning of the CTA's career or consistently throughout the CTA's entire career. You'll easily be able to see if you need to be lucky and guess when to invest or whether you can invest anytime because the performance is consistent.

"GIVE ME ANOTHER 3 MONTHS . . ."

When you have money in a managed account or a fund and you're unhappy with the current performance, you may be trying to decide when and if to cash out your investment. At that time, your broker or CTA may ask for another few months to get things going. If this happens to you, you can easily compare the 1-month, 3-month, or 6-month time intervals and immediately see what you can expect. Does this CTA perform well over the short term? If you calculate the percentage of profitability over the different time intervals, you will know if it makes any sense to put off your decision to liquidate.

WHAT THE TERM "DUE DILIGENCE" MEANS

In a legal sense, it means undertaking a study of a person or an entity to uncover as much background as possible. The word *diligence* carries the connotation of perseverance and determination—an un-wavering drive to uncover the essence of the subject being studied.

When preparing a "due diligence report" on CTAs, learn as much as possible about these traders, their systems, and their performances. A study of this sort is done to make sure their track records can be relied upon as an accurate representation of their trading. Additionally, a due diligence study provides valuable insights into how certain CTAs will help reach investment goals. Also learn if they are compatible with you. Can their staff (back room) respond to the challenge of trading more funds?

One of the best places to start is the disclosure document. This instrument should contain all the information that is pertinent to investors who are considering investing in a particular CTA or a fund. For a fund or limited partnership, the document is called a prospectus. In addition to information about the futures traders, the document also includes the risk disclosure statements required by the Commodity Futures Trading Commission. It also includes background on other entities—such as the organizer (commodity pool operator) and clearing firm (futures commission merchant)—that will play a major role in the investment.

Your goal in examining the disclosure documents is to read between the lines and to validate all salient points. Keep in mind that the offering documents are written by attorneys who are paid to interpret the facts of any case or argument in light of their clients' best interests.

The unfortunate part of this situation is that these documents have grown longer and more complicated each year. The investing public would be better served if the CFTC stressed simplicity and understandability, as well as risk disclosure, in these documents.

Prior to being made available to prospective investors, these offering documents are sent to the CFTC for review. The CFTC reserves 21 days to make comments and order required changes. If the promoter of the offering doesn't hear from the CFTC within this time period, it can begin the selling process. Depending on the specific type and size of the offering, this process may include reviews by the secretaries of state of the various states in which it is to be sold. Many of these investments are considered a security during the selling process. Therefore, they are under the jurisdiction of the Security and Exchange Commission or each state's secretary of state at this stage. Once they begin trading futures, the jurisdiction is passed to the CFTC and the National Futures Association.

The CFTC and state and federal regulatory bodies can still require changes or additions to these documents even if the 21-day review period by the CFTC has expired and the offering document has been printed. Therefore, from time to time, you may find additions or changes pasted or bound into an offering document.

WHAT TO LOOK FOR

There are various levels of due diligence investigations. Take the examination of a CTA's track record as an illustration. Professional due diligence studies might use accountants to test the CTA's track record, just as you would test a company's accounting records. They would randomly select specific periods of trading for review. The CTAs would be asked to produce the order tickets (the NFA requires members to retain each order ticket for 5 years) covering the period. These would be checked against records of the range the market traded on that day to make sure the trade was possible. The accountants would track the trade until it was closed, calculating the profit or loss for all trades for the period. This would then be compared with what was presented in the performance tables.

The analysis of the rate of return and how it was calculated is another example of a less intensive, but equally important, level of investigation.

To help this due diligence process, there is so much more in the offering document than the track records. It is possible to review the backgrounds of all the principals: CPO, general partner(s), advisers, clearing firms, etc. Do they have enough experience to satisfy you?

As you study the offering document, write down your questions. Don't hesitate to call or write the administrators of the investments (their addresses and phone numbers are in the front of the documents) with your questions.

Another important area covers the conflicts of interest. Are they acceptable? For example, if the advisers receive per-trade commissions, as well as management and/or incentive fees, will they have the tendency to overtrade?

The fees involved critically affect performance. Think of them as drawdowns of equity. It is money paid out of the trading equity and can no longer be used to generate profits. If the fees are unreasonable, they drain the equity. Reasonable fees are needed to compensate all those involved for the work and risk assumed in bringing the investment to market.

Do your homework before you invest. Most investments that sound too good to be true are! You are the only one who can make the decision to invest. Take care that you have looked over the entire offering very carefully.

DIVERSIFYING CTA TRADING SYSTEMS

When you or the investment vehicle you are considering uses more than one CTA, consider the concept of using CTAs that have diversified trading systems. Just as the prudent trader has a diversified portfolio, the prudent investor does not invest in CTAs that use similar trading systems.

The reason is simple. If all the CTAs in a fund are trend followers and the trend takes an abrupt change of direction, they all get caught in the move. If one CTA is a trend follower and the second a contrarian, the trend change just described may not impact the investment as severely.

There are several other ways of looking at diversification with regard to CTAs managing futures trading accounts. Futures portfolios should normally be diversified in accordance with the markets in which they are traded. The risk involved in trading all of one's equity in one or two markets is great.

The second test for diversification among multiple CTAs sharing management responsibilities for a managed account program is negative correlation, discussed earlier in this chapter. Analysis of the long-term trading results of the different CTAs would need to indicate they do not incur drawdowns at the same time. This gives the program balance.

Your objective in creating diversity in a group of CTAs is to understand how their systems trade the market.

CTA SELECTION SUMMARY

In review, the steps you should take when you select a trading adviser are:

Step 1

Locate a group of CTAs that interest you. Since futures trading is very speculative and involves such a high degree of risk, you naturally expect a high return for assuming the risk. Therefore, the first number to look for is the rate of return.

There are several methods of calculating ROR. Using the compound annual ROR method is preferable. This was the formula that utilized the present value and the future value to determine the ROR over the length of the track record in years.

Avoid or at least be very wary of track records that are shorter than 3 years or are hypothetical. Simulated or hypothetical performance tables are often generated to test trading systems developed through "paper trading." These track records have certain limitations, such as eliminating the human emotional factor that comes into play when a trader is actually risking personal or client money. Any offering memorandum, such as a prospectus or disclosure document, reviewed by the CFTC requires hypothetical performance records to be clearly stated as such and to carry a special disclosure statement.

Step 2

High ROR is not the most important factor to consider when selecting CTAs. A stable and consistent performance record is more important than an occasional astronomical ROR figure. Be much more comfortable with a trader who produces a 40 percent or 60 percent return year in and year out than with one who produces a 100 percent or 200 percent return one time with equally high drawdowns.

Remember the loss-recover table in Figure 10.1. To recover from a 70 percent loss, the CTA needs a 233.33 percent gain or a 900 percent gain to recoup a 90 percent loss. Whenever the equity is seriously depleted, chances of success geometrically decline.

Review the pros and cons of various methods of evaluation—ROR, VAMI, Sharp ratio, Sterling ratio, CTA batting average, and time-interval analysis. The batting average usually is the best.

Step 3

Once you isolate CTAs that have acceptable trading records and whose performance is stable and consistent, you can move on to the more time-consuming analysis. Start with the analysis of the numbers because it is the easiest information to obtain. You'll find it in each CTA's printed disclosure document distributed to prospective clients. Check the date on the cover to make certain you are dealing with current numbers. The CFTC requires the CTA to update the disclosure document every 6 months.

This step involves due diligence—learning as much as possible about the integrity, trading acumen, and operations of the CTAs under review. You'll want to check with the National Futures Association Information Center (800-621-3570) to see if it has ever disciplined the CTAs. Request client and professional references from the CTA.

Study the CTA's trading system. If it is a trend-following system, how well does it adjust to trend changes? What impact has it had on the ROR?

By telephone or in person, interview the CTA and/or commodity pool operator in the case of a fund, limited partnership, or pool. What kind of people will you be dealing with? Will they be responsive to any questions you may have?

Also, take a look at the CTA's back room, if possible. The back room is where the paperwork for the trading takes place. Are the orders handled efficiently? Is the operation well staffed and equipped? What quote equipment is being used? If you're investing in a fund that will give a CTA another $500,000 or $1 million to trade, can the increase in volume be handled without problem? How has volume increases affected ROR in the past?

Are fees in line with industry standards? Keep the loss-recovery table (Figure 10.1) in the back of your mind. Money paid out as management fees is not any more available to trade than equity loss trading. Exorbitant fees can cripple traders as fast as a large drawdown.

Step 4

You are now down to a short list of CTAs that have passed all your tests. As always with futures trading, diversify. Select more than one CTA or invest in a fund that uses more than one. Match your CTAs so they are negatively correlated.

Step 5

Develop an ongoing monitoring procedure. One of the best is time-interval analysis. Keep your eye on the target of increasing your equity.

All of the above is the minimum you should do when selecting a professionally managed futures trading program, but it is not a foolproof way of making money. Even the best CTAs experience drawdowns. You may well have your money with them when they do. You have heard it before—*only invest what you can afford to lose.* The high rewards associated with futures trading are matched with the high losses that can also be sustained.

Knowing Your Rights and Recourse as an Investor in the Futures Markets

Key Concepts

♦ Investing Advantages in a Federally Regulated Industry
♦ Knowing the CFTC and NFA Regulations for Protection against Swindlers
♦ Sorting the Ethical from the Unethical Commodity Broker
♦ Asking 15 Key Questions Before You Invest
♦ Communicating with Your Broker
♦ Recognizing Three Cardinal Sins Committed by Brokers

If you understand your rights before you become a participant in the futures market, you'll have a far better chance of being successful than if you plunge into it without fully understanding the risks. Over the years, most individual traders have been net losers, but the opportunity to make a 200 percent or 300 percent or more return on one's money in a few months, weeks, or even days brings a steady flow of investors to the pits.

If you do lose, whose fault is it? Should you accept the blame no matter what? Or is your broker, the IB, the clearing firm, or the exchange completely or partially responsible? If so, what can you do about it? How can you evaluate what you are being told? How can you protect yourself against swindlers? What action can you take if you ever feel you have been cheated or mistreated? What are your rights in relationship to the FCM and the exchanges?

CHECK WITH THE NFA WHEN IN DOUBT

The first point to remember when you consider futures and/or options on futures (also known as *exchange-traded options,* as opposed to some metal options that involve the cash metals market that are unregulated) is that the futures market is regulated by the National Futures Association. It is an industry-supported organization authorized by Congress via the Commodity Futures Trading Commission.

No person or firm can engage in any business involving the buying or selling of futures contracts for the public without becoming an NFA member or associate member. In other words, to conduct any futures business you must be an NFA member, and members can only do business with other members. An exception is the associated person (AP), who deals with the customer. APs are commonly known as commodity brokers.

Most APs work for introducing brokers. The IB introduces the person or firm that wishes to trade to the futures commission merchant. The FCM is the entity that enters orders into the market through floor traders. The floor traders are the ones that do the actual trading in the pits of the exchanges.

The FCM is also responsible for the back-room operation. This operation deals with the accounting involved in maintaining the trading account of each person or entity that is trading. Each exchange has a clearing operation to balance each day's trading.

If you are approached by anyone regarding an investment in the futures market, that person must be a member or an associate member of the NFA. To check a person's standing, i.e., a salesperson (broker) or firm (IB) that sent you a letter about opening an account, all you need to do is make a toll-free call to the NFA (1-800-621-3570, or 1-800-572-9400 from Illinois) and ask.

If the person or firm is not registered with the NFA, tell the NFA's representative exactly what was sent or offered to you, and the NFA will investigate. Don't do any business with a salesperson or firm until you clear up, to your satisfaction, this point. The type of investment being promoted may sound like it should be part of the futures industry, but if it isn't, it doesn't require NFA registration. If the product is not federally regulated, you will more than likely have difficulty getting satisfaction if something goes wrong.

If the person or firm soliciting you is registered with the NFA, you know that person or firm must adhere to all NFA and CFTC rules and regulations. By reviewing the guidelines the NFA has set down for promotional material, you'll know if the firm that is soliciting your business is in compliance. If its advertising clearly violates these dictates, you should consider yourself forewarned. Also, if you ever have problems with the firm, you can use its disregard of NFA rules in your formal complaint. The specific NFA rule governing promotion is Rule 2-29. Its broad definition of promotional material includes the following:

"1. Any text of a standardized oral presentation, such as a sales script, or any communication for publication in any newspaper, magazine, or similar medium, or any broadcast over television, radio, or other electronic medium, which is disseminated or directed to the public concerning a futures account, agreement, or transaction

2. Any standardized form of report, letter, circular, memorandum, or publication, such as a newsletter, which is disseminated or directed to the public

3. Any other written material disseminated or directed to the public for the purpose of soliciting a futures account, agreement, or transaction, such as a seminar or class."

In general, you can consider just about all communications with you, the public, as promotional activities or promotional material.

NFA PROHIBITIONS ON PUBLIC COMMUNICATIONS

The NFA has three general prohibitions that apply to all communications with the public. They are (1) fraudulent or deceitful communications, (2) high-pressure communications, and (3) the statement that futures trading is appropriate for everyone.

Rule 2-29 requires anyone selling futures trading to provide a balanced discussion of the profit potential and the risk of loss. Whenever the possibility of profit is mentioned, an equally prominent statement of the risk of loss must accompany it.

To make this determination, the NFA analyzes the overall impact of the promotional material. The NFA takes into consideration the number of times each word is used, the size of the type, and the amount of time or space devoted to each. But these are not the only considerations.

Remember that the mention of profit can take many forms and is not limited to the word *profit*. Charts and graphs showing the growth of an account, for example, are considered statements about profits.

There are two separate cautionary statements that are required to be disclosed if actual results or hypothetical results are used in the promotional material. These are separate and distinct requirements.

The question of balance is particularly important in video and other oral presentations. For example, a 60-second commercial with only 5 seconds discussing loss or superimposing a disclaimer at the bottom of the screen is not acceptable to the NFA.

This holds true for telephone sales as well. The AP can't talk about profits for 10 minutes and then say, "Past performance is not indicative of future results," and let it go at that. That AP would be in clear violation of Rule 2-29.

High-pressure sales tactics are a serious breach of the NFA's customer protection program. The NFA considers the following as the principal characteristics of high-pressure selling:

1. Exaggerating profit potential
2. Exaggerating past results
3. Exaggerating the qualifications of an AP
4. Exaggerating the need for urgency in making the investment decision
5. Constantly badgering the prospect
6. Belittling the prospect for not investing
7. Emphasizing profits that have been missed
8. Using courier services to deliver and pick up account papers
9. Downplaying the importance of the paperwork as mere regulatory red tape
10. Providing poor service to the customer after the sale

"Hypothetical results" are records of the results of trading that actually did not take place. They were constructed from computer simulations or some other mechanical method. When presented with a trading track record of a broker, CTA, or system, the first thing to do is to check to see if the results are labeled as hypothetical. It must be done in a manner that any reader would be able to immediately and clearly understand.

NFA Rule 2-29(b)(4) requires any hypothetical results (including graphs) to be accompanied by a cautionary statement from CFTC Regulation 4.41(b)(1), which describes the limitation of hypothetical results.

> Hypothetical or simulated performance results have certain inherent limitations. Unlike an actual performance record, simulated results do not represent actual trading. Also, since the trades have not actually been executed, the results may have under- or over-compensated for the impact, if any, of certain market factors, such as lack of liquidity. Simulated trading programs in general are also subject to the fact that they are designed with the benefit of hindsight. No representation is being made that any account will or is likely to achieve profits or losses similar to those shown.

The creator of the track record must be able to demonstrate to the NFA the basis for the hypothetical results and keep records to prove how the record was calculated. Real and hypothetical results should never be mixed on the same track record. The NFA believes this is confusing and misleading.

Are the rules any easier if actual, rather than hypothetical, results are used? The person promoting the track record must be able to prove the results using actual account statements. The accounts selected must be representative of all the accounts the person controls. The CTA can't just show you the best account. The NFA will check equity runs and do all the detail work needed to compare the accounts used with all other accounts, if and when it audits the CTA.

If different types and sizes of accounts are traded, using a representative account becomes more difficult because the NFA will want an explanation of the selection and how it compares with a "typical" account. Some of the differences taken into consideration are size, margin rates, trading strategies, markets, and commissions.

Also, beware of advertising that uses a lot of high-powered adjectives, such as *largest* or *best* or *fastest*. If superlatives are used, the user may have problems with the NFA. The NFA's position is that such claims may be regularly used in other industries, but they cannot be used by NFA members without detailed substantiation.

In the eyes of the NFA, the use of qualifiers, such as "one of the fastest" or "one of the largest," does little to alter the need to document the claim. Whatever is said in sales and advertising must be proved if questioned by the NFA.

When it comes to promoting exchange-traded options; there are additional considerations. The NFA takes exception to the use of the term *limited risk* when referring to options. The broker must make it clear that the risk is limited to the entire amount of the premium plus transaction costs. The term *transaction costs* means the commission and fees; and the term *fees* means NFA, exchange, and FCM fees.

If a broker is promoting a third-party controller (a CTA), some promotional material prepared by the CTA may be used. This does not reduce the broker's accountability in any way.

The NFA looks at the responsibility to police the industry as a two-way road. In other words, if a broker is promoting a CTA and the sales literature is misleading, the broker will be held responsible along with the CTA if the NFA gets involved in a complaint. Every party that prepares or uses promotional materials is responsible for compliance with NFA Rule 2-29, including the supervisory organization.

Live TV or radio interviews done by APs or CTAs do not fall within the strict definition of promotional material, but the registered person doing the interview is always subject to the three general prohibitions: fraud, high pressure, and inappropriateness of futures trading for all investors. In addition, if the show is paid for by the NFA member and this fact is not disclosed, the NFA will call it fraud. The NFA strongly discourages shows that "pretend" to be news.

The newsletter *Commodity Traders Consumer Reports* and other independent sources that rate CTAs are often used as promotional materials. The person using the material still has a lot of responsibility and must be sure that the report is accurate and that proper disclosure is made regarding the limitations of the results and rating.

This means that rates of return must be calculated in a manner consistent with CFTC regulations [Rule 4.21(a)(4)(ii)(F)]. The user must be able to show to the NFA that the calculations comply with the rules. Lastly, all the information available to support any numerical data must be available to the NFA if it requests it.

The overall position of the NFA is very clear. From time to time, interpretation of borderline cases can cause consternation between broker and customer. By and large, however, there is little room for confusion with the NFA.

If you are solicited by a broker who is using some type of advertising that delivers an unbalanced presentation of the enormous profits to be made from the futures market with little or no mention of risk, this should send up at least two red flags: The material is in violation of NFA Rule 2-29, and you should beware of whoever is presenting the materials. If this initial overture is so out of tune, the rest of the song will probably be as well. The next refrain will be a high-pressure sales presentation most likely.

Advertising that is balanced and informative can be very helpful to you in deciding if you are suited for futures trading and if you want to learn more. As you absorb these types of messages, you'll learn how much risk you'll be accepting and have a more complete picture of profit opportunity.

INVESTING IS SERIOUS BUSINESS

Once attention is aroused, most buyers begin the next stage of the sales process, the search for more information. Investing is serious business. Therefore, as interest in a product or service grows, you will want to learn as much as you can about it.

At this stage, you often see a big difference between the ethical broker and one who plays fast and loose. The former will spend time with you, send you information, such as newsletters, and be sincerely interested in learning about your investment needs. The wheeler-dealer's objective is to raise a prospect's greed level to such a fever pitch that money is sent immediately. This is high-pressure sales. There's no time for thought and reflection. You'll hear lines like this:

- "An opportunity this good only comes by once in a blue moon!"
- "If you don't get $2,000 to me by noon tomorrow, you'll miss your chance to turn it into $10,000 in the next two weeks!"
- "Gold is going sky-high tomorrow!"

From ethical brokers, you'll hear descriptions of opportunities won and opportunities lost. The legitimate AP will tell you that sooner or later another good, solid trading opportunity will appear. You'll also be provided with a balanced presentation of the risk, something you won't hear from "deal peddlers." A futures trade that sounds too good to be true probably is, as the saying goes.

In its booklet *Before You Say Yes,* the NFA lists 15 questions that can help you distinguish qualified investment salespeople from swindlers. The following is a paraphrased version of those questions:

1. What is the commission rate? Other costs?
2. What are the risks?
3. Can you send me a written explanation of the risk involved?
4. Can you send me copies of your sales literature?
5. Are you selling futures contracts sold on the regulated exchanges?
6. Which governmental or industry regulator supervises your firm?
7. Specifically, where would my money be held?
8. When and where can we meet in person?
9. How and when can I liquidate my investment if I so desire?
10. Will you send me your entire proposal in the mail?
11. If a dispute arises, what are the means available to resolve it?
12. Where did you get my name?
13. Would you mind explaining your proposal to my lawyer?
14. Would you give me the names of your principals and officers?
15. Can you provide references?

Experience has shown that the dishonest salespeople usually resist or are not prepared for this type of interrogation. Their "marks" are impulsive buyers who make entirely emotional decisions. The answers you get are vague and evasive. For example,

QUESTION: How much are commissions?

RESPONSE: They're never a problem.

QUESTION: If I have a complaint, what can I do?

RESPONSE: Don't even worry about that. I'll take care of you personally.

By gathering a lot of information and taking some time making your decision, you can protect yourself from the majority of swindlers, but not all. The clever ones mimic legitimate sales operations, but their tactics can be uncovered if you do your homework and control your emotions.

The next step of the typical sales process is the evaluation of alternatives. Only the most experienced investors take the time to do this. Most people, if they decide to trade, go with the person or company in pursuit of them. Be selective. You need someone who will provide synergism to your trading effort and who will help you overcome your limitations. Use due diligence. As far as checking on a specific broker, call the NFA on its toll-free number. Explain that you want to check the status of an AP and ask the following questions:

1. Is the broker currently registered?
2. With which firm?
3. How long has the broker been registered?
4. Has the NFA taken any public disciplinary action against the broker?
5. Has the broker been registered with any firm that has been cited for compliance problems?
6. Is there anything else you can tell me about the broker I'm considering?

This toll-free call takes about 5 minutes and tells you if the AP in question has ever had problems with the NFA. You'll also get some facts about the broker's experience which you can compare with what you've been told.

You can also check the website of the Commodity Futures Trading Commission to see if a broker is under administrative sanctions. The telephone number is 202-418-5508. The address of the website page is www.cftc.gov/proc/admsanclst.htm.

Another source to check is the *NFA Manual*. It includes a section, which is well cross-referenced by broker name, detailing the disciplinary hearings conducted by the NFA. It is published by Prentice-Hall Information Services (800-562-0245). Your public library may have it or might order it for you. It costs about $78 per year and is updated periodically throughout the year.

Once you make your broker choice, you formally make your selection by completing the account papers. Your broker should ask you to read them carefully and fill them out in your own handwriting. The reason for you to do it in your own hand is so the broker is assured that you saw them and had the opportunity to read them. The broker will ask you if you understand them and have any questions. Remember, even account papers should describe the risks you are assuming.

If the broker offers to fill them out for you ("I'll just get them typed up for you"), consider this a warning signal. The easier the broker makes it for you to fill out the account papers, the less likely you are to study them. They are worth the time and effort it takes to understand what you are signing because they define the risk you face in great detail.

The last phase of the sales process is called the *postpurchase period*. What happens after your account is opened and funded?

Most accounts begin trading at this point. To place a trade, you call your broker or your broker calls you. The broker has your order relayed to the order desk of the proper exchange, which passes it on to the pits. Once filled, it moves back through the chain, culminating with your broker calling you with your "fill."

A written confirmation is mailed to you the next day from the FCM's back office. On a monthly basis, you receive a summary report of your trading.

At this stage of your relationship with your broker, what should you be protecting yourself against? The first thing is simple, clerical errors on the part of the back room (accounting) of the FCM. Many rifts occur because customers paid no attention to these documents. The broker has very little or nothing to do with the preparation of trade confirmations or monthly statements. They are generated at the headquarters of the FCM, and depending on its policy, the FCM may or may not send a copy to the broker. Carefully examine all paperwork at the time you receive it. Verify that:

1. The commissions charged to your account are those to which you and your broker agreed.
2. The fill price is the same as the one your broker gave you.
3. Any money you deposited in your account has been properly credited.
4. The trade you made is the same as the one on the statement, particularly that you are on the side (long or short) that you want to be.
5. The mathematics is correct, and all debits and credits have been properly applied.

The broker does get a preliminary run of all the trades made each day. It is the broker's responsibility to check it and to make the FCM aware of any discrepancies. The corrections may or may not get made before the trade confirmation is mailed to you. If a correction was not made before the confirmation was mailed, the correction is mailed separately, which you would receive the following day. In these cases, your broker would normally alert you, but you must double-check to see the error is corrected. If it doesn't get corrected, contact your broker to see that the correction is made.

COMMUNICATIONS ARE THE KEY

The glue that holds the customer-broker relationship together is good communication. The most professional brokers set up guidelines early on so you are aware of what to expect and what is expected from you. They want to know:

1. Time of day you are most easily accessible.
2. Whether you are to call in or whether your broker will call you.
3. What steps will be taken if you can't be contacted (e.g., should your broker put stops in the market, close out positions after 4, 8, 12, or 24 hours of not being in contact, etc.).
4. What steps will be taken if the account goes into debit? (Do you plan to wire money into the account? Transfer from another account? Overnight a check?)
5. How trading emergencies will be handled.

6. What hours you are available and whom to contact when you are not available.

7. Normal office hours and any evening hours your broker is available.

8. Your home phone number, if that's the only way to stay in touch with you.

9. A contact person who can reach you quickly if you are not always near a phone.

10. Provisions for unusual situations, such as when you are traveling or taking a vacation.

Don't get out of touch with your broker no matter what. If a situation arises where you are not going to be available, either put stops in the market or close out the positions or even the account. Do not risk trading when you cannot be reached. If your broker doesn't mention this, be sure you do.

THE THREE CARDINAL SINS

Three very serious offenses sometimes committed by brokers are misrepresentation, unauthorized trading, and churning.

Misrepresentation usually revolves around the broker not telling the prospective client enough about the risk of futures trading. As mentioned earlier, the NFA is very stringent about this, but it can happen anyway. One day a customer opens the mail to find a $2,000, or $5,000, or $10,000 margin call. The broker had told the customer this would never happen because stop-loss orders were to be used religiously. Unfortunately, the futures market being traded made limit moves against the client's position for a day or two and no trading took place. As a result, the stop orders could not be activated. When the smoke cleared, the customer was seriously in debt. The customer had not been warned about the possibility of limit moves.

Another common misrepresentation is representing a hypothetical track record of a trading system or showing a track record without noting that commissions have not been deducted. When they are, the track record is negative or substantially less attractive.

Unauthorized trading occurs when a broker places trades for a customer's account without the customer's authority, knowledge, or consent. Usually, this is a breakdown of communications. The broker makes assumptions about what the client wants to do, or "thinks" it was discussed and approval implied. Worse yet, the broker deliberately placed trades without talking to the customer, solely to generate commissions. For these reasons, you must carefully review the trade confirmation and monthly statements. Do you remember discussing and approving each trade?

The professional broker guards against this eventuality by tape recording all orders placed by customers. Some firms have tape equipment that records every conversation. The order desks of the exchanges record all conversations. Check with your broker in the beginning to learn if taping equipment is used. When there is a question, ask your broker to play back the conversation. You may also want to tape your conversations with your broker. If you do, be sure to inform the broker you are doing so.

Churning or overtrading an account is another serious violation by brokers. This is measured by calculating the commission-to-equity ratio over a specific period of time, usually a month. If $1,000 in commissions is generated in an account with $10,000 in equity during a particular month, the commission-to-equity ratio would be 1:10, or 10 percent. How high is too high? When has your broker violated NFA rules?

First, if you are calling all the trades, there are no grounds for complaints. You can trade as much as you want as long as you maintain the proper level of equity. If, on the other hand, you have turned over trading discretion in your account to your broker by signing a limited power of attorney, your broker's supervisor, the FCM, and the NFA should be checking the trade volume. There is no set ratio figure that automatically triggers a churning violation, but once the monthly commission-to-equity ratio gets into the 15 to 25 percent range, regulators and supervisors take notice. They may require an explanation of why the ratio is so high.

Sometimes there are legitimate reasons for the high ratio. You may have agreed to have your broker trade a certain day trading system. These are very short-term positions that are opened and closed during the same trading session. No positions are carried overnight. Day trading systems, because they are so short term, often generate a lot of commissions. If they are making money, customers like them because the customers do not assume the risk of holding a position overnight.

However, if there are no obvious explanations and the broker is churning an account just to bolster personal income, regulators can step in and take disciplinary action. The customer can file a complaint as well in hopes of recovering commissions and equity.

ONLINE BROKERS

Futures trading online only heightens all trading concerns. There are no instructor-brokers to direct you and keep you out of trouble. The ride may be exhilarating, but it is fraught with peril.

In preparation, you need to question the prospective broker about how the firm's system works. Is it fast enough to give you fills during fast markets? Or will it overload and leave you out in the cold? How quickly are trades confirmed? What are the commission fees for online? Will trading online save you money? This is only the beginning of what you need to know. Many of the more established brokerage firms offer online trading now, but as one analyst has said, "It's a brand-new paradigm."

MANAGING YOUR COMPLAINT

Futures trading is a very complex and fast-moving investment. Thousands of things can go wrong. Most are accidental, but a few may be intentional. There are procedures to deal with them all.

Naturally, the simple complaints involving obvious errors on statements can be resolved with a call to your broker. What do you do though if you feel you have suffered some serious loss or damage at the hands of your broker? What recourse do you have? The possible eventuality of this ever occurring is one of the strongest arguments for only investing in federally regulated investments, such as futures. With these types of investment vehicles, a wide array of options are open to you.

The first step, as always, is discussing the problem with the broker and the broker's supervisor. If you get no satisfaction, you can turn to the regulators for help.

The first level in the futures industry is the NFA. Call the NFA on its toll-free number 800-621-3570, or 800-572-9400 if you live in Illinois. Explain your situation and the NFA will outline your options. One of the questions it will ask is whether you signed the Pre-Dispute Arbitration Agreement, included in your account papers.

You were not required to sign it, but if you did, it binds you and your broker to accepting arbitration of disputes by the NFA. This can be to your advantage, particularly if you are a small investor, because it reduces the expense and time of litigation. You won't have to hire an attorney and you can request nonindustry arbitrators on your panel. You'll get a square deal, particularly if you are in the right. The only negative aspect is that you may be waiving further rights to sue in a court of law. If you didn't sign the Pre-Dispute Arbitration Agreement, you can still turn to the NFA for help and take advantage of its arbitration facility.

You can also file a complaint with the CFTC. If you are considering this approach, contact the CFTC for a copy of its free booklet *Questions & Answers about How You Can Resolve a Commodity Market-Related Dispute*. The CFTC has basically three reparation procedures: voluntary, summary and formal.

The voluntary procedure is used for claims under $10,000, and CFTC-appointed judgment officers administer it. Both parties have an opportunity to uncover facts ("discovery") and present their arguments in writing. There is no oral hearing. Decisions are final, and no appeal is permitted. A nonrefundable $25 fee is required.

The summary procedure is similar to the voluntary one, but it allows for both a limited oral presentation and a written presentation and takes place in Washington, D.C. Further, you can appeal the decision beyond the CFTC to a court of law if you are still not satisfied. The CFTC handles complaints of $10,000 or less and requires a $50 nonrefundable filing fee.

The formal procedure is designed to handle major complaints, over $10,000. A courtlike hearing is conducted in one of twenty locations throughout the United States before an administrative judge. An attorney can represent you if you wish. Appeals to the CFTC and the courts are possible. A $200 nonrefundable fee is required to file.

Besides the NFA and the CFTC, you can take a complaint to the American Arbitration Association, or you can file a civil suit. In addition, if you think your broker or firm has committed a criminal offense, you can contact the Federal Bureau of Investigation. If the U.S. mail was involved, contact the Chief Postal Inspector of the United States Postal Service. If you invested in a limited partnership or a fund, you may be able to appeal to your local state attorney general or the federal Security and Exchange Commission. Other places with which you may check are the Better Business Bureau and the Federal Trade Commission.

For help deciding your most effective alternative, you should probably sit down and discuss choices with your attorney. It is hoped that you will not get to this stage if you have kept in mind two very critical considerations: Your most effective protection results from systematically conducting due diligence research when selecting a broker. Act rationally. Don't get caught up in an emotional response to the potential the futures markets may offer. Stick to investments that are federally regulated. This gives you a better dispute resolution process than unregulated investments.

The most beneficial arbitration is usually done between brokers and clients. Once it goes beyond this stage, the costs and complications seem to outweigh the results. Work hard at this level to keep the lines of communication open. Efforts in this area pay dividends in better trading, fewer errors, and more enjoyable trading.

INDEX

Page references in *italics* indicate additional display material

Russell R. Wasendorf, Sr., is chairman and chief executive officer of Peregrine Financial Group, Inc., a futures commission merchant in Chicago. He also heads Wasendorf & Associations, Inc., a research firm specializing in managed futures investment, and is president of Wasendorf & Son Company. Wasendorf is the author or coauthor of five books: *Commodity Trading—The Essential Primer, All about Futures, All about Options, All about Commodities,* and *Foreign Currency Trading.*

Since 1980, Wasendorf has written and published the market letter *Futures and Options Factors,* which was ranked as the number one newsletter in 1997 by *Commodity Traders Consumers Reports.* He is also the founder of the Center for Futures Education, and is a former director of the Commodity Education Institute.